THE STONES OF CHRIST CHURCH

The story of the buildings of Christ Church, Oxford

THE STONES OF CHRIST CHURCH

The story of the buildings of
Christ Church, Oxford

Judith Curthoys

PROFILE BOOKS

First published in Great Britain in 2017 by
Profile Books Ltd
3 Holford Yard
Bevin Way
London WC1X 9HD
www.profilebooks.com

1 3 5 7 9 10 8 6 4 2

A CIP catalogue record for this book is available from the British Library.

ISBN: 978 1 78125 812 5

Text design by Sue Lamble
Typeset in Photina by MacGuru Ltd

Printed and bound in Great Britain by TJ International, Padstow

Contents

Illustrations

Except where otherwise indicated, all illustrations are from the Christ Church Archives and are reproduced by permission of the Governing Body of Christ Church. Abbreviated sources refer to entries in the bibliography on pages 261–9.

Endpapers

Front: Detail from a plan of Oxford by David Loggan, engraved and published in 1675. Christ Church (marked as '13') is shown slightly to the right of the centre. The key has been adapted: it appears elsewhere on the complete plan, at a different scale and within a more ornate frame.

Back: The buildings and grounds of Christ Church in 2015. (Drawn by Jeremy Bays, www.art-work-shop.co.uk. © 2015 Steward of Christ Church)

Colour plates *(between pages 144 and 145)*

Portrait of Cardinal Thomas Wolsey by an unknown artist, late sixteenth or early seventeenth century.

Decorative moulding beneath the oriel window at the south end of the St Aldate's front.

Wolsey's emblems decorating the interior of the Hall roof.

The Hall after the major repairs and restoration of the roof in 2014–15. (Photograph by Ralph Williamson)

The sports pavilion after refurbishment in 2014.

The stairs from Tom Quad to the Hall. (Photograph by Ralph Williamson)

Black and white illustrations

Introduction and acknowledgements

This book deals primarily with the history of the buildings of Christ Church and its predecessors, Cardinal College and King Henry VIII's College. The story of St Frideswide's Priory and its church up to their dissolution should constitute another volume, so there is only the briefest of discussions about the medieval development of the site. Nor is there an in-depth analysis of the cathedral within these covers. The cathedral is not, in fact, dealt with, outside the introductory chapter, until the major refurbishment of the nineteenth century. It is included only as diocesan seat and college chapel, except where its earlier history directly impinges on our understanding of Christ Church.

The book's arrangement puts the history of each building, from beginning to end, in one place. So the history of Peckwater Quadrangle will begin and finish in the chapter devoted to the eighteenth century, and that of Tom Tower in the seventeenth-century section. I hope this will be easier for the reader than a purely chronological approach, which would mean constantly flicking back and forth between the index and the text.

Pevsner famously pronounced that a bicycle shed was a building, but a church was architecture.[1] Needless to say, scholars have contradicted him, and this book aims to follow in the footsteps of those gainsayers and show that the buildings of Christ Church, built with care for both design and function, whether grand or humble, have much to tell about the history of the site and the institutions that have occupied it. In the main, Christ Church's buildings are splendid: a visitor in the mid-seventeenth century commented that 'it is more like some fine castle, or great palace than a College'.[2] The already grand site was enhanced during the eighteenth and nineteenth centuries by ever more imposing structures, and in the twentieth by buildings of a more functional, but still interesting, nature. Although there were three, often long, principal building phases – the mid-sixteenth century, the late seventeenth and entire eighteenth centuries and the second half of the nineteenth – there can barely have been a year throughout Christ Church's five centuries when there was no scaffolding at all. After the era of Cardinal Wolsey, the main periods of construction were initiated or carried through by the three 'builder deans': John Fell, Henry Aldrich and Henry Liddell. At whatever date, the struggle to provide for the changing needs of academics and residents while honouring the history and beauty of Christ Church has been constant.

Some buildings are far better recorded than others. The college archive includes accounts for the building of Tom Tower, and the Library's construction is well documented. Contracts with the mason and plumber who worked on Peckwater Quad are detailed, and the papers on Blue Boar voluminous. Meadow Buildings, on the other hand, barely get a mention; no drawings survive, and correspondence is minimal.

Previous works on the college and cathedral buildings have tended to be rather perfunctory. Henry Thompson wrote a small chapter, more a tourist guide than a serious study, in his 1900 history of Christ Church; S. A. Warner and E. W. Watson concentrated on the cathedral; and the volumes of the *History of the University of Oxford* included Christ Church's buildings in its chapters on the physical setting for the academic community.[3] General architectural studies of Oxford also cover the colleges to a greater or lesser extent. Tom Tower has a work devoted entirely to the plans for its construction, written by W. D. Caröe, and the building accounts of the Library were edited by the late John Mason and Jean Cook.[4] The indefatigable Geoffrey Bill researched and wrote much, particularly on the nineteenth-century restoration of the cathedral and construction of the Wolsey Tower, which has now been published some years after his death. But there has not been a systematic account of Christ Church's buildings investigating why and how they changed from generation to generation. It is time that that was put right. I hope I do so in the pages of this book.

To compensate for my shortcomings as an architectural historian, many experts have come to my aid. At Christ Church, Jon Down, House Surveyor, has advised constantly with good humour and patience. A hi-viz jacket and hard hat have become new staples in my wardrobe. The Clerk of Works department, under the leadership of Tony Morris and Keith Aldridge, is always helpful. The astonishing knowledge of Matthew Power and Jim Godfrey on all aspects of the cathedral is indispensable. Graham Keevill, consultant archaeologist to Christ Church, has contributed much on both the buried and the vertical archaeology of the site, and is always keen to show me new discoveries in muddy holes! Julian Munby offered his assistance as soon as the book was first mooted. Geoffrey Tyack read a long and ultimately unpublished chapter for my previous book on Christ Church, *The Cardinal's College*, and gave it the thumbs-up; he then graciously took on the whole present text, giving generously of his time and expertise. Both Julian and Geoffrey are wonderful supporters of this amateur in the field. Other scholars, working in more specific areas, have also been generous with their research: Michael Hall and Peter Howell deserve particular mention. As ever, my colleague archivists are always ready to help and to advise; particular thanks must go to Julian Reid, Robin Darwall-Smith, Mike Riordan and Rob Petre.

Needless to say, the wonderful team at Profile Books are worth their weight in gold for their encouragement, support and commitment. My colleagues in the Library, too, are indispensable, particularly Rachel Pilgrim for her friendship and ability to nag nicely. Alina Nachescu and Dave Stumpp give their time and talents freely, for which I thank them unreservedly. Nothing would ever appear in print were it not for the Development Office, particularly Simon Offen and Sandra Harrison, who bend over backwards to help whenever they are asked. Deans Christopher Lewis and Martyn Percy have been more than kind in their support. I am also very grateful to Christ Church not only for allowing me to take time out to study architectural history at Rewley House but also for funding the course. My tutor, Paul Barnwell, deserves much credit for ensuring that parapets and purlins, Palladian and Picturesque, are terms that I can use with slightly more assurance than was previously possible. Hopefully, his teaching and ever helpful advice will have eliminated the worst of any errors. Those that remain are most definitely mine.

Judith Curthoys
Oxford, December 2016

1

A college-in-waiting: St Frideswide's Priory and its environs

L egend has it that St Frideswide's Priory, the small religious house that from the early eighth century occupied the site where Christ Church now stands, was founded by Frideswide, a local noblewoman, in thanksgiving for her deliverance from her energetic and persistent suitor Algar. Little is known about the beginnings of this monastery. It was possibly a

The statue of St Frideswide that stands on the west face of the north transept, drawn in the 1830s. It is now very badly eroded.

The remains of a stone-paved ford were found during the foundation excavations for Meadow Buildings sixteen feet below the current ground level.

Of the Saxon foundation, just a single floor tile survives. James Park
Harrison and James Parker, after excavations at the east end in the 1880s,
entered into vigorous debate about the possibility that the early church
may have had a Byzantine-style apsidal form dating either from the eighth
century or immediately after Aethelred's refoundation after the fire.

Harrison (1891)

double house, of both monks and nuns, and was here before Oxford was
laid out around 900 (by either Alfred, Edward or, possibly, Aethelflaed), its
presence prompting the town's development.[1] Positioned at the southern
end of a gravel island or spit, which was much more prominent then than
it is today, and between two Thames crossing points, nothing now remains
of the Saxon church or the early monastic site, which was, in all likelihood,
a simple gathering of timber buildings with a strong stone tower, within a
defined enclosure.[2] After the monastery and all its documents were destroyed
by fire in December 1002, during the revenge massacre of the Danes on St
Brice's Day, King Aethelred confirmed all its charters, rebuilt and enlarged
the church, and refounded the house as a priory of secular canons.

Later, in the early twelfth century, the canons – now regular Augustinians, under the governance of Gwymund, chaplain to Henry I – began to
close themselves off from the burgeoning city. The king granted permission
for the canons to build to the south of the priory church, on the street that
ran around the inside of the town's defences, and for all the entrances to the
precinct to be closed, making it fully enclosed for the first time.[3] It was also at
this time, not long after Henry's refoundation charter of c.1120, that Robert
of Cricklade, the prior of St Frideswide's, began a complete reconstruction
of the monastic buildings. Rather than pulling everything down and starting with a blank canvas, Robert did things in stages. The first new buildings
were the eastern side of the cloister, including the Chapter House with its
classic Norman chevron design around the door, and then the chancel.[4] The

The priory church, now the cathedral, from the north-west, as it was in the later medieval period, drawn by F. Mackenzie and engraved by John Le Keux.

prior then worked his way west and north. The progression of his labours suggests that the old church, left intact until all else was completed, stood slightly to the north of the main body of the present cathedral, its site partly underneath the present north transept and a small square precursor to the Latin Chapel. This small square chapel – half the size of the present Latin Chapel – was ready for the translation of St Frideswide's relics into a raised shrine in 1180, from a grave at the east end of the church.[5] The crossing tower and north transept were completed during the 1180s and then, after another, less calamitous, fire in 1190, the nave and the cloister were finished, with the door of the Chapter House being extended downwards.[6] The original west end of the church – demolished in the 1520s – was uncovered during excavations in 2005 under the present flagstone terrace.[7] The rest of the north-east corner was probably just about complete by the end of the thirteenth century, with finishing touches taking until the 1330s. It was

*The Chapter House door in the 1820s, showing its classic
Romanesque decoration, and the steps to the raised east end.*

only a small church, by the standards of Durham, for example, although quite large enough for its community, but the form was exactly what would have been expected, with the three vertical stages of arcade, triforium and clerestory, albeit arranged in an unusual giant order – with the triforium contained within the arcade – to give an impression of height in a building that is actually quite low by contemporary monastic standards. Its spire was one of the first in the country to be built in stone, *c.*1225, with pinnacles reminiscent of Normandy.[8] The proximity of the city wall, tight against the east end, meant that the Lady Chapel – in early English Gothic – was to the north, rather than in the more traditional location beyond the main altar.

Other alterations and additions followed in the centuries that followed, including the lovely fifteenth-century 'watching loft' (which is actually more likely to be a chantry chapel with the tomb of the patron below and an

4

*The 'watching loft' or chantry chapel, close to the
shrine of St Frideswide, seen in the 1830s.*

upstairs chamber for a priest, the lierne vaulting and openwork pendants
above the chancel from the late fifteenth century, and a new window in the
north transept, dated to the early sixteenth century.[9]

To the west and north of the priory church were the graveyards for the
priory community and for the small parish church or chapel of St Frideswide, lost beneath the extensions to the priory church.[10] Part of one cem-
etery may have fallen out of use, as a later medieval, beautifully crafted
garderobe (water closet) was uncovered in the recent excavations just to the
north-west of the cathedral. This must have been associated with another
building of some sort, perhaps guest lodgings, constructed over this part of
the graveyard.[11] To the south of the church were domestic buildings, including the prior's lodgings, the dormitory, the refectory and the kitchen. The
monks' infirmary may have been on roughly the same site as the present
Meadow Buildings, close to the edge of the precinct, with a small adjoining

*The east end of the priory church (from 1546 the cathedral)
between the fourteenth and the nineteenth centuries, with its
traditional thirteenth-century Decorated window.*

chapel especially for services for the sick. Anthony Wood, the famous seventeenth-century Oxford antiquarian, suggests that the infirmary chapel became the Audit House at Christ Church, where, apparently, the canons were accustomed to take their meals.[12]

The Priory House

Much of the present Priory House and the east range of the cloister south of and above the Chapter House occupy what was the monastic dormitory. If there was a night-stair directly into the priory church, there is no surviving evidence except, perhaps, the curious indentation at the foot of the pillar beside the door to the sacristy. Part of the Norman construction,

As recently as the 1490s Robert Sherborne, fellow of New College and dean of St Paul's, had funded the complete renewal of the cloister from the ground up. The new building was in a late Perpendicular style, and its construction had required alterations to the doorway up to the monks' dormitory so that the shafts for the vault should be symmetrical. Intriguingly, many of the bosses in the vault are of women: aristocratic and secular women at that. In a male monastery (as it was then) eyebrows may have been raised at such decoration, but the chantry that was established at the same time as the rebuilding was partly to commemorate a Mrs Halman, a shopkeeper with a premises near Carfax that appears to have been a specialist ecclesiastical retailer. It is feasible that Mrs Halman was one of a group of pious, older ladies (the hairstyles shown in the bosses are a bit dated) who were members of a consorority for St Frideswide. Regardless of the lateness of the work, Wolsey's demolition of one side of the cloister would suggest that the destruction of the remainder was on the cards.

Munby (forthcoming)

the day-stair led up to the dormitory from the cloister through a doorway slightly to the north of the current Priory House entrance.[13] The dormitory, or a portion of it, may have been rebuilt in the thirteenth century, and then again in the very late fifteenth, when the cloisters were rebuilt by the mason William Orchard, under the watchful eye of Robert Sherborne.[14] The door was moved to its present position and the staircase given a dog-leg, a small quatrefoil window in the old door-frame to shed a little light on to the stairs, a tiled floor to the new landing, and a stone handrail. The walls were painted in dramatic broad grey and red stripes.[15] At the same time as he was redesigning the cloister, Sherborne altered part of the mid-thirteenth-century dormitory to form a residence for the prior and built a new house or extension to its south.[16] The residence was probably used subsequently by the deans of both Cardinal College and King Henry VIII's College, and then by the first dean of Christ Church, Richard Cox, until the present deanery in the Great Quadrangle was made fit for habitation.

In addition to his changes at the entrance to the dormitory, Sherborne extended the property further south, connecting with some of the remaining monastic buildings.[17] Recent archaeological investigations have found timbers dating from the mid-thirteenth century being reused as joists.[18] The Chapter House roof was replaced in 1261, so these may well be part of the original – too good to throw away. They were no doubt held on to by the clerk of works for repairs and maintenance. More timbers date to Sherborne's alterations, and more to work around the construction of Cardinal College in 1525.[19] A tremendously thick wall at the southern end of the Priory House probably indicates the conclusion of the Norman construction, with the late fifteenth-century extension to the south drastically altered in the 1630s.

From the early twentieth century, and probably before, the Priory House was usually the lodging of the Lady Margaret professor of divinity.[20] It had been proposed in the 1930s that the rooms over the Chapter House be adapted for the use of the choir, but this did not happen. It was not until 1970 that the Playne Vallance architectural partnership modernised the whole property, creating a new self-contained ground-floor flat entered from the cloister.[21] Further changes were made in 1985, just before Rowan Williams, the future archbishop of Canterbury, moved in as the Lady Margaret professor, and as John Norsworthy was appointed cathedral registrar; offices were created out of the part of the Priory House that extended over the Chapter House.[22] After the death of Canon Peter Hinchliff in 1995, the residence was divided in two the following year, and the more southerly portion became known as Cloister House.[23] The plan allowed for one of the canonries in Tom Quad to be made available for college use.[24] At the same time the Pococke Garden, for the use of staff, was created out of the huge garden attached to the house.[25]

Just around the corner from the dormitory, occupying the south side of the cloister, was the refectory, rebuilt in the late fifteenth century, probably at the same time as the cloister.[26] A fine building, with storage underneath, it included a pulpit for the reading of the scriptures during meals. The entrance to the undercroft was at the west end – an engraving made prior to its conversion into student rooms in the late eighteenth century shows the

Alterations were made to the choir practice room, off the Chapter House, in 1985. The room is said to have been created by William Tresham, a canon of Christ Church from 1546 to 1560, soon after the foundation of Christ Church in 1546. While the work was being done on the Priory House, a new garden, designed by Mavis Batey in 1985, was laid out in the cloister which included all twenty-four plants shown in the borders of Wolsey's lectionary (the Library's MS 101).

grand west window with a porch beneath. The monks' entrance was from the cloister passage at the east end, closer to both dormitory and church.[27] Separate from the refectory, but conveniently placed between it and the infirmary, the monastic kitchen was probably on the site where Wolsey's grand replacement now stands.

The exact size of the whole precinct (which would have been surrounded, at least from the twelfth century, by a wall) is not known, but it extended westwards to the gardens or yards of the properties on St Aldate's, to St Frideswide's Street on the north and to the city wall and the edge of the river terrace to the south.[28] Outside the city wall was the Meadow, with the monastic fishponds in St Frideswide's (now Merton) Grove. The grange – with its stables, pigsties, cattle pens and grain stores – was east of the ponds.[29]

So by the early years of the sixteenth century this small, enclosed community was tucked almost invisibly into a corner of the city of Oxford, surrounded by the city walls on two sides and hemmed in by shops, houses, inns and schools on the west and north. The stubby and ancient spire of the priory church may have been the only feature visible over the surrounding tenements and other properties.

To the north, St Edward's Street (now Alfred Street) ran towards the priory from the High Street, between the Bear Inn on one side and Peckwater Inn on the other, and was closed by a small gate which guarded one entrance to the priory churchyard.[30] Further east, Shidyerd Street (now Oriel Street) made its way from the High too, continuing south – through

*The cottages on the Meadow by the Rose Lane gate, around 1830. Little is
known about these houses, except that they probably stand on the site of the
medieval grange, and that they were leased to Corpus Christi College from
1690 until the mid-nineteenth century, when they were taken back in hand.
The cottages were the subject of much dispute between the two colleges as they
fell gradually into disrepair. In 2016 a new greenhouse was built alongside.*

what is now Corpus Christi's staff car park – until it reached the bastion
and postern gate behind the priory church.[31] For a few years around 1517
much of this eastern boundary would have been occupied by the construction teams building the new Corpus Christi College. Running slightly to the
north of the centre of the present Tom Quad, a small street called St Frideswide's Lane turned off what is now St Aldate's to join up with St Edward's
Street just outside the churchyard gate.[32] It was busy with shops and houses,
with their accompanying refuse pits, privies and outhouses. Some properties
had been, and possibly still were, used as academic halls of residence, such
as Burnell's Inn and Greek Hall; others were pubs or shops, or both. Rooms
in one of the inns in the lane – either the Dolphin or the Pike – were used
in the twelfth and thirteenth centuries as a synagogue.[33] Many of the city's
fishmongers used St Aldate's to sell their wares, and the slaughterhouses
belonging to the local butchers were spread out along the present Brewer
Street, also known as Sleying Lane. The several inns would have added
their own aromas, noise and mess, and the various streams of the Thames

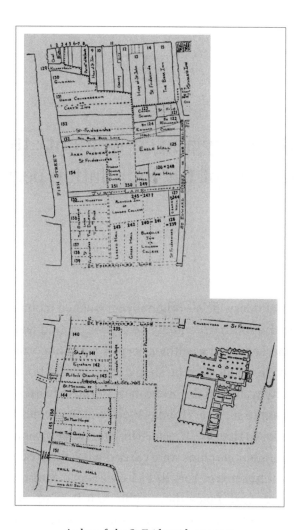

A plan of the St Frideswide precinct.

(including Trill Mill Stream, which flowed close to the city defences past the workshops of fellmongers and slaughtermen before it entered the Meadow) were undoubtedly polluted and unpleasant. And where the city wall joined St Aldate's, at the south gate, in the midst of the midden and racket, was the tiny church of St Michael.[34]

11

2

'So goodly and convenient': the buildings of the foundation period

So by 1524 St Frideswide's – originally an isolated monastic community perched on the southern end of the higher ground above the Thames flood plain – had become a wealthy priory of some importance to the university, hemmed in on all sides by shops, inns, private houses and halls of residence, the city walls and the brand-new Corpus Christi College.[1]

But it was not to survive. Thomas Wolsey, at the height of his influence as Lord Chancellor to Henry VIII, sealed its fate. Wolsey was an indefatigable builder, and his ambitious plans were carried out nationwide. As soon as he was appointed archbishop of York in 1514, he began work on the province's London residence, York Place (later Whitehall Palace), and at Hampton Court, on which he had taken a ninety-nine-year lease. In 1522 Wolsey, by now a cardinal, acquired The More and Tyttenhanger, both in Hertfordshire, with the abbacy of St Alban's, and in 1523 Durham Place – next door to York Place on the Strand – with the bishopric of Durham. In 1529 he exchanged the bishopric of Durham and its palace for Winchester with its residence at Esher. Hampton Court was probably complete by 1525, when Wolsey handed it over to King Henry, but York Place kept him occupied until his death in 1530.

To tackle all these projects Wolsey maintained a vast works department. There was a central office based in Battersea, which dealt with his London projects, a second group handling works at The More, Esher and

Tyttenhanger, and a third office, under Thomas Cromwell, employed by the cardinal, which managed all business relating to his collegiate buildings in Oxford and Ipswich.[2] Towards the end of Wolsey's life a fourth department was established, to handle works at Cawood and Southwell, both properties of the archbishopric of York. Wolsey was tireless, working not only on his own projects but also on the king's, including the extraordinary temporary palace at Guisnes for the Field of the Cloth of Gold.[3] The arrangement and size of the tent-palace show remarkable resemblances to Christ Church's Great Quadrangle, and it is more than likely that Wolsey had a hand in the latter's design.[4]

These private schemes, however, were not enough for the cardinal, who harboured a passion for education. Wolsey had been planning an Oxford college for a while when John Longland, the bishop of Lincoln and a contemporary of Wolsey at Magdalen College, wrote to him in 1522 to say that both the king and the queen, Catherine of Aragon, approved of his idea.[5] The site was easily chosen, and St Frideswide's was dissolved by papal bull in April 1524; Wolsey wasted no time, beginning work on Cardinal College almost immediately, certainly by January 1525, even though the royal licence for its foundation was not granted until July of that year. In fact, papers were still being accrued relating to the college's property in 1527.[6] Money was evidently to be no object.[7]

Wolsey's overall educational scheme was immense in its scope; his new college would be at the centre of a web of feeder grammar schools (as Winchester was to New College, for example) in all corners of the country, and the accommodation that he planned was to be no less impressive. The priory site formed only the core of a much larger college precinct. Portions of the city wall, the church of St Michael at the South Gate and all the tenements on St Aldate's, where the new frontage was to go, and on the adjacent alleys were demolished, including two that had belonged to Balliol College (for which no compensation was ever paid).[8] Outside the priory grounds, new land was acquired and brought into the precincts of Cardinal College. Two little streets – St Frideswide's Lane and Jury Lane – were closed and the properties pulled down, and a new road, Blue Boar Lane, was constructed further to the north in compensation, entailing the demolition, at least in part, of the Blue Boar pub and its associated residence, and parts of two other inns, the Unicorn and the Bull, which had belonged to Oseney Abbey.[9]

Throughout the medieval period, across St Edward's Street and at the end of St Frideswide's Lane, stood Peckwater Inn. Very little is known about the inn, but it was big, occupying perhaps two-thirds of the block between St Edward's Street, Shidyerd Street and Shitebarn Lane.[10] To its east had been several tenements, all of which were acquired by Canterbury College in the later fourteenth century: one from Godstow Priory, one from Thomas of Gloucester, four from St Frideswide's, one from Abingdon Abbey and one from Balliol College.

Canterbury College was one of five monastic colleges in medieval Oxford, and had been established in 1362 by Archbishop Islip exclusively for Benedictine monks from Canterbury cathedral priory. The college consisted of a single quadrangle opening on to Shidyerd Street, the construction of which began in the 1370s and continued for another eighty years, concluding with its library in around 1450. On the west side was the hall; on the south was the chapel; and chambers occupied the east and north. The hall seems to have had a finely built porch; evidence of buttresses that would have framed the steps into the building and ashlared string courses were found in recent excavations.[11] Accommodation for the warden of the college was in the south-west corner, between the refectory and the chapel. The kitchen was probably tucked in behind the hall.[12] The library adjoined a garden, raised up at first-floor level, and was well stocked with two to three hundred chained volumes. W. A. Pantin suggests that it was built, in the 1450s, to the west of the hall, which would place it, coincidentally, under the present Christ Church Library. It had a stone-paved floor, glazing and a stone-tiled roof. The rooms below were rented out, often to monks from Bath.[13]

On the northern side of Shitebarn Lane were larger properties, including: Vine Hall, which had housed a grammar school and had a stone-built garderobe; Solar Hall, belonging to New College; and St Edward Hall, which belonged to Oriel College. Even in these tiny backstreets many of the properties had shops on their street fronts.[14] Many properties on these boundaries

Only the gatehouse survives of Wolsey's first 'feeder school' for Cardinal College in Ipswich. It was under construction during 1529, but at Wolsey's fall most of the stone was shipped to Westminster. Its foundation stone was discovered and given to Christ Church in 1789. Christ Church also holds a portion of the statutes of Ipswich School.

The foundation stone of Ipswich School, donated to Christ Church in 1789.

were already owned by the priory, which made Wolsey's life a little easier when he came to plan his college. At least they were his to knock down without much in the way of qualms. The remainder, though, had to be acquired by compulsory purchase.

Cardinal College was the third new college to be built in Oxford in the early sixteenth century. First there had been Brasenose, in 1509, and

As monastic colleges, neither Canterbury nor any of the other four –
Gloucester College, for Benedictine monks of the southern province;
Durham College, for northern Benedictines; St Bernard's, for Cistercians;
and St Mary's College, for Augustinians – survived the Reformation, in spite
of new building encouraged by Wolsey at the latter as late as 1518. Rewley
Abbey, a studium for Cistercians, was dissolved in 1536. Although Canterbury College was probably within Wolsey's sights, it survived until the late
1530s, when it was taken over by the king for his successor college.

then, just eight years later, Corpus Christi. Both of these took over the site
of academic halls. These halls had once been pre-eminent as lodgings for
undergraduates but were now in drastic decline. From a high point of fifty
such halls in 1469, by 1511 there were twenty-five or so, and by 1514 only
twelve. Monasticism, too, was retreating, and Tudor alterations to the medieval colleges, such as Merton, were designed to make life more comfortable
and the buildings more beautiful. Grandeur, however, was not on the agenda
of the founders of either Brasenose or Corpus.[15] Corpus Christi was, in fact,
originally planned as a monastic college for the monks of St Swithun's in
Winchester, but following Henry VIII's costly war with France and the rise
of a younger and more belligerent circle about the king, Bishop Fox saw that
the greater need was to educate able servants of church and state, rather
than just the monks of his cathedral priory. Though modest in scale, the
college was generously endowed, and Fox took advantage of his connections
with the court to introduce to Oxford some of the ablest craftsmen in the
country, including the master carpenter Humphrey Coke.[16]

Cardinal College was on a different scale altogether. Begun only eight
years after Corpus Christi, it was still conventional in its style but at a completely new level in terms of ambition, designed to outdo Wolsey's *alma
mater*, Magdalen. The college's annual income was to be in excess of £2,000,
which would fund a foundation of 176 people.[17] To build such an edifice
required a deep pocket and a huge workforce.

Soon after the end of the Christmas holiday, during the week after

Epiphany 1525, Henry Redman and John Lubyns, Wolsey's chief architects, with William Jonson, their deputy, were on the site 'to see the platte [flat area] with the grownde and devysyng the beylding'.[18] Humphrey Coke, said to be the greatest carpenter of his time, in royal service from 1496 until his death in 1531, had worked alongside Redman at Eton, designing the cloister there. He had been responsible for the timberwork at the Field of the Cloth of Gold and at neighbouring Corpus Christi College. At Cardinal College he was responsible, with his warden, Robert Carow, for the roofs of both the new chapel and the dining hall; the latter has been described as Coke's 'greatest work [and] the last great work of medieval carpentry, uncontaminated by Renaissance influence'.[19]

By the end of January 1525 tools were being purchased, and in February masons and labourers were already hard at work, housed in Peckwater Inn, specially acquired and converted both as their lodgings and as workshops.[20] Although all of Wolsey's building projects were located close to water, which made for cheaper and easier transportation of materials, one of the first tasks to be tackled was to improve the appalling condition of the roads into Oxford, which had been terribly neglected. Funds were designated specifically.[21]

The first six months of preparation and building are recorded in an account book kept by the first dean of Cardinal College, John Higden.[22] In

---

Henry Redman and John Lubyns were significant men in their trades. Redman's father, Thomas, had been master mason at Westminster Abbey, and Henry had followed in his father's footsteps. He built the nave and chancel of St Margaret's Church, then worked at Eton College and for Henry VIII at Greenwich and Windsor. He was Wolsey's principal architect at York Place (Whitehall Palace) and Hampton Court. When Redman died, in 1528, he left his projects in the hands of John Lubyns (sometimes Lovyns or Lebons), who had been employed as one of the king's masons by 1506 and was evidently the man in overall charge at Cardinal College. After Wolsey's fall, Lubyns continued to work for the king at Hampton Court.

ODNB

---

those early months there were 32 masons, 16 rough-layers and 64 labourers on site, overseen by William Staunton, who may have had particular responsibility for the lime kilns, as well as the surveyor, Nicholas Townley, and Townley's assistant, Rowland Messenger, who were appointed to work alongside Wolsey's senior craftsmen.[23]

At the end of this initial period the foundation stone was laid on 17 July 1525.[24] Wolsey was not in attendance, and his place at the ceremony was taken by John Longland, bishop of Lincoln. As far as we know, Wolsey never came to Oxford to see the progress of his grand design.

The design of Cardinal College was not new, just on a grander scale than any predecessor – the 'apotheosis of that plan of the "closed quadrangle"'.[25] The main quadrangle measured seventeen perches in each direction, and the intention was evidently to have a cloister of one perch depth all around.[26] The effect would have been similar to that at St Stephen's Chapel at the Palace of Westminster, another design by Henry Redman and his then partner, William Vertue. At Magdalen accommodation extended over the cloister, but Cardinal College's cloister would have been free-standing. Not only would the whole effect have been lighter, but the design allowed for longer staircases, bigger windows and larger, airier rooms.[27] Architecturally, the quadrangle contains nothing surprising; it is Perpendicular Gothic with square-headed mullioned windows (albeit larger than those in contemporary colleges), which were probably glazed from the outset. The doorways, gateways and cloister arches are typically four-centred. But although there

This account book is Corpus Christi College's MS 565. It is battered and much nibbled by sixteenth-century mice, and its presence in Corpus Christi may have been the consequence of the plague in Oxford. Cardinal College's dean and some of the canons took refuge at Poughley in Berkshire, a small priory among those dissolved for the foundation of Cardinal College (and, until recently, the home of the commander of RAF Welford). It was decreed that any moneys delivered to Oxford for the building work during their absence should be handed to John Claymond, the president of Corpus Christi.

St Stephen's cloister, Westminster. These cloisters were rebuilt between 1526 and 1529, and give a good indication of what the cloister around the Great Quadrangle would have been like, had Wolsey ever completed his project. The triple shafts with moulded capitals and bases and the decorative moulding between the shafts at the corners are identical.

is considerable decoration, particularly around the main gate, there is no significant indication that Wolsey intended to branch out into more Renaissance styles with, say, terracotta roundels, such as those at Hampton Court. Perhaps they did not fit the academic style that he wanted to emulate as well as develop. The only hint of Renaissance influence is the carving of the putti in a small panel below the first-floor oriel window on the south-west tower.

Wolsey's desire for his college to be bigger and better than its exemplars meant that the usual arrangement of dining hall and chapel end-to-end on one side of the quadrangle was abandoned. At Cardinal College the dining hall took up half the southern side of the quadrangle, and the chapel, apparently planned to be slightly longer than the one at King's College in Cambridge, was to have occupied the whole of the north side.

Higden's account records that stone – freestone and rag – was sourced

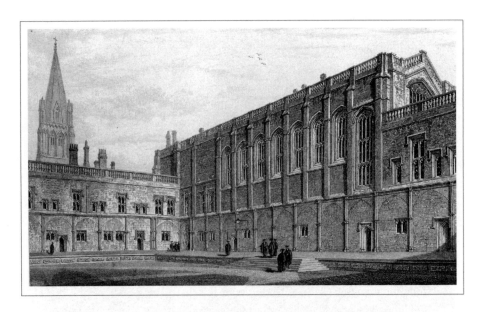

*Mackenzie and Le Keux's illustration of the Hall before the major
alterations of the nineteenth century. The wall between the Hall and
the staircase tower was probably built in the 1630s. John Fell replaced
the original castellation in the 1660s with the balustrade.*

from local quarries in Taynton, Headington, Barrington and, just over the
county border in Gloucestershire, Sherborne. Taynton freestone could be
quarried in large blocks and was useful for quoins and dressings; it was
used in Oxford at least from the early fourteenth century, at Merton, and
probably for the spire on the priory church of St Frideswide.[28] Headington
stone, for which Wolsey purchased half an acre of quarry, was more difficult to trim into neat blocks but was harder and more durable.[29] The first
load of 100 tons – at 1s. 8d. per ton – of Barrington (deep yellow) and
Sherborne (white) stone was selected by Dean Higden and John Lubyns in
person on 28 June 1525.[30] Stonesfield 'slates' – in fact, a variant of the
same limestone rather than true slate – are found only around the village
of that name, in north-east Oxfordshire, mined from thin seams via hill-
side adits, and became ubiquitous for local houses and Oxford colleges.[31]
Similar tiles, known as Cotswold slates, were acquired from the area around
Stow-on-the-Wold.

20

Cardinal College was built of local limestone. The quarries at Headington and Holton (Wheatley) were the closest, but Burford stone was also used in huge quantities. Roofs were covered with split tiles of the same limestone.

Later, the same stones were used to build Peckwater Quad (with Barnsley stone from slightly further west in the Cotswolds for the decorative features) and Canterbury Quad. The Library, too, was constructed with Headington stone, but in both hardstone and freestone, which gave interesting variations in colour and texture. Tom Tower was of Taynton, selected personally by Christopher Wren from the quarry belonging to the mason Christopher Kempster. The only variation was to be for the statues – in Portland stone – for the niches on either side of the tower, but these were never made.

By the early nineteenth century the problems with soft Headington stone were becoming evident, and architects looked further afield, using Bath stone for many of Oxford's Gothic revival structures, including Meadow Buildings. The arrival of the railway, however, opened up new opportunities, and Clipsham stone from Rutland became the medium of choice, with just a brief flirtation with Doulting from the Mendips. Clipsham was more resilient than the local limestones to the growing pollution in the city, and became almost ubiquitous, being used for repairs and new buildings from the late nineteenth century right through to the 1960s.

Christ Church ventured away from the traditional yellow limestones when it commissioned Powell and Moya to design Blue Boar Quad and the Picture Gallery. Both were constructed in concrete and with decorative Portland stone facings over brick. The white/grey finish was in cold contrast to the familiar warm stones of old, but was the height of fashion in the 1960s. The Library's major restoration, around 1960, required a change of medium too. Even if Headington stone had been available, it had proved its fallibility, so the original colour contrast was maintained with Clipsham (for the yellow) and Portland Shelly Whitbed (for the massive white pilasters).

In modern times the trend has been away from Clipsham, and attempts have been made to find better matches for the original limestones. When the Wolsey Tower was restored in the 1980s, the surveyor opted for stone from the Savonnières quarries, in the Meuse region of France. These efforts continue today for all repairs made to the masonry.

Howell, in Brock and Curthoys (2000), 749; Arkell (1947)

Five lime kilns, often operated by women, kept the masons supplied, and it was not long into the building programme before the first slaters were called in. By the end of June, still before the formal foundation of the college, there were eight men, each receiving 6d. a day, with five servants, working with the slates from the Rissingtons, just over the county boundary in Gloucestershire. Timber was acquired from Abingdon, courtesy of the abbot, whose own servants were paid to find and mark the trees to be felled. Trees were also supplied from Cuddesdon, The Shawe, Cumnor, Beckley, Shotover and Forest Hill. Carting the timber was a major expense, particularly if it was brought overland. Each load cost a shilling or more to move. In contrast, timber that arrived at 'the bridge at Oxford' (presumably Folly Bridge) by river cost just 8d. per load. In April 12,000 laths, at 2s. per thousand, were delivered, and wainscoting and glass were also arriving at the site in mid-April, so at least some of the buildings must have been at an advanced stage within only three months. After the laying of the foundation stone in July, it would seem that Higden handed over the administration of the building and of the landed estate to a college accounts clerk. The staff already included a high steward, a clerk of the lands, an under-steward, bailiffs and receivers, all of whom would have been involved directly with the management of the endowment provided by Wolsey. The transfer of power from the prior to the cardinal must have been smooth, and possibly barely noticed by the tenants in the scattered estates.

The Great Quadrangle

The lodgings

Progress on the new college was astonishingly quick. By the end of 1526, after only two years' work, Dr John London, warden of New College, wrote to a Mr Larke describing the buildings as they stood.[32] The west-side lodgings were complete and ready for occupation, with only the battlements to be added. Already coloured and gilded representations of the king's and Wolsey's arms decorated the stonework and the timberwork inside.[33] Five sets of principal lodgings were created within the quadrangle: three on the east

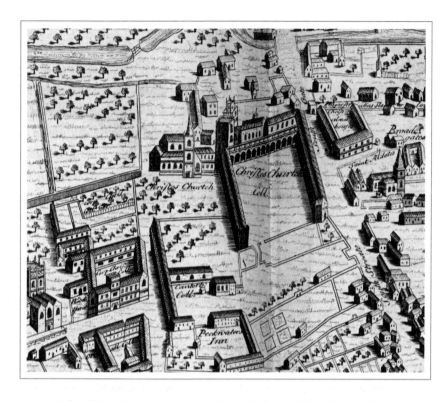

A detail from Ralph Agas's map of Oxford, dated 1578, showing Christ Church, perhaps not entirely accurately, with the Great Quadrangle unfinished but with Palmer's tower already over the Hall stairs. The cathedral is separate and rather isolated behind Wolsey's quad. Peckwater Quad has three sides – north, south and west – and Canterbury Quad is little more than a hall and a chapel. Behind the kitchen and down to the meadow are odd ranges and domestic buildings. Across St Aldate's, the almshouse is impressive.

side, one in the south-west corner and one immediately to the north of the main gate.

Wolsey's statutes allowed for a dean, forty senior canons and sixty junior. Plainly the later arrangement of the Great Quadrangle as it is now, in effect a cathedral close, was not the plan for Cardinal College. However, eight of the senior canons had to hold doctorates, and it was these men who formed the Governing Body: the sub-dean, who was to deputise for the dean whenever necessary, with four censors responsible for the education and discipline of junior members of the college and three bursars to manage all financial matters both external and domestic. Perhaps the principal lodgings were to be used by these senior administrators.

The history of the deanery and the canons' lodgings is difficult to trace. No significant records survive after the initial building, as the residences have always been considered private. The dean and canons have been fairly free (until modern times and the imposition of listed building regulations) to do much as they wished with the interiors. Only the exteriors and anything structural came within the remit of the Chapter or Governing Body.

Not long after the foundation of Christ Church (Henry VIII's ultimate replacement for Wolsey's college) in 1546, a decree was passed allocating the lodgings by seniority with, unsurprisingly, the newer residences chosen by the most senior men.[34] The best was considered to be the lodging next to the deanery, followed by the lodging on the north side of the great gate. The third and fourth lodgings in order of preference were the residences next to the church (in front of the remainder of the priory church nave) and the residence described as 'next to the Hall', probably the Priory House. The house in the Chaplains' Quad was considered the fifth-best (probably the residence later destroyed by fire, in 1669), then the one in the south-west corner, occupying the turret and rooms alongside, and finally the lodgings in Peckwater Inn and Canterbury College.[35] Once installed in their respective residences, the canons needed furnishings. Much of the furniture, as in any house move, would have been brought from canons' previous houses, but the accounts record that carpenters were called in to make shelves, desks and tables, and to panel the walls.[36] A great press with its own locks and keys was fitted into the sub-dean's bedchamber in 1583.[37] Each residence had a water pump installed in the garden.[38]

In theory, as a canon rose through the ranks, so he moved from an inferior residence to a superior one. By a decree confirmed in 1593, the canonries (or residences) were, as we have seen, allocated by seniority or long service rather than by stall.[39] Any attempt to circumvent the rules was frowned upon. If the most senior man chose not to move when a better residence became available, it was made available to more junior canons. The constant shifting from one house to another would have been unpopular, particularly for those canons with families, so it was not long before residences began to be passed to one's successor in the canonical stall without any sense of the 'ancient order for antiquities'.[40]

There were evidently great debates over this seniority issue; early in the seventeenth century Thomas Thornton drew up an account of the allocation of lodgings.[41] The document recites the first resident of each lodging, recording whether he had acquired the residence by 'antiquity', as Thornton perceived was correct, or just by being appointed to the same stall (named after the seat that the canon occupied in the cathedral). To a certain extent, the document seems to be a defence of Thornton's brother's use of his own canonry, disguised as a general defence of Christ Church's unwritten constitution.[42] Thomas had been 'upgraded' from the lodgings by the church to the residence next to the great gate, but, as his old residence was apparently unwanted, he allowed his brother Richard to use it free of charge. In support of his case, Thornton's paper also mentions an exchange that occurred in 1591 between John Weston and John Kennall in which Weston seems to have swapped his lodgings – the least desirable residence, in Canterbury Quad – for one in the Great Quadrangle. Formal letters of exchange were drawn up, but the temporary swap between two individuals became rather more permanent than the rules permitted. In 1632, at a hearing before the Lord Keeper, Thomas Coventry, the exchange was later to be overturned.[43]

In spite of tradition, it would appear that the allocation of lodgings was never as simple as it should have been. In the mid-nineteenth century (shortly before two canonries were suppressed) the holder of the first stall (the sub-dean) was housed in the north-west corner of the Great Quadrangle, the second stall in the Priory House, the third in Killcanon, the fourth on the east side next to the deanery, the fifth (the regius professor of divinity) at the south end of the east side (before the refurbishment of the cathedral), the sixth (the regius professor of Hebrew) in the south-west corner, the seventh in Peckwater Quad and the eighth at the east end of the north side of the Great Quadrangle. But in 1933 Kenneth Kirk, the new regius professor of moral and pastoral theology, refused to move into the lodgings next to the deanery on account of its bad state.

Financing the maintenance of the canons' lodgings was always a bone of contention. On several occasions between the seventeenth century and the twenty-first the matter has been the subject of Chapter and Governing Body debate. In 1650, after damage caused by the court and the army, the canons were reimbursed from the corporate pot for any repairs that were needed to the residences.[44] In 1716, however, a fresh decree was issued requiring all bills to be approved before any payment would be made.[45] This decree was just a warning shot across the canons' bows; a year later an act from 1631 was renewed, laying down stringent terms and conditions, as much for the treasurer as for the canons. The treasurer should not, it stated, 'have power to disburse annually of his own authority towards the reparations of the Dean's Lodgings etc above the summe of £4, of the canons above the summe of 40s, of a Student's or Chaplain's above the summe of 6s 8d. If any greater summes be requisite, the treasurer is to have the Dean and Chapter's assent.' Repairs to leads and slats over the lodgings, outhouses and stables of the dean and canons could be paid by the college, but only a shilling was to be permitted for each load of gravel supplied.[46]

By 1756 the rules had been simplified: no repairs were to be done to the deanery and canonries at Domus expense (with the bills settled by the Chapter) except outside work on walls, chimneys, slatting, roofs and leadwork.[47] Similarly, in 1896, the Estates Committee recommended that the House (i.e., the college, so named from its Latin nickname 'Aedis Christi' or

The terms 'Student' and 'alumnus' have always caused problems at Christ Church. A Student (always with an upper-case 'S') is now the equivalent of a Fellow. Before 1858, Students were stipendiary members of the academic establishment, whether graduate or undergraduate. Only the Dean and Chapter were the Governing Body. The remainder of the Students could be tutors, or studying for higher degrees, or just pupils. Non-stipendiary undergraduates were called noblemen, gentlemen commoners, commoners or servitors. 'Alumnus' was the Latin equivalent for Student, and did not mean an old member of the college, as it is commonly used today.

'The House of Christ') would pay for no repairs except those that were strictly structural, external decoration or anything related to the drains. This was reiterated in 1946, when the Governing Body accepted liability for ensuring that lodgings were in a 'state of good tenantable repair' at the beginning of any occupancy and at fourteen-year intervals. Forty years later, in 1986, and again in 2009, the division of labour between Domus and the occupant was made clearer, and in the latter document, and for the first time, such matters as building regulations and Listed Building Consent were specifically included in the rules.[48]

The south-west lodgings

The intended use of the south-west turret and the lodgings of which it formed a part is uncertain and the subject of debate. They could have been for the deanery. During the medieval period the head of a college was often lodged over the main gate with the treasury above, accessible only through the lodgings for security. This was the case at New College. However, the Warden of New College was seen more as a patron than as a guardian of the college's assets, and was expected to receive important and influential guests in sumptuous surroundings, feeding them from his own kitchen rather than at the common table. The treasury there was later separated from the lodgings. In Cambridge it was not uncommon for the lodgings of a head of house to be adjacent to the upper end of the dining hall.[49]

An alternative suggestion is that the south-west turret was to be an audit room, treasury and muniment room.[50] Wolsey's statutes certainly stated that the muniments and treasures were to be kept in chests in the tower, behind a door with three keys.[51] Perhaps Wolsey was intending to combine these different styles and traditions; the dean would be both custodian of his college's treasures and records and a lordly host in comfortable and impressive lodgings, the only building to be given fashionable new decoration.

In spite of their apparent grandeur, after Christ Church's foundation the south-west lodgings were considered to be only the sixth out of eight canonries. Perhaps the noise of the city street and the proximity of the south gate made them unappealing. The first occupant, from 1546 to 1557, was James Courthope, a former fellow of Corpus Christi and a career clergyman. He was a canon not only of Christ Church but also of Lincoln, and later dean of Peterborough, so perhaps rarely in residence.[52] Courthope was followed in the lodging by William Chedsey, a Catholic who flourished in the brief reign of Mary Tudor but lost his positions soon after the accession of Elizabeth.[53] After Chedsey came John Kennall, who swapped the south-west lodgings for the least favourable lodgings in Canterbury Quad with John Weston, who became a Student in 1562 and a canon in 1591. To move from what appeared to be the grandest to the meanest must hint that the south-west canonry was far less appealing than it may have looked from the outside.

After Weston the residence was allocated to the regius professor of Hebrew and occupied first by John Morris, whose bequest still benefits the Library, and then by Edward Pococke, perhaps its most famous early inhabitant. It was Pococke who planted the plane tree in the Priory House garden and the fig tree in his own back garden, scions of which still survive.[54]

Architecturally, little happened in the south-west canonry between the sixteenth century and the nineteenth. The south gate of the city, in a terrible state of repair, probably ever since Wolsey demolished St Michael's Church and the surrounding tenements, was supposed to be rebuilt in 1617 between the southernmost turret and the Brewer Street corner of the almshouse. However, in spite of the Dean and Chapter's approval for the rebuilding, the work was never undertaken.[55] In 1726, under the care of Robert Clavering, bishop of Llandaff and then Peterborough, the east turret was repaired, and in 1742 the windows were mended and re-leaded.[56]

But in 1809 Christ Church was struck by fire.[57] Probably the result of a careless candle or an unguarded grate, a spark catching either the bressumer, or main beam, over a fireplace or a nearby roof timber, it broke out at midnight on 3 March near the south-west lodgings. The reservoir at the centre of Tom Quad, now known to all as Mercury, after the statue in its centre, was immediately called into action, but its contents were insufficient to quell the flames, which were leaping from the rooms between the

Hall and the south-west lodgings. Fire engines were called in from colleges all around, and from the city, and many individuals leapt to help. Portraits and valuable furniture were cleared from the Hall and stacked up in the Chapter House in case the wind changed; the local militia, the Oxford Loyal Volunteers, ensured the maintenance of law and order and protected the rescued furniture from looters. By seven o'clock in the morning the fire was under control and everyone was safe from harm.[58] A calm night meant that the conflagration had not spread, although the firemen had evidently been extremely, or perhaps excessively, diligent in their work, damaging rooms quite some distance away. Barré Charles Roberts, an undergraduate, was called back to Oxford as his rooms in either Tom 4 or 5 had been affected. Roberts was not best pleased; all that had happened was a slight singeing of his ceiling but, with considerable irony, he said, 'it was necessary to break all my furniture, spoil my books, and steal my wine in order to prevent my being a sufferer from the flames ... I sincerely wish the rooms had been destroyed, in which case the Chapter would have built me much better ones.'[59]

Others were less lucky. The south-west lodgings, then occupied by Joseph White, were gutted along with those of four students, two of whom had been in residence for less than a month. Eight further rooms in Tom 1 and 2 were damaged, with the total loss estimated at £12,000.[60] Complete reconstruction was the only option. The celebrated architect James Wyatt, who had been responsible for the design of Canterbury Quad and alterations to the Hall stairs, was called in to supervise what would be his penultimate project.[61] He estimated that the structural work could be completed by the end of June if the old stone was reused; new bricks could not be obtained quickly enough. The timber and glass could be acquired locally, and locks were supplied by Standley and Gale in Birmingham. Roofing lead was recovered from the ashes as far as possible, but new material was purchased from the church of Fyfield.[62] Wooden staircases were rebuilt in stone, and the balustrades replaced in iron.[63] The bulk of the work was done by the local architect John Hudson, who was employed by the Dean and Chapter throughout the first half of the nineteenth century; the final accounts show that Hudson received in excess of £10,000. The total cost of the repairs came to £14, 272.[64]

A set of drawings showing the destructive results of the fire were published by William Crotch. Within a couple of days the Dean and Chapter publicly thanked in the local paper all who had come to help and, as they had done after the 1669 fire, tried to ensure that such destruction would not happen again by buying a fire engine of their own, to be kept in the Lodge. The treasurer had been instructed to purchase one just a year earlier (a reiteration of an order of 1785), but had disastrously failed to do so. Dean Jackson gave a personal gift of £1,500 to enable water to be brought from the city water works into Peckwater Quad and the canonry gardens on the north side of the Great Quadrangle. He also suggested that gates should connect all the gardens so that fire engines could pass freely around the buildings.[65] Edmund New's early twentieth-century sketch of Christ Church suggests this work was carried out.

By the beginning of the twentieth century the stonework on the St Aldate's frontage was beginning to show the effects of time, weather and pollution. W. D. Caröe was commissioned to take on this work, which of

William Douglas Caröe (1857–1938) was a Liverpool-born architect of Danish descent. He graduated in mathematics from Trinity College, Cambridge, and was immediately articled to a local architect. After assisting John Pearson with the design of Truro Cathedral, his own practice grew, and he was appointed in 1885 as architect to the Ecclesiastical Commissioners and to the Charity Commission. Caröe worked all over the country and beyond, but is best known at Christ Church for his restoration work on Tom Tower and the west front between 1908 and 1910, for his extension to the kitchen and for the construction of the 'rabbit-hole' stair between the Common Room and Hall.

Other colleges were also undertaking major repairs at this time: between 1902 and 1906, for example, Hawksmoor's towers at All Souls were practically rebuilt.

ODNB

Published in 1809, Six Etchings by William Crotch from Sketches by Mr O'Neill *showed the total destruction of the interior of the south-west corner of the Great Quadrangle by the fire of that year.*

course included the structure of the south-west canonry. But little was done on the interior, except for minor redecoration and minimal modernisation, for another century.[66] In 2006, however, when Canon Oliver O'Donovan, regius professor of moral and pastoral theology, left Oxford for Edinburgh, it was noted at a Governing Body meeting that the canonry had been neglected completely for twenty-seven years, while all the other canonries had benefited from recent refurbishments.[67] Considerable debate took place over costs and how to reduce them, and over the possible need for a conservation architect and archaeologist, given the premises' Grade 1 listing, but time was of the essence; a new canon professor, who would require the residence, was to be appointed within the year. The architects Ridge and Partners, of Woodstock, were called in to prepare plans and to oversee the

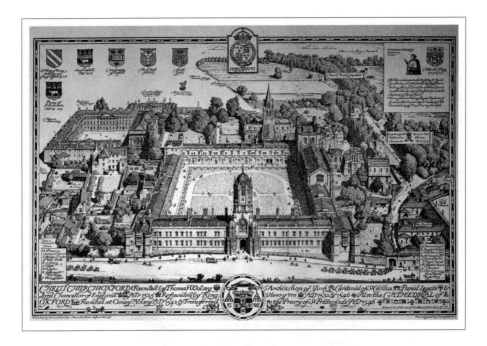

Christ Church, c.1915, drawn by Edmund Hort New. New's drawings,
engraved by Emery Walker, were known as the 'New Loggan Prints' as
they were drawn in the same style as David Loggan's mid-seventeenth
century illustrations, using a bird's-eye view and including many
small details of Oxford and college life. New worked with William
Morris for the Kelmscott Press and taught T. E. Lawrence to draw.

work, which was to include complete redecoration, soundproofing, a considerably upgraded kitchen and central heating. An agreement with Feltham Construction was signed, and work began on 11 June 2007 to be ready for the arrival of the new regius professor just four months later.[68]

The east-side lodgings

On the east side three similar residences occupied the whole length of the quad, stretching across the front of the partially demolished priory church. When Dr London wrote his letter to Larke, in 1526, the demolition of the first bays of the nave had already taken place and the new buildings were well under way, with the walls complete on the inside of the quad and the beginnings of the planned cloister evident.[69]

Furthest north on this side is the deanery, which, according to the map of Oxford drawn by the professional surveyor and map-maker Ralph Agas in 1578, terminated just before the chapel site. The lodgings probably became the deanery very soon after the foundation of Christ Church or just a few years later, when the theologian Peter Martyr was moved, to ensure his safety from Oxford's mob, into the Priory House in the early 1550s.[70] Thomas Thornton, writing around 1617, described the first occupants of the east-side residences: Canon Thomas Day chose those in front of the cathedral, and William Haines chose the lodgings next to the deanery, the implication being that the dean lived at the northern end from earliest times.[71]

It has been mooted that the east side of the Great Quadrangle was not used as the deanery and two canonries until into the seventeenth century. Rather, so the suggestion goes, the whole of the east side could have been taken up with accommodation for royal visitors, with a long gallery running its complete length, culminating in an elevated walkway, or bridge, from the first floor to the ante-hall. This is very unlikely and seems only to have been proposed as Elizabeth I used a temporary bridge of this kind from the lodgings at the south end (from the now blocked but still visible doorway) to the Hall.[72]

There has been much debate about where Wolsey's buildings on both east and west faces were left unfinished. The west-side conundrum was solved during work in 1896, but the extent of the deanery still has to be solved. Agas's map, although perhaps not entirely accurate, shows both west and east sides of the quadrangle finished up to the foundations of the barely begun Wolseian chapel. The end wall of the deanery, however, looks a bit more finished, with a wall taller than the others, and it seems feasible that the only portion of the deanery added when John Fell completed the building of the Great Quadrangle in the early 1660s was the bay containing today's study – with its elegant garden window and the upstairs parlour or drawing room. A small room was added over the passage to Peckwater to form, eventually, the first floor of the Fell Tower.

In 1621 Dean Goodwin's will revealed that the deanery consisted of twelve rooms: a hall, great parlour, little parlour, an 'entree' and larder, the

A stereoscopic image of the Killcanon passage through from the Great Quadrangle to Peckwater, without Fell Tower. The photograph was probably taken around 1870, as the tower was added to the deanery in the 1870s. The statue seen here was replaced by another of Fell on the Great Quad side and one of Dean Liddell on the north side. The original was moved to the grounds of Nuneham House, a few miles outside Oxford.

menservants' chamber, the old chamber, middle chamber, maids' chamber, new chamber, great chamber, Mr Edmond's chamber (perhaps for the dean's manservant) and kitchen. Outside were a woodshed, a capon house and a stable.[73]

As with the canonries, little is known about work on the deanery. Only when work was paid for by the Chapter or, later, the Governing Body is there any consistent record. Francis Atterbury, Christ Church's abominable early eighteenth-century dean, continued to annoy the Chapter even as he left in 1713, taking with him the locks to his residence, which had been paid for from the corporate purse. According to Canon Stratford, small tasks in the lodgings for which the dean had been responsible from his own pocket had been skimped: new window seats installed by Atterbury had been left completely unpainted where there were to be cushions. Stratford scornfully remarked that he must have saved 'all of five farthings'.[74]

A little later, in 1729, the Chapter, now more content with the Crown's choice of dean (then William Bradshaw), was happy to meet the cost of repairing the wainscot of the dining room's bow window. In 1732 John Conybeare, appointed to the deanery at Christmas that year and evidently concerned that the New Library would be an intrusion, requested that a wall be built to separate his garden from the building site. The lodgings were also given new glazing in the parlour, and the whole house a fresh coat of whitewash.[75] The Chapter minutes record a constant stream of minor but essential jobs: roof repairs, glazing, new doors and locks.[76]

In June 1783 £300 was allocated to the dean for pulling down the 'offices' in the deanery garden and rebuilding them in a more commodious place and manner. The old ones had been demolished in 1717 at the beginning of the Library construction, but, in spite of a Chapter decree requiring that replacements be erected at once, it appears that the dean had been using facilities in the old Canterbury College building at the bottom of his garden. But these too had to go to make way for the final stage of the sumptuous new quadrangle. It is possible, too, that the exceptionally hot summer months that year – caused by the eruption of Laki in Iceland – had made the need for new privies even more pressing.[77]

As far back as 1744 Mr Green the plumber had been commissioned to organise a water supply to Mercury and to the deanery – the city's pipes from the Hinksey conduit were in need of repair – and he was paid £6 for creating a supply to the Bell Yard.[78] In 1829 notice was given to the directors of the city water works that the Dean and Chapter had had enough: the agreement for the supply of water to the Great Quadrangle was to be ended at the following Lady Day, and they wished to treat for new terms.[79] Evidently the Chapter met with no satisfaction and went ahead alone.[80] In 1831 the college plumber was ordered to bring river water to the kitchen, the Priory House and the lodgings on the east side of the Great Quadrangle. However, the polluted state of the Thames and the Cherwell at the time – soon to be identified by Henry Acland (Dr Lee's Reader in Anatomy) as the principal culprit in the outbreaks of cholera that swept through Oxford – makes this seem a rather bizarre idea. It may, of course, have been a safety measure born of the devastating fire in the south-west lodgings in 1809. Certainly later the same year another fire engine was purchased to be kept in the Lodge.[81]

When Henry Liddell arrived in the deanery in 1855, he took the opportunity to alter the accommodation to his own taste. It was he who panelled the drawing room and hall and opened out the long gallery to make an additional reception room. His most famous addition to the deanery, however, was the 'lexicon staircase', paid for from the profits from the Greek dictionary he compiled with Robert Scott.[82]

While Liddell was busy on the rest of the Great Quadrangle during the 1870s, he commissioned George Frederick Bodley to build the Fell Tower in the north-east corner of the quadrangle. Possibly planned two centuries earlier – but not executed – by John Fell to provide the base for astronomical observations that he had originally wanted in Tom Tower but which Wren had scuppered (see below), the tower was embellished on the Tom Quad side with a statue of Dean Liddell, paid for by the dean's indefatigable right-hand man Thomas Vere Bayne and the judge and MP Sir John Mowbray. On the other, the Killcanon face, is a representation of John Fell, erected in 1877 at Liddell's expense.[83]

Throughout the twentieth century, and into the twenty-first, alterations and repairs have taken place, often coinciding with the arrival of new deans or to adapt to changing circumstances. New services were installed, beginning with electric lighting in 1901 at the same time as it was going into most residences and student rooms, and then, at the recommendation of Dean Lowe's doctors, engineers Handisyde and Weatherfoil replaced malfunctioning radiators and installed a new boiler in 1952.[84] The garden frontage was restored in 1930, and then again in 2011. Soft furnishings – carpets, curtains, linoleum – were also replaced in 1930, and there was some building work in the Fell Tower.[85] After approval from the city and county authorities, on the condition that it was invisible from anywhere other than the deanery garden, an office was built at the north end of the deanery in 1970; in 1980 the whole residence was replumbed, rewired and redecorated, and its kitchen reorganised; and in the mid-1980s the north and south chimney stacks, shown to be in a perilous state during the decennial survey, were taken down and rebuilt.[86] Most recently, modern accoutrements such as an en suite bathroom have been added.

Liddell and Scott's dictionary, still a standard reference work, was published in 1843, before Henry Liddell became dean. Robert Scott was an exact contemporary of Liddell as a Student at Christ Church, matriculating in 1830. The staircase was part of wider 'improvements' to the deanery, and was installed in 1856. The interior alterations were carried out by Joshua Robinson Symm, and the woodwork installed by Baker's, of Lambeth.

Probably the least altered of all the lodgings, and certainly of those on the east side of the Great Quadrangle, is the central residence. Traditionally occupied by the canon of the fourth stall, it was considered to the best residence after the deanery. Certainly being next to the dean would have come with a prestige all its own, but the lodgings would also have been warm and quiet. Its garden may have been a little dark, on the north side of the cathedral, but a raised walkway (or perhaps a bowling alley) would have been lit by the morning sun at least.[87]

The last resident of this lodging was Claude Jenkins, regius professor of ecclesiastical history and librarian of Lambeth Palace. Jenkins was an eccentric, not given to washing (his bath is said to have been used to store his files on the *Church Quarterly Review*, of which he was the editor) or to disposing of anything.[88] The residence was in desperate need of attention by the mid-1950s, when it was found to be riddled with dry rot (it had been bad enough in 1933, when Canon Kirk refused to take up residence there).[89] Not long after Jenkins died in 1959, the Chapter and the Governing Body came to an informal agreement: the choir school needed to expand into 1 Brewer Street, lately used for student accommodation, so it was decided that the Chapter would take over the Brewer Street property for the school and the college would acquire the canonry as graduate accommodation. In the early 1970s the wish for new accommodation for the Law Library prompted a more formal arrangement. Discussions were held, and the Accommodation and Estates Committees came up with a number of proposals:

1. That Tom 9 (Canon Jenkins's lodgings) be converted into offices, the

The hallway of Canon Jenkins's lodgings (now Tom 9). The state of this residence was instrumental in the reorganisation of the canons' residences in the 1930s and 1970s.

Law Library be moved into the Treasury and Steward's offices under the Hall, and Canon Demant's house on the north side of Tom Quad be divided into two to create an additional canonry;

2. That the Law Library and the offices would move into Canon Demant's house, leaving Tom 9 and 8 St Aldate's as canonries;

3. That just the offices would move to Canon Demant's house, with the Law Library moving into the old offices, and Tom 9 and 8 St Aldate's retained for the canons; or

4. That the offices would go into Tom 9, and the Law Library into the east end of Canon Demant's house, with the west end of the residence and 8 St Aldate's as canons' lodgings.

In the end, it was decided that reconverting Tom 9 back into a canonry would be far too expensive, so option 1 was selected and permission sought from the Visitor for the permanent alienation of Canon Jenkins's lodgings from the Chapter.[90] The Steward's Office, occupying the ground floor, almost doubled its floor area (from 650 square feet to 1,170), a huge improvement on its rather cramped corner taken out of the Treasury when the office was created in 1867. The Treasury, upstairs, lost 90 square feet.[91] The conversion of Tom 9, which still reveals its domestic origins, was done by the builders Symm.[92]

Wolsey had demolished the first three bays of the priory church's nave when he began the construction of his college, and the southernmost residence on the east side stood across the remnant of the nave with a narrow passageway between the lodgings and the cathedral. Fifty years after the closing of the cathedral's west end someone brought up the inconvenience of the single small entrance through the cloister, and proposals were made in 1617 to create a 'new way to the church'. The 'lodging that now standeth desolate' in front of the cathedral was the subject of a Chapter meeting on 31 July that year.[93] If the kitchen in the residence of the regius professor of divinity, John Prideaux, were demolished, a doorway more fitting for the university 'coming to and going from sermons' and solving the problem of 'The une[v]eness of the same way for carrying of Coarses, Etc.' could be created.[94] The minutes of the meeting are delightful, being an extremely rare, if not unique, account of the persuasive arguments of the sub-dean, Leonard Hutten.

Hutten presented the plans. Canon Thomas Thornton argued that they would deprive the lodging of its kitchen. Hutten countered that the Chapter would incorporate Dr Prideaux's kitchen into Thornton's lodging and build Prideaux a new one elsewhere. All well and good, said Thornton, acknowledging that the first part was feasible, but where would Prideaux's new kitchen be built? Hutten 'took him by the hand and lead [sic] him to the place, and showed him ad oculum wher both he should be provided and wher the dore should be for the ease of Dr Howson and there side of the colledge'. Thornton agreed to the work being done; his brother Richard

The building firm Symm & Company has been active in Oxford since 1815, working on an extraordinary number of University and college buildings. It is, perhaps, the company on which Thomas Hardy based Jude the Obscure's employers. Joshua Robinson Symm first worked at Christ Church in the 1860s with the architect T. N. Deane, on the construction of Meadow Buildings. The company was the principal contractor for the restoration of the cathedral between 1870 and 1877, and then for alterations to Tom Quad. Both the Wolsey Tower and the Fell Tower were constructed by Symm.

In 1881 the company was responsible for the new drainage system; in 1893 it built the new choir school; and in the early years of the twentieth century it undertook the restoration of crumbling stonework from Tom Tower and the St Aldate's front to Peckwater Quad. Further external repairs and refurbishments were done across college from 1960 into the 1980s, including repairs, both major and minor, to the cathedral spire and to the Wolsey Tower.

Law (1998)

had earlier described the residence as spoilt, both inside and out, so perhaps Thomas saw the chance of a more general refurbishment.[95] But perhaps Prideaux objected to the loss of *his* kitchen, in spite of the promises to make improvements, for the new entrance to the cathedral, in just the same place, was delayed for another 250 years.

Only the usual repairs and renovations took place between 1617 and the mid-nineteenth century; it was not until Dean Liddell commissioned George Gilbert Scott to restore the cathedral that anything significant happened to this canonry. Perhaps the most important part of Scott's work was the connection of the cathedral to Tom Quad by its extraordinary 'tunnel'.[96] From 1525, as we have seen, the only public entrance into the cathedral had been the south door in the cloister. It was evident that the £12,000 that Scott had estimated for the full renewal of the west end was never going to be forthcoming, and Scott realised that a complete reconstruction, although wonderful for the cathedral, would be far less so for the college. A compromise solution was reached, and Scott constructed a new bay between the existing west end and the lodgings of the regius professor of divinity in a very plain Romanesque style to echo (but not copy) the original Norman design, and then broke through to the quad.[97] Lecture rooms and senior members' offices were created in the detached portion near the Hall archway (which became known as Great Quad or Tom 8), with a Jacobean fireplace, purchased by Robert Faussett, the Treasurer, from Grimbly and Hughes, a high-class grocer's shop on Cornmarket, introduced into one.[98]

The west-side lodgings

In the sixteenth century the residence on the north side of the main gate was considered the second-best, but its history as a canonry is barely documented and it was almost forgotten until the very recent alterations to the Porter's Lodge in 2014, when the original grandeur was partly revealed. Heavy structural posts, moulded ceiling beams and Tudor fireplaces with four-centred arches show the quality of Wolsey's building.[99] The canonry's extent is shown on William Williams's 1730s plan of Christ Church,[100] although it had already ceased to be used as a single residence by then. Perhaps it fell out of use soon after the construction of the north-side lodgings in the 1660s. Throughout much of its history staircase 5 had only two rooms and staircase 6 no more than four, so these were either fairly substantial sets or the staircases were used for other purposes too.

A porter's lodge definitely existed in 1727, when a Robert Wilkins was paid for work there. It was whitewashed in 1745 and was large enough to house the new fire engine, 'with proper pipes and hoses', purchased in 1831. In 1932 a new porter's lodge was built at Tom Gate, but this was little more than a larger version of the present custodians' kiosk within the gateway, not a more substantial reconfiguration of the Tom 5 rooms.[101] The old kiosk was moved to Canterbury Gate, and the even smaller one that had been there was given to the choir school to use as a scorer's box on the cricket field.[102] The Head Porter had a 'house' on the south side of the gate.[103]

In 1972 the Governing Body decided that improvements to the lodge were long overdue. The architects Bosanquet and Perryman drew up sketch plans to convert Tom 5 into a bedroom, and sorting and collection rooms for mail. Bathroom and kitchen facilities were to be improved and the 1930s kiosk replaced with something small again. The architects reckoned a cost of £8,000. A year later, in November 1973, when the costs had risen to between £10,000 and £20,000, the Governing Body referred the plans back for more detailed drawings. The scheme was still being mulled over in 1975, when the decision was made just to provide a bedroom (Tom 5:1) and then give the rest a quick lick of paint.[104]

By 1983, however, colleges were becoming much more attuned to the needs and expectations of visitors. Guests arriving at Tom Gate had to queue, in the perishing wind which always seems to howl through, regardless of the temperature beyond the tower, to make their enquiries through a small window in the wooden box. Two men were now on permanent duty there, and a proper walk-in lodge was considered essential. A budget of £20,000 was set aside, but the Governing Body found, to their dismay, that the lowest tender for the work was £45,527. There was no option; if Christ Church was not to look too much like the poor relation to other colleges, something had to be done, and most of Bosanquet and Perryman's ideas from 1972 were implemented. The work duly won an Oxford Preservation Trust award.[105]

In the early years of the twenty-first century, however, it was evident that it was time for a complete rethink. The vacation conference business and the expectations of students now paying considerable sums to come to college have prompted many colleges to redesign their lodges to offer a more stylish and professional entrance. Christ Church followed suit, taking advantage of the redesign to make the lodge more accessible. The entrance created in the 1980s, up a steep flight of stairs under the tower, is narrow and impossible for those using a wheelchair. After discussions with the City Conservation Officer and with English Heritage, and the granting of Listed Buildings approval, Knowles & Co. began work in 2014 to extend the lodge over the whole of the ground floor of Tom 5, to the designs of Robert Montgomery Associates. Tudor features that had been covered were revealed and the space opened out to provide a much grander reception area, with pigeon-holes for student post, a mail room, a luggage room and an office for the Head Porter, as well as improved kitchen and toilet facilities. The steep staircase under the tower was given a glass door. The Tom 5 entrance was retained and a new one added from the Tom 6 staircase, with ramps for easy access. While the work was under way, the porters decamped to a large Portakabin just inside the quad which was clothed with a *trompe-l'oeil* representation of the cloister arches and windows.[106]

The rooms of the rest

The main residences that occupied much of the Great Quadrangle were for just the privileged few. In one or two staircases of the main quad and, presumably, in buildings yet to be constructed Wolsey intended to house his hundred students. Where many of these rooms were to be requires speculation. Peckwater Inn, used by Wolsey to house his builders, must have been a potential site. Perhaps he had Canterbury College, too, in mind, even though it was attached to a rich and flourishing priory, technically *not* available for dissolution. But many of St Frideswide's buildings were still to be demolished: the cloister, Chapter House, prior's lodging, refectory, the courtyard known as Chaplains' Quad from the earliest days of Christ Church and, of course, the priory church itself. The grand staircase tower up to Hall has remarkably shallow foundations on its east side, which has prompted the idea that a residential block was to be built alongside it, buttressing the tower as well as having a practical use.

The Cardinal College statutes stipulated that rooms were to be shared by two men: one senior and a junior, who had the use of a roll-out truckle bed. Slowly the monastic dormitory tradition was being eroded by a growing desire for privacy. It was not long before room-sharing was abandoned altogether at Christ Church, probably when the Peckwater buildings were improved at the end of the sixteenth century and beginning of the seventeenth.[107] Other rooms were set aside for the barber, the treasury and the estates clerk, and one for making candles.[108] Also important was to be the sacristy, where all items relating to the chapel were kept: its plate, vestments and books.

Because of the proposed cloister, rooms at Cardinal College could be bigger than those in any other college. Windows were bigger and glazed, something that was not inevitable elsewhere. The new fashion of panelling, in part to keep out the draughts, was probably adopted at Cardinal College right from the start.[109] It was certainly in place in some rooms before the sixteenth century was out.[110] In the front range, fireplaces were positioned on the inside walls to allow the chimneys to be partially concealed by the crenellations and to allow for large impressive windows facing the street.[111]

The gate

An imposing entrance was crucial. The main gateway on St Aldate's stood as high as the roof of the lodgings either side by the time of Dr London's 1526 letter; perhaps its final appearance would have been a stone version of the great west gate at Hampton Court, a larger version of the gate towers built at many other colleges, from New College in the fourteenth century to Wadham College in the seventeenth. David Loggan's mid-seventeenth-century engraving certainly shows something that may be the lower portion of an oriel window. By the time of Wolsey's fall the gateway was two storeys high, with flanking turrets decorated with Wolsey's arms and other heraldic emblems. The entrance was closed with immense oak doors, the northerly one punctured by a wicket gate.[112] The keys for this were held only by the porter and the dean.

The decorative treatment of the front matches that in other up-to-date royal works, such as the Henry VII Chapel at Westminster Abbey, and the gate-tower shows no lack of ambition in its size and massiveness. Cardinal College was making a very definite statement about Wolsey and his omnipresence.[113]

The chapel

Wolsey's new chapel, a replacement for the priory church, was to be immense, occupying the whole of the north side of the Great Quadrangle stretching from St Aldate's in the west possibly as far as the back of the east range, which would have made it approximately 300 feet long. The footings suggest that it would have been 33 feet wide, marginally narrower than that of King's College, Cambridge, but a few feet longer. In 1526, according to Dr

*An undergraduate room in 1906 (Tom 2:3). Before the changes
to the constitution in 1867, this room would undoubtedly have
been for the use of a nobleman or gentleman commoner.*

London, the foundations were in place and the first decorative layer of stone-work evident, later sketched by the seventeenth-century polymath John Aubrey. Massive footing-walls – 8 feet thick and 5 feet deep – interpreted as the foundations of the great west end, were uncovered in archaeological excavations in 1962, and a pillar base or turret foundation was found at the east end during the digs of 2005–7.[114]

Work on the chapel roof was continuing apace, off-site at Sonning under the watchful eye of Humphrey Coke, but little else was happening on that side of the quadrangle.[115] There may have been plans for a discrete chapel or a vestry at the east end or even a special place for the shrine of St Frideswide, once the priory church had been demolished – the strange kink on Agas's engraving suggests that the later passage wiggled its way around

*A reconstruction of the west gate of Hampton Court before its
height was reduced by two storeys in the eighteenth century.*

some heavy-duty footings. It is easy to forget that, at the time of the building
of Cardinal College, England – and Wolsey – were still Catholic.

There has been considerable debate over the west front and whether a
turret matching that on the south corner of the frontage was planned for the
north end. If this was part of the plan, then why was it not begun at the same
time? Was something different planned for this corner? Arguments have
raged over the possibility that Wolsey might have chosen something completely asymmetrical such as a low ante-chapel, in complete contradiction
of the usual Oxford practice. Some have proposed that the west front would
have been balanced and the chapel extended further east to give Wolsey the
length he wanted (to be bigger than the chapel of King's College) and to
allow a 'proper' east end with a grand window.[116] A matching tower would
have created an imposing narthex or ante-chapel. However, if this had been

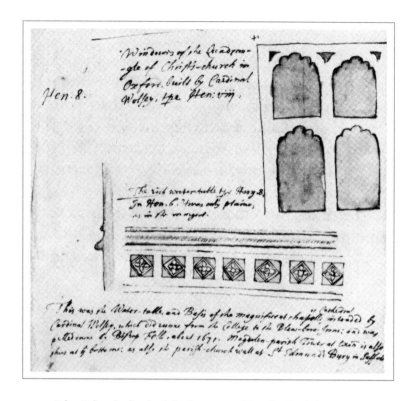

John Aubrey's sketch of the footings and first levels of the chapel.

the plan, how would access to the more northerly part of the college site have been arranged?

There has also been much discussion over Wolsey's intentions towards the priory church. Did he intend to demolish it completely or not? There is evidence to suggest that work may have been done, particularly to the chancel roof, early in the sixteenth century, when payments were made for the 'making, framing, and kerving of the new vault of the roof of the quere'.[117] It is hard, though, to justify the evident plans for an immense chapel if the priory church were to be retained (unless a small portion was to be kept as a royal or private chapel), but it is quite easy to argue that these payments were actually made to the craftsmen working on the roof of the new chapel. Even though the priory church was still in full use and, by all accounts, had high-quality services (the music of which was led by the

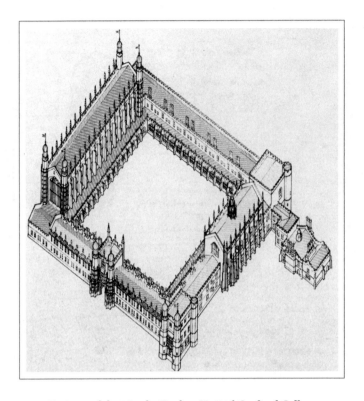

Conjectural drawing by Daphne Hart of Cardinal College.

incomparable John Taverner from the middle of 1526), at least three bays of the nave, and possibly more, were demolished to allow the construction of the east side of the quad, and scaffolding was purchased to take down the spire.[118] Recent archaeology has shown the west end of the priory church extended to about halfway across the present terrace. Vestments and chapel books, including missals, processionals, hymnals and so on, were brought to Cardinal College in October and December 1525 and June 1526, and Robert Amadas, the royal goldsmith, supplied gilt candlesticks, censers, chalices and a pyx.[119]

The seventeenth century saw what little there was of the planned chapel finally and ignominiously removed: in the 1640s, when Dean Samuel Fell first thought about finishing off the north side of the quadrangle; then during the Civil War, when most of the stashed building materials were commandeered for the city's defences; and finally in the early 1660s, when John Fell picked up where his father had left off, not least to fulfil his promise to his friend Richard Allestree to provide him with decent new lodgings.

The belfry

Without the church spire, the bells would have needed to be rehoused. If Wolsey intended the tower over the Hall stairs to be a belfry, a *pro tem* solution was necessary, and excavations in 1871 revealed the possibility of a bell-tower in the old monastery cloister.[120] Temporary or not, this would have been a large wooden structure, with foundations of rough mortar and rubble masonry – which varied in depth depending on the solidity of the gravel bed beneath – intended to take considerable weight. The stone base measured 42½ feet across to the ends of its buttresses. Its design is uncertain, but the engraving of King's College, Cambridge, by David Loggan shows a structure that Wolsey may well have intended to mirror.[121]

Surely the remainder of the priory's buildings – not just the church – were destined for destruction too. After all, almost immediately after taking control of the site, Wolsey's men had dismantled one side of the recently refurbished cloister to make way for the staircase up to Hall.

The Hall

The two greatest completed structures of Cardinal College were the dining hall and the kitchen. Only eighteen months after construction began in 1525, the dining-hall foundations were already around 6 feet above

---

The stone foundations of the possible bell-tower were exposed in 1871, during Gilbert Scott's restoration of the cathedral and cloister. They were reburied in the 1980s, during further work on the Chapter House and the laying-out of the garden. It is possible that this temporary belfry was constructed to house the abbey's bells after the diocese of Oxford was moved from Oseney Abbey to Christ Church in 1546, until either a permanent belfry or the cathedral spire was made stable enough to take the large ring.

*Engraving by David Loggan of the bell-tower at King's College,
Cambridge (on the far left). This is the only indication of
what Wolsey's temporary tower may have been like.*

ground. Even allowing for the size of the college, with its hundred canons
or fellows, the Hall was huge, measuring 115 feet long by 40 feet wide, and
50 feet high.[122] It is an eight-bay building buttressed on both sides, grand
and well constructed – in 1720 William Townesend said that 'there never
was in England a better building for fineness and curiosity as well as for
strength and the goodness of the materials' – with fine ashlar blocks, even
in areas where the masonry would not be seen.[123] The windows are mainly
four-light and four-centred, but there is an oriel window with a fan vault
and pendants in the second bay on the south side and a slightly projecting
window in the west bay of the north face. The roof is a hammerbeam of
eight bays pairing with the window reveals, which rest on decorative stone
corbels.[124] The fire, around which students were allowed to gather on the

coldest nights, was centrally placed, and there was a louvre in the roof to filter out the smoke.[125]

The Perpendicular windows are immense, with stained glass that, like much of the panelling, was originally decorated with the arms and emblems of the founder and his monarch. Once again, Wolsey turned to the best in the business, James Nicholson. In 1529 Nicholson was paid £28 for forty-seven sets of Wolsey's arms and for 246 'bends or poses called *Dominus Mihi Adjutor*'. These showed the coat of arms, cardinal's hat, crosses from the archbishopric of York and his papal legacy, the pallium or cross-keys of York and other emblems of Wolsey's ranks and office, including the blue leopard heads and Tudor roses.[126] The west window, which holds the only remaining sixteenth-century glass, shows two rows of shields with the arms of Durham, York, Lincoln, Bath and Wells, and St Albans, as well as the royal arms and those of Clare.[127]

Just in case anyone was still in any doubt about the name and importance of the founder of the college, the central roof bosses show the arms of the see of Winchester encircled with the Order of the Garter; above the roof plate are the badges of Wolsey and a line of shields showing either T. E. (for 'Thomas Ebor.') or T. W. (for 'Thomas Winton.'). Further down, the wainscoting is embellished with the arms of the University, the arms of Wolsey (which became those of the college), a Tudor rose, the arms of Henry VIII, a portcullis, a fleur-de-lys, the arms of Oseney, the pastoral staves (or croziers) saltire and pillars saltire.[128]

The arrangement of the Hall was similar to that in other colleges: a high table on a dais for the most senior members, with the more junior men arranged below, according to status. The first major work in the Hall after its construction was prompted by over-enthusiastic choirboys. Assisting with the burning of the Christmas decorations on the central fire at Epiphany 1720, perhaps they threw on too much, or the fire became too big, but sparks from the fire caught in the dry and rotting lanthorn. Nothing happened immediately, but evidently the embers smouldered away for some hours before finally catching in the early hours of the morning. Wolsey's glorious creation caught fire, and it remains a mystery how the blaze was

James Nicholson was a master glazier originally from the Netherlands who, with colleagues such as Galyon Hone, was encouraged to come to England to work on the building projects of Henry VIII and Wolsey. These incomers fell foul of the Worshipful Company of Glaziers, who resented the foreigners with their new and exciting artistic narrative style. But they thrived under the patronage of wealthy, influential and powerful men. Nicholson had worked at Hampton Court and in the chapel at King's College, Cambridge, before coming to Oxford.

Fifty-two pieces of Nicholson's glass remain, most in the south bay and west windows of the Hall, and two in the Chapter House. *Dominus mihi adjutor* was Wolsey's motto.

http://vidimus.org/issues/issue-11/feature/

extinguished at such a great height. But quelled it was, and less of the roof was burned than might have been expected.[129] The louvre, however, collapsed. The master mason William Townesend, who was at a loose end during a lull when no funds were coming in for the new library, redirected his attentions to the replacement of the roof, which he thought was of a most curious design, and the building of proper fireplaces with chimneys.[130] Dendrochronological survey has shown that repairs were made to portions of the roof using timbers felled in the spring of 1716. These may well have been timbers prepared for use in the library, construction of which was just beginning, but diverted by Townesend for the emergency repairs. George I contributed £1,000 to the immense cost of replacing the damaged parts of the roof, matching the original but without its louvre. New stone paving and vaulting under the floor were intended to protect the Hall from any future disaster.[131] How much work was done at this time is not recorded, but a later eighteenth-century writer said that the 'new state and magnificence' of the hall were due to David Gregory, first canon and then dean. Gregory evidently liked to finish things off properly; it was he who ensured that the library's interior was completed in all its splendour, and he who was the main force behind the construction of the Anatomy School.[132] In the summer of 1740

Ingram's engraving of the Hall in the early nineteenth century.
The fire surrounds shown here were installed in 1805.

the Hall was completely reglazed and new glass installed in the windows along the passage between the ante-hall and the kitchen, which must have helped keep food warm on its way up to Hall.[133]

Changes were made everywhere during the nineteenth century, beginning with Wyatt's alterations to the entrance to the dining hall. At some point in the late eighteenth century, estimates had been obtained for wainscoting the east end and sides of the Hall with Ionic pilasters. If that was done, then by 1799 it had fallen out of favour, for Wyatt removed four Ionic columns with bases and capitals, with six pilasters and entablature, replacing them with the present doorway.[134] Just a year or so later he installed the doors at the head of the Hall stairs and at the top of the stairs leading to the kitchen. In 1805 the present fireplaces were installed, replacing those from 1720.[135]

There was further modernisation once Henry Liddell was firmly

Late eighteenth-century proposals for a reworking of the Hall
interior in a classical style, probably by James Wyatt.

established in the deanery. In 1856 warm-air heating was installed in the
Hall, followed by gas lighting in 1862.[136] New painted-glass windows by
Horwood Brothers, in a rather sickly shade of green, replaced the old glass
on the north side of the Hall in 1872, and new stained glass was installed in
the oriel window on the south side in 1878.[137]

By 1900 only the large west window and the 'noblemen's' south oriel
had any remaining sixteenth-century glass. The window at the south end of
the dais was given by Archdeacon Clerke in commemoration of the Prince
of Wales and the Crown Prince of Denmark, both undergraduates at Christ
Church; the one on the north end was presented by Edward Francis Sampson
(a Student of Christ Church since 1865), and the noblemen's oriel, on the
south side, was presented by Herbert Salwey (Student from 1860), all three
in the late nineteenth century. Shortly before his death, and just after the
renovation of the Hall in 1905, Thomas Vere Bayne suggested a scheme that
incorporated the shields of the deans, four to each window, in all the south
side windows east of the noblemen's oriel, offering to pay for the first two.[138]
In the event, only these two were done – one to either side of the entrance
and including the shields of the first twenty deans.

Candle and gas lighting, together with gas heating, caused their own
grubby problems over the years, so in 1905 all the wooden panels were renovated, at a cost of £528. The pinnacles on the Hall, erected in the 1880s

The firm of Horwood Brothers was founded by Edwin (1833/34–1892) and his younger brothers Harry (1838–1917) and Mark (1840–1904), who were born in Mells, Somerset. Their careers in glasswork probably began at the craft school run in their home village by the rector. By 1871 they had moved to Frome and established their own firm, employing four men and a boy. By the time of his death in 1892, Edwin was the only brother left working in the business. The firm was on occasion used by William Butterfield, but how it came to be commissioned at Christ Church is impossible to say. No business or family archive survives.

as part of G. F. Bodley's renovations in Tom Quad, were restored in 1936, but the first major work in Hall during the twentieth century was the construction of the new servery in 1949. The Steward had apparently wanted a 'mechanical escalator' from the kitchen to the Hall but could not find what he wanted in the country (buying from overseas was difficult in the years immediately after the Second World War) and so settled happily for a lift and a conveyor. On 9 January 1950 Dean Lowe opened the new servery; the editor of the Christ Church Annual Report said that the 'contrast of it with the medieval squalor and inconvenience of the old scullery, which few of us had ever ventured to enter, is quite extraordinary'.

The most recent changes to the Hall were begun in 1980, when the panels and heraldry were renovated, new doors were placed at the east end and the Horwood green glass was replaced by new designs executed by Patrick Reyntiens.[139] Reyntiens, a prominent stained-glass designer, is probably best known for his work for the new Coventry Cathedral in the late 1950s but has worked the length and breadth of England and Wales, and overseas, often in partnership with John Piper. John Mason, then Librarian and Curator of Common Room, whose brainchild the new windows were, had several examples of Reyntiens's work within easy reach, including the single window in the chapel at Ripon College, two windows at St Bartholomew's Church in Nettlebed and a series of five for the chapel of Nuffield College. These were all modern: some figurative, others abstract.

But at Christ Church the Governing Body wanted designs that would fit in the 1520s hall, complementing the windows that were to remain, including the Wolseian glass in the large west window, the oriel windows and the Victorian examples by Burlison and Grylls, installed by Bodley. It took eleven years for the Governing Body to decide to remove eleven windows, but, once agreed, Reyntiens came up with a scheme that combined Tudor strapwork with Baroque borders in gentle shades.[140]

The new windows feature portraits and the coats of arms of deans and famous old members of college. Each celebrates the two founders with a monogram and crown representing Henry VIII and a cardinal's hat for Wolsey. There was much correspondence between Reyntiens and members of the Governing Body, who worried excessively over the minute details of the heraldry and portraiture, even writing to the College of Arms to ensure that the depictions were accurate. Reyntiens was evidently irritated, but the final result was much appreciated: the dean wrote that the designer should be 'aware of the House's gratitude and admiration'. On the north side the men are divided into rough subject groups: clergymen, statesmen, medics, scientists and artists. On the south are the deans arranged chronologically, from Henry Aldrich (dean 1689–1710) to Cuthbert Simpson (dean 1959–69), portrayed by their coats of arms, and further portrait medallions illustrating other famous alumni such as the naturalist Joseph Banks, John Guise, who gave Christ Church his collection of Old Master paintings and drawings, and the poet W. H. Auden.

The fifth window on the south side celebrates Charles Dodgson's creation *Alice's Adventures in Wonderland*. The medallions show the 'real' Alice (Dodgson's muse, the daughter of Henry Liddell) and Dodgson himself. Around the edges are representations of Tenniel's characters from the Alice books.

In 2014 Humphrey Coke's roof, celebrated throughout history, was found not to be quite the absolute triumph its heralds had always proclaimed. Early one July morning, after a severe thunderstorm, the Hall staff discovered that one of the main purlins had sheared off, fortunately resting on the principal roof tie below rather than crashing straight to the floor.[141]

The consequent repair work on this purlin revealed that the junctions of the trusses and purlins across the entire roof were too perfunctory, and there was considerable evidence of Victorian repairs. A full examination of the roof ensued, and it turned out that Coke had miscalculated the pitch of the roof. Most hammerbeam roofs have a pitch of 45 degrees, but this is far shallower. As a consequence, the hammerbeam could rotate, allowing the lanterns to drop and pushing the walls outwards. The walls on the quad side, which has thinner buttresses, had deflected by 3½ inches, and those on the south side by 1½ inches. Perhaps Coke had tried to be too ambitious in his design, but nevertheless the roof has been there for half a millennium. While work was undertaken to repair the roof and to stabilise it for the future, the opportunity completely to clean and restore the timberwork was too good to miss. A birdcage scaffold was erected inside the Hall for the second time in forty years, and the work was undertaken by Cliveden Conservation after consultation with the local conservation officer and Historic England. A full archaeological investigation was made along with a hi-tech laser survey to make the college records as up-to-date as possible. Odd artefacts found among the timbers, such as a pair of ancient shoes, an eighteenth-century cartwheel penny and some musket balls (probably from the Civil War), were transferred to the archive to be replaced by a new time capsule containing articles that may look equally bizarre when the next repairs come to be done.[142]

Choir school and Common Room

The space underneath the Hall, which in similar establishments in earlier times would have been used as storage for provisions, later became the grammar school for Christ Church's choir boys in 1525. It was not until the nineteenth century that the cathedral school expanded to take boys other than those who sang the cathedral services, so for many years this space was used purely by the eight young choristers and their *informator*, who was charged with teaching them not just music but also all their grammar and other essentials. Graffiti scratched into the walls suggests that the boys were no different from any other schoolchildren.

*The Old Grammar School, drawn by John Buckler; it is now the
Law Library. The most easterly window is now blocked and is inside
the cellar extension created by Cecil Handisyde in 1949.*

The boys had the run of the place for nearly two centuries, but at least
two men – the Treasurer and Richard Busby, headmaster of Westminster
School – restricted their space considerably. After the 1720 fire in the Hall,
when the new stone flags and vault were installed, the treasurer eyed the
newly strengthened rooms as ideal for a secure vault, and a portion of the
space under the Hall was converted for the safe-keeping of Christ Church's
cash and treasures. Doors and windows were made secure, under the direction of the ubiquitous Townesend, and an iron chest procured.[143] The other
end of the ground floor under the Hall had been set aside in 1667, by the
gift of Richard Busby, to be the Senior Common Room. However convenient
the new vaulting was for a secure Treasury, it must have made the Common
Room an awkward place for social gathering. Certainly when William Corne
(Student 1793–1810) died, his coffin was squeezed 'between the pillars in
the middle of the room'.[144]

The schoolboys were gradually edged out – although reminiscences

*The old Treasury and Steward's Office under the Hall during their
conversion into the Law Library in 1976. Both Wolsey's masonry
and the new vaulting built after the 1720 fire are evident.*

from old boys suggest that at least a portion of the room under Hall was still used into the 1850s – until the Chapter built new accommodation for them just south of the lane to the Meadow.[145] Part of this survives in 'Mrs Potts's Cottage', now the Clerk of Works' offices, but most was demolished after the school had moved to Brewer Street in 1892 and when the land was reused for the Memorial Garden in 1920.[146]

The Treasury and the Steward's Office remained at the east end until 1976, when Tom 9, the central residence on the east side of Tom Quad, was converted into offices. In their place was created a new Law Library. The quantity surveyors were Biscoe-Taylor and the architects Bosanquet and Diplock, both firms that Christ Church used frequently during the 1970s.[147] Under the careful attention of Edward Burn, the law tutor who invigorated and modernised the study of the subject at Christ Church, the vaulted rooms were rapidly transformed into a modern facility. The work was not without controversy; the door from Tom Quad was moved slightly within its 'cloister'

> The first Law Library had been in Tom 4:1, a room that had been an under-
> graduate reading room from the mid-nineteenth century until its books
> were reincorporated into the main library in the 1960s.
>
> Many old members contributed both to the creation of the new library
> and to its refurbishment in 2004 to the designs of Luke Hughes. It was
> renamed the Edward Burn Law Library.
>
> Cartwright and Burn, in Butler (2006), 158

arch, a decision that met with disapproval for its alleged disturbance of the original appearance of the quad. A successful appeal against the planning decision allowed work to begin in 1975, and the Library was opened by Lord Justice Eric Sachs on 26 June 1976.[148] Slowly but surely, the needs of the college were overtaking the traditional capitular spaces.

The Students made further moves on the south side of the quad in the 1860s: the New Common Room, once the rooms of J. A. Stewart, had been acquired in 1860.[149] In the 1870s the inconvenient vaulting installed after the fire of 1720, which made the room look like a crypt, was removed and replaced with steel girders encased in oak, and the passageway was moved to its present location (between the Common Room and the Law Library), with the old passage from Tom Quad to School Yard converted into the but-ler's pantry. The little garden to the south was enclosed at the same time. A smoking room was added in 1890, after three years of furious discussion:[150] Charles Dodgson, the Curator at the time, was vehemently against smoking in the Common Room.[151] Further alterations were made under the super-vision of Caröe in 1909/10, when the 'rabbit-hole' staircase was created between the Common Room and the Hall, allowing the senior members to appear at High Table suddenly, in a delightfully Carrollian manner, for dinner.

The wonderfully named 'Domestic Comfort Committee' was established in 1982 to make the rooms more amenable, beginning with the premise that there was no comfortable sitting room. The committee decided that the Old

Common Room was the best place in which to establish one, and so drew up plans and visited possible furniture suppliers, including Charles Hammond of Sloane Street, Harrods, Geddes of Oxford and Wesley-Barrell in Witney. Over the course of five years all three rooms in Tom Quad were refurbished and considerably tidied.[152]

The Hall stairs and ante-hall

Obviously the stairs connecting the Great Quadrangle to the Hall were important, and Wolsey had been anxious to complete their construction, paying overtime to ensure that the work was done even when he must have seen the writing on the wall. However, when he finally fell from favour, only the entrances and windows were complete; there was no internal structure or roof. How the staircase up to the Hall was to be arranged is impossible to say; according to Mavis Batey and Catherine Cole, the positions of the windows suggest a staircase up against the south wall, and smaller than the current one.[153] There was also, certainly in the early eighteenth century, a small stone spiral staircase, which now goes up to the Victorian belfry above the staircase tower but which then opened on to the hall staircase.[154] There is an obvious area of rebuilt wall in the corner of the first landing, but it is hard to believe that such a small and insignificant stair would have been Wolsey's original intention as the access to the Hall. Its existence does, however, lend some credence to the idea that the floor above the stairs was to be used for something that required only limited access. A belfry seems the obvious suggestion. Security would not have been great enough for an archive or treasury.[155]

Unfortunately there are no images of the staircase prior to Wyatt's Gothicisation of c.1800, except for Thomas Rowlandson's cartoon, but Williams's eighteenth-century plan shows the opening onto the spiral staircase with a few steps onto a landing, and two stairs rising from the ground floor towards the same landing as there are today. Perhaps the doorway was knocked through at a subsequent date, after Wolsey's fall, and before money was available to complete the staircase, or as a convenient entrance from the Library. Although traditionally the stair to a great hall was a single flight

– like the one at New College – it would appear that Cardinal College's stair always, or from a very early date, consisted of two.[156]

In 1559 Thomas Palmer, the auditor, left £20 towards the completion of a tower over either the great gate or the Hall stairs, provided that the work was begun within three years of his death. It was the Hall stairs that received attention. John Bereblock's engraving of the Great Quadrangle, drawn as part of a series to celebrate the visit of Elizabeth I to Oxford in 1566, is the earliest representation of Christ Church.[157] In spite of its inaccurate perspective, the engraving clearly shows the new tower, which also appears on Agas's map of 1578. Sampson Strong's portrait of Cardinal Wolsey from 1610 shows a battlemented tower considerably higher than the ante-hall. But this tower evidently did not last for long, as it does not appear on later drawings. Either that, or Bereblock's engraving is even less figurative than has previously been acknowledged.

The stairs and the tower remained unfinished until the 1630s. Dean Samuel Fell was a born administrator, with a particular talent for building projects.[158] At some time either during his predecessor Brian Duppa's time as dean (1628–38), while Fell was still a canon and the Lady Margaret professor, or soon after his own appointment as dean, he masterminded the construction of the fan vault over the stairs to the Hall by, according to Anthony Wood, an unidentified mason called Smith. No evidence survives in the archive for the creation of the vault: account books are missing for most of the 1630s, and so there has been much discussion about which talented Smith was commissioned for the work. One suggestion is that it was Robert Smith, who was a mason *privilegatus* of the University and had been commissioned to work at St John's College, possibly vaulting the passage between the Front and Canterbury quadrangles. He definitely laid marble paving at Queen's.[159] There may be a connection between Juxon's commissions as president of St John's and his bishopric of Hereford, where he may have been inspired by the beautiful octagonal chapter house supported by a single central column.[160] The similarities, says the architectural historian Mark Girouard, are tempting. And Robert Smith's partner, Hugh Davies, produced models for the Bodleian staircase. Another possibility is William

The Hall stairs, drawn by Augustus Charles Pugin and engraved by
Daniel Havell, soon after the alterations to the staircase by Wyatt.

Smith, Warden of the Masons' Company in London and neighbour of the
chief benefactor of the project, Paul Bayning.[161] Whoever it was, the staircase and its vault filled a space that Wolsey had left unfinished, in spite of
all his efforts. Described by a visitor in the 1730s as 'a very curious piece of
architecture being extremely large and only supported by one single pillar
which is not at all heavy and yet has the strength sufficient for its office',
the staircase was part of, depending on how one views it, an early Gothic
revival or late Gothic survival in Oxford and Cambridge where the style was
considered to be more in keeping with the medieval buildings of the colleges
and university than the emerging Baroque.[162]

 This 'curious piece of architecture' was not considered perfect, however,
so in the early years of the nineteenth century James Wyatt, who had turned
his hand from Classical to his preferred Gothic across the University, was

called in to make alterations to both the Hall and the staircase.[163] Wyatt may have been intending much more elaborate and dramatic changes, but ultimately his principal alteration was to move the lower flight of steps eastwards, reducing the size of the first landing considerably, so that the graceful pillar supporting the fan vault could be seen from top to bottom, emphasising its height and elegance. At the same time, the area at the foot of the stairs was reconfigured with new arches and doorways. One doorway to the cellar was blocked, only to be opened again in 2011 to allow for the construction of a lift up to the ante-hall, and another was vandalised in 1829 with the words 'No Peel', in a dramatic show of high political feeling.[164]

The ante-hall, with its buttery and cellars beneath, was part of Wolsey's scheme, providing a grand meeting place and central location for the payment of board and lodging bills, known as battels, at the buttery door.

The kitchen

From the ante-hall a covered stair led down to the kitchen. Aside from this short passage (or pentice), the kitchen was completely detached, as was customary, from the rest of the buildings. It was immense: a 40-foot cube with three great fireplaces and rooms off, housing bread ovens and other necessities. The building was constructed in fine ashlared stone with low battlemented gables. The roof has three bays with king-post trusses and is more elaborate, with curved braces and decorative spandrels, than such a practical room would suggest.[165]

Stone-built kitchens from the fourteenth century incorporated their hearths in the outer walls and supplied them with proper chimneys, but having fireplaces on three walls, rather than grouped together to keep the heat and smoke to one area, was quite rare. Hearths typically tended to be quite shallow, contained within the walls, or there were strong relieving arches built over the fireplace.[166] Both techniques seem to have been used at Cardinal College. In spite of the provision of three fireplaces in the walls, there was still a central hearth in the classic medieval style; the surviving gridiron is a rare large example, which may originally have had wheels so that it could be rolled over hot embers. This was a fast and easy way to cook large joints.[167] An account of a visit to Christ Church in 1772 commented that the gridiron, 'tho made in the time of Henry the 8th does not seem much the worse for the wearing'.[168] The main spit-range in the kitchen could roast forty legs of mutton, or seventy chickens, at the same time. In addition to the three fireplaces there was a separate oven for bread and pastries. It was this latter oven that produced the meringues made famous in Dorothy Sayers's *Gaudy Night*.[169] Built to feed a large establishment, the kitchen was completed in time for Christmas dinner in 1526, with only the central ventilating louvre remaining to be finished.

A water supply was probably never a problem in Oxford, and Cardinal College was sited on the end of a gravel spit surrounded by river streams with a water table not far down. All the principal lodgings had wells and pumps from the earliest days. The kitchen was sluiced through regularly with clean water, and rainwater collected from all over the site was fed through a 'goodly vault' into a tank in the kitchen so large that a man had to climb right in to maintain it.[170] Somewhere there would have been a *gurgitum*, or sump, to take excess water and muck away.

In his letter of 1526 Dr London described the ancillary buildings that stretched towards the Meadow: 'larder houses, pastry houses, lodgings for common servants, slaughter and fish houses, with such other necessary buildings substantially and goodly done in such manner as no two of the best colleges in Oxford have rooms so goodly and convenient'. There is no sense at all that Wolsey was making do with the old monastic buildings. The kitchen and its subsidiary buildings show distinct parallels with those at Hampton Court, another Wolseian creation. There, where a community of perhaps a thousand people had to be fed on a daily basis, there were fifty-seven rooms or buildings associated with its kitchen.[171] Christ Church's kitchen was not so huge but still contained all the principal elements, including the bread oven in a separate room, offices, stores (probably with secure stores for spices or other expensive ingredients) and serving hatches close to the stairs to Hall, with sufficient space to allow the chef to survey the dishes before they were taken for consumption.

The kitchen is not mentioned very often in the college's expenses, which suggests that the building fulfilled its purpose very well for several centuries. In the eighteenth century it was described as a 'noble room' with 'a great many commons drest in it every day'.[172] Rudolph Ackermann's engraving from 1814 shows the room much as it was soon after completion in 1526. Basic maintenance throughout the seventeenth and eighteenth centuries included spicks for the kitchen and new spits for the fires, made by a John Showell, who also mended the locks to the pastry room and a cupboard, cut a new key for the kitchen garden, mended the pump irons and the pothooks and repaired a skimmer.[173] It took nine months for Showell's account, dated January 1678, to be settled.[174] A new grate was installed, together with stoves and a smoke jack, in 1716–17, and the kitchen coalhouse, evidently a target for pilfering, was moved to a more secure place.[175]

In 1739 the lanthorn was taken down for repair, and in 1740 the windows in the pentice were glazed, doubtless doing much to improve the warmth of dishes arriving in Hall.[176] Doors were placed at the top and bottom of these stairs in 1777. The first major modernisation seems to have been in 1778, when a new grate and stoves were installed by Thomas Browne of Woodstock. The chimney was to be altered using only Stourbridge brick – Stourbridge clay was particularly renowned for its fire-resistant properties – at the back of the grate.[177] Labouring in the kitchen was evidently uncomfortably hot, as the manciple recorded the expenditure of 16s. for ale for the workmen, and the costs generally appear to have made the treasurer a bit hot under the collar; he was given permission to dispose of old college plate to the value of £100 to fund the project.[178]

It was not until the early twentieth century that further major works were undertaken. After Caröe had designed the stone spiral staircase between the Senior Common Room and the Hall, he planned improvements and extensions to the kitchen. The Steward, Major Arthur Slessor, had brought the need to rebuild and extend the kitchen and scullery to the Governing Body during the summer of 1910, and a committee was established at the beginning of Michaelmas term.[179] Objections were raised by Dr Lee's Readers (the tutors in chemistry and physics), who used the laboratory – once the Anatomy School – next door; they were concerned that the

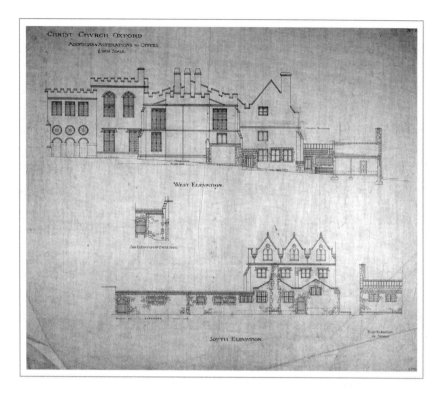

W. D. Caröe's elevations of the kitchen extension.

kitchen might begin to encroach on their space, so a plan was drawn up to build the extension south towards the Meadow, rather than westwards. The yard behind the kitchen was modernised, and space was provided for coal sheds, refrigerators, larders, ventilation and toilets.[180] Caröe's drawings were incredibly detailed, right down to the studding on the back door, but this was no mere tidying or dressing up. New modern structures, of steel and concrete, were designed by Homan and Rodgers. The total cost was £7,209 13s. 7d.[181]

After the Second World War, attention returned to catering. The Undercroft refectory was created, to be useful for club dinners and servants' events, and the new servery off the Hall made life much easier for both kitchen and Hall staff. A little later the kitchen, less glamorously, acquired a second-hand marine boiler, its predecessor having been condemned by

The baron of beef cooked to celebrate the end of meat rationing after the Second World War. This was one of the last occasions on which the Tudor fireplaces were used.

the insurance assessors in 1956.[182] It was not until 1962 that the kitchen's cooking equipment was upgraded. The Steward's recommendations included alterations to the large fireplaces, including the Tudor spits, so the dean and censors felt it was necessary to call in the college's 'authorities' on ancient monuments. Both J. N. L. Myres, the librarian, and E. G. W. Bill, the archivist, were duly consulted. Both expressed some dismay at the proposed modernisation but were overruled; the Governing Body decided that the recommendations 'were desirable and in the interest of the House'.[183] In the early 1970s another general refurbishment was undertaken, including yet another replacement of the boiler, a new cold store, new lavatories for kitchen staff and redecoration. The lifts from the kitchen, deemed to be completely insanitary by the health inspectors, with their rough brick walls, which were harbouring dirt and vermin, were also renovated.[184]

Externally, too, the kitchen was beginning to show its age. In 1981 the redundant chimney stacks on the west and south sides were removed for safety, with the west one, considered architecturally important, being rebuilt.[185] And in 1987 the east wall was completely refaced.[186]

In 1992, not long after the appointment of John Harris as Steward, £400,000 was allocated for a complete overhaul of the catering facilities.[187] The Hall, Hall servery, dishwashing area, pastry room, main kitchen, pot wash, vegetable preparation area, chilled and frozen food stores and dry stores were all to be modernised. It had been acknowledged for ages that the work was needed, but it had been resisted until new food legislation enforced it. The work was to be done in a crash programme over the long vacation, during which time the conferences were fed entirely from the servery and the McKenna Room. The new kitchen was opened formally by Her Majesty the Queen on 3 December 1992.

The arrival of a new chef, Chris Simms, in 2009 prompted a new round of renovations and renewals, including state-of-the-art equipment in the kitchen (soon to embrace induction cooking and *sous vide*), new serveries in the Hall, new changing facilities and freezer rooms in Caröe's ancillary buildings.[188] A kitchen that was celebrated in the eighteenth century remains equally star-spangled today.

* * * * *

As there is no surviving plan of Wolsey's college, it is impossible to know *exactly* what he intended, but, even so, much of the cardinal's scheme is apparent. None of Wolsey's major building projects in Hertfordshire and London was begun from scratch, so he must have seen Cardinal College as his great opportunity, perhaps the pinnacle of his creative career. But Wolsey's magnificent scheme was never completed. He threw money and men at it: in the spring of 1527 there were 122 freemasons, 25 hard hewers, 47 roughlayers, 32 carpenters, 4 slaters, 12 sawyers, 2 clerks, 3 purveyors and 228 labourers. The bill for labour was a high and significant part of the total costs: in the fortnight ending on 6 April 1527 over £140 was expended, of which only £26 was on materials.[189] Wolsey had never been troubled by budgetary constraints, but in the late 1520s mutterings against his extravagance grew louder. Thomas Cromwell advised him to slow down a little, but the appeal fell on deaf ears.

During 1528 large quantities of lead were purchased from Derbyshire, suggesting that roofs were being covered and the plumbing installed, including the pumps for the deanery and all the lodgings, and glaziers were busy on windows.[190] By the end of the year the ceiling in the Hall and its huge central louvre were being painted and gilded: £102 3s. 4d. was spent on 'workinge and kervynge the Halle Rouff of the sayde Colleage with catars spannderells orbes lyntells and other ornaments so Garnysshede by conuencion'.

As the decoration was added to the Hall, most of the east, west and south sides of the Great Quadrangle were completed. Such was Wolsey's attention to the sumptuousness of his college that he arranged for blue velvet wall hangings, counterpanes, and a bed and bolster from his own private household to be sent to the deanery.[191]

It is astonishing quite how late in the day Wolsey was still working on and negotiating for his college. In June 1529, just as Henry was beginning to turn against his friend and adviser, Wolsey asked, successfully, for the site of the priory of St Mary de Pré in St Albans, dissolved in 1528, to be added to Cardinal College, and he was still requiring royal servants to use all their diligence to ensure that the college was properly established. In September of that year Cardinal Lorenzo Campeggio issued a licence to allow Wolsey to take timber from Sonning manor, and a month later, even after the writ of praemunire had been issued against the Cardinal, accounts were prepared for stone, the carriage of gravel, the repair of the lime kilns, the transfer of lead from Poughley, the painting of the hall and the construction of the roof timbers of the almshouse. Wolsey was not giving in easily. But by December the king had declared his intention that Cardinal College was to be dissolved. In no time at all, inventories of fixtures and fittings were being drawn up, including twenty-two silk hangings purchased especially for the college, a bed that had originally been designed for the royal visit to Guisnes (the Field of the Cloth of Gold) and a counterpane of verdours (probably a tapestry showing lush green vegetation) for the dean. Throughout 1530 Wolsey appealed to the king and to his courtiers and officials, each letter phrased differently to appeal to each individual.[192]

But it was all to no avail. Cardinal College was dissolved, and its premature end meant that its successor, Christ Church, was left without elements, such as a library and a muniment room, that one would have expected from a benefactor whose commitment to education and whose talents for administration were so evident.[193] The residential sides of the great Gothic quadrangle – which measured 264 by 261 feet, the largest in Oxford – were all but finished up to the planned chapel.[194] However, only the foundations and the first row of decorative masonry of the chapel were visible. The cloister was barely begun: only the shafts to support the vault – paired and decorative in each corner – and springers, heavily restored by Dean Liddell over three centuries later, survive to suggest the intention. Tom Tower did not rise over the front gate until 1681. Of the monastic buildings other than the church, three-quarters of the old cloister, cluttered with the foundations for a bell-tower, the prior's house, which served briefly as the deanery, the old refectory and the chapter house were still standing.[195]

At the time of Wolsey's death in 1530 work was still continuing on his northern projects, but there is evidence that his skilled workers and labourers were going unpaid, in spite of a gift of £1,000 from the king, and he left considerable debts. In just the first two years expenditure on Cardinal College approached £9,000.[196] Unlike Corpus Christi, which was given a rubble finish, Wolsey's masons worked in the finest ashlar, even in places where the stonework would not be seen. Cromwell remarked to Wolsey in April 1528 that 'Every man thinks the like was never seen for largeness, beauty, sumptuous, curious and substantial building' and Dr London had commented that the work of the masons and carpenters was 'as clean wrought as ever we saw done in any place'.[197] The total cost of the construction is unknown, as some of the accounts no longer survive, but another £8,400 was spent between November 1528 and October 1529. Something in the region of £22,000 seems likely, and there was so much more still to be done.[198]

In all things Cardinal College was impressive. Dr London was in awe, even as early as December 1526:

> I think Almighty God is not more duly, more devoutly nor better served in any church in Christendom, both working day and holyday, and in

their learning they be the flower of my Lord's University, they be lights to all other places, and it cannot be but they do prosper in virtue where God is so truly served, and the gifts of the Holy Ghost among every one of them be so abundantly relucent. In the ordering of their lands, all other places may and do take example of them. If you were a continual dweller in Oxford, and did take a watchful regard unto that young college, but yesterday in manner begun, ye should not think but it were a very old foundation, established in everything as though it had been founded two hundred years past, only the buildings not yet finished sheweth it to be a new foundation.[199]

3

The almshouse: 'an original endowment close to our Gate'

The almshouse, now the lodgings of the Master of Pembroke College, across St Aldate's from Tom Gate, was also part of Wolsey's foundation. Established by the cardinal's statutes as a home for thirteen poor men and a female servant, the almshouse was not completed before his fall. The timber frame, presumably for the roof, was under construction at Kirtlington in the summer of 1529, but the slates did not go on until 1546. The core of the building is sixteenth-century, with two storeys and attics. Originally, there were two blocks: the main one on the street and a smaller one behind, to the west, but these were joined in the early nineteenth century. The details of the windows and doors are sixteenth-century Perpendicular, with four-centred lights and arches.[1]

Both Wolsey and Henry VIII took their charitable concerns seriously, and it seems that, while construction work may have stopped during the brief period of King Henry VIII's College (1530–46), there was never any intention of abandoning the idea of an almshouse. When Christ Church was founded, the number of almsmen to receive pensions was increased to twenty-four.

The residents seem largely to have administered themselves, but every now and again there were cases requiring discipline. In 1732 part of the almshouse was sublet as a brewhouse; the brewer was given six months to move out, but records suggest that he was still conducting his business there six years later.

The almshouse in 1819, before its renovation. Drawn by
John Buckler, and engraved by Joseph Skelton.

The almshouse, and the almsmen, seem always to have been something
of a thorn in the Chapter's side; so, late in the nineteenth century, a vigorous debate broke out over its future.[2] Pembroke College had long coveted the
property and had approached Christ Church, unsuccessfully, in the eighteenth century to acquire the site for a new chapel.[3] In 1831, by which time
the almshouse was in a state of severe dilapidation, Pembroke tried again
– this time to clear the unsightly building out of the way and, allegedly, to
open up Pembroke's east frontage. Pembroke's offer included the provision
of land, or a money grant, towards the building of a new almhouse, but
there were one or two voices among the Chapter suggesting that this was an
ideal opportunity to get rid altogether of the bedesmen, who were of 'little
use and no ornament'. The treasurer, Henry Woodstock, had all sorts of
ideas about the premises: one suggestion was that the schoolmaster and
choristers could move in. Alternatively, it could be fitted up for the chaplains,
if Fell's Buildings and Chaplains' Quad were ever demolished. He felt that the
new buildings erected in the place of Fell's and Chaplains' 'might be deemed
too good for the chaplains'.[4]

Instead, plans were developed to demolish the almshouse and to move

The quadrangle of the almshouse before its alterations in 1834.

the almsmen to new lodgings into a converted stable on the other side of the road.[5] In the end, legal advice scuppered the scheme; to lose the almsmen altogether would require an expensive Act of Parliament. It would be cheaper to renovate. So in 1834 the local architect and builder John Hudson was paid nearly £1,500 for rebuilding and extending the north front, installing new plumbing, repairing the roof and erecting new gables and chimneys. Fourteen kitchen ranges were fitted and new regulations put in place obliging the almsmen to take care of their improved residence. But the debate about the men's future was soon to begin again. The Cathedral Commission of 1852 aimed to revitalise cathedral life and included provisions to involve the bedesmen in the everyday running of their cathedrals. Most cathedrals found tasks for their almsmen, including cleaning, lighting and extinguishing candles, and acting as precinct constables or as doorkeepers, for example. But at Christ Church, as always, things were different. When the constitution was revised in 1867, the opportunity to sever the link between

*The almshouse during refurbishment. Health and
safety were evidently not an issue.*

cathedral and almshouse was taken. A petition to Chancery was filed, and
an order granted, with the rooms finally being vacated in 1876 and the men
paid off with an increased annual stipend.[6]

The building was immediately converted into a residence for the treasurer.[7] Faussett demonstrated his interest in antique furnishings, acquiring
a wall panel for the almshouse drawing room from a farmhouse in Chal-
grove. An ornamental chimney-piece, door-heads and an oak staircase were
retrieved from properties in Brewer Street, and the panelling in the attics
came from old houses on St Aldate's demolished to make way for the post
office. The sundial was from the garden of a demolished house in Swerford.

A few years later, in 1886, Pembroke College renewed its application
to buy the almshouse. A committee was established, chaired by the dean, to
discuss the pros and cons of the sale. It would be a neighbourly thing to sell
the property to Pembroke, whose site was rather confined with no obvious

site for extension, to say nothing of the fact that Christ Church's finances were in a rather dire state and the income received from the sale would be very useful. A valuation of £10,000 by the college surveyor prompted the Almshouse Committee to recommend sale to Pembroke College. But Thomas Vere Bayne, an ardent Wolseian, was vehemently against it and prepared a report for the Governing Body. Not only was the house 'coeval with the foundation' and mentioned in the Charter of Dotation, but much had been spent on it to put it into good repair for the almsmen, and then for its conversion into the treasurer's lodgings. Even if the property were too big for a single tutor or officer, the house could still be used for undergraduate accommodation, as lecture facilities or as a reading room. Bayne felt that members of the Governing Body were merely trustees and should not exercise their 'temporary power in reducing the original area of Ch.Ch. by parting with our earliest and closest possession ... we have no moral right to deprive our successors of a plot of ground and a building so advantageously situated ... it is lèse majesté against the House to part with an original endowment close to our Gate'.[8] It was another year before any decision was made. The Almshouse Committee, now renamed the Treasurer's Lodgings Committee, resolved that plans should be drawn up to convert the house either into two tutor's residences or one house with two or three lecture rooms.[9] A motion was put before the Governing Body on 8 February 1888 with an amendment offering the option to sell advantageously to Pembroke College. Bayne tried again to persuade the Governing Body not to sell, but he lost the fight and the Governing Body approved the sale on 22 February by fourteen votes to nine.[10]

4

A cautious start: Christ Church at the end of the sixteenth century

After Wolsey's fall in 1529, Cardinal College was refounded as King Henry VIII's College. The canons of this apparently interim institution had an income that was small in comparison with that of Cardinal College and of Christ Church, but still substantially larger, at over £700 per annum, than that of many of the other colleges. The college had retained all the land that had belonged to St Frideswide's and to the monasteries of Littlemore and Daventry. Even so, the canons must have been conscious that they had no resources to continue the great scheme for some time.[1]

Little was done to the buildings except essential finishing off, such as the installation of windows and roofing to make the surviving monastic buildings and the new structures suitable for habitation. The northern end of the west front, where it would have joined Wolsey's new chapel, was closed and a north-facing window installed.[2] A new window was installed on the north wall of the west face, and the masonry finished – Wolsey's proposed chapel was definitely not within the budget. In 1832, when alterations were being made on staircase 7, a cross-wall was revealed which included this mullioned window and a cornice running the depth of the building, all worn as they had been exposed to the weather until the 1660s.[3]

But the number of men at King Henry VIII's College was tiny compared with Wolsey's intended house. The few residents would have found no difficulty in accommodating themselves within Wolsey's completed works. But

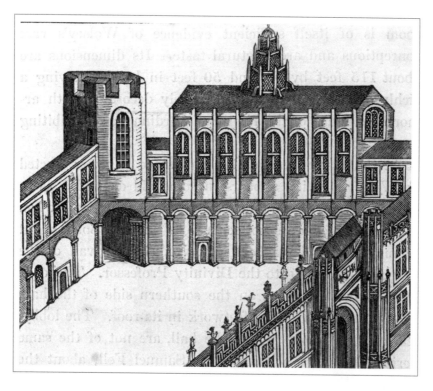

*Bereblock's drawing of Christ Church, one of a series made
for the visit of Elizabeth I to Oxford in 1566.*

in 1546, when Henry VIII created Christ Church – his own immense and
unique combined college and cathedral – the situation was very different.
The king died very soon after the foundation, leaving no statutes by which
to establish the new college-cum-cathedral. As a consequence, it was Wolsey's scheme that was re-adopted, although whether by accident or design
is hard to say. The buildings once again had to house a Student body of one
hundred and all the staff. The grand lodgings in the Great Quadrangle were
definitely not sufficient.

Curiously, the building site on the north side of the quad was not filled
in to create additional accommodation but was left empty, with just the
footings of Wolsey's chapel and the muddy remains of a cobbled street –
an extension of the present-day Alfred Street towards the medieval priory

*Tom Gate. New paving was laid in 1582 in a vain
attempt to keep the quadrangle free of mud.*

– used as a thoroughfare by the townspeople.[4] With the public now regularly visiting the newly designated cathedral, the Great Quadrant, as it is often called in early accounts and decrees, needed constant maintenance. A labourer to sweep the quad was employed on a permanent basis, and the porter kept a dog – the only one permitted in college – to keep swine and cattle out.[5] No one, of whatever standing, was allowed to keep a horse anywhere except on the Meadow.[6] But still the mud by the gate must have proved intolerable: 792 square yards of paving were laid by Thomas House before the great gate in 1582.[7]

The earliest map depiction of Christ Church is on Agas's panorama of the city of Oxford, produced in 1578. It shows the unfinished Great Quadrangle and, just in outline, Wolsey's planned chapel. The residences around the quad were now occupied by the dean and canons, taking the place of

Wolsey's senior officers. Palmer's tower stands over the Hall stairs, with an array of buildings to the south, including the kitchen with its tall louvre. The site of Canterbury College is marked by three structures and a long wall, and Peckwater Quad, still called an Inn, by three sides: north, west and south. The site is open and rather sparsely populated; Oxford was at its lowest ebb, but on the verge of renaissance.[8]

So where were the one hundred Students, the staff and the commoners – who started to arrive very soon after the foundation – to be housed? There was the small, medieval Chaplains' Quadrangle tucked in behind the kitchen and a few rooms in the Great Quadrangle, but many more would be needed.

Rather than starting a new building, the Dean and Chapter immediately called into service Peckwater Inn, used by Wolsey as lodgings and workshops for his builders, to provide rooms for Students and commoners, except for one corner, which was occupied by a canon. Further to the east was Canterbury Quad, the remains of the medieval Canterbury College, which Henry VIII had incorporated into his foundation after the dissolution of Christ Church in Canterbury. From 1582 Peck and Canterbury were separated by a gate and wall, and then another gate led into Merton Street.[9]

Much of the timber and stone for new work and for repairs was recovered from Oseney Abbey. The asset was just too good to lose, and the fear of theft encouraged the Dean and Chapter to make arrangements for the safety of the resources that could be scavenged from the decaying monastery.[10] In one trip alone in 1582 fifty-seven loads of freestone were shifted and stacked in a storehouse in the Timber Yard behind the cathedral.[11]

Some of this salvage was to be used immediately for a far more salubrious project than just the patching up of existing buildings. A substantial quantity of the stone was immediately put to use replacing the wooden shuttering at the west end of the cathedral, which must have stood for the best part of twenty years. The wall, with its new grand window, took about eighteen months to finish. The centring for the window was installed by William Pickhaver at the same time as he was less glamorously employed repairing a grate in the privies, and the ironwork was made ready for the glass.[12] Other tasks were being done in the cathedral while the scaffolding was up and the

A rather romantic view of Oseney Abbey in ruins, engraved by Thomas
Dale in 1820. Much of the abbey's stone and lead, as well as the bells,
were taken for work at Christ Church under a decree made by Henry VIII.
During the Civil War the abbey buildings were used as an ammunition
store, and an explosion in 1643 damaged much of what was left.

place full of builders: the Dean and Chapter purchased new wainscoting
for seats so that the canons and doctors might 'have roome to sit & heare
sermons', the seats in the Lady Chapel were repaired, four new pendants
were carved for the choir roof and the remainder fastened in place to complete the work that had been begun in the mid-fifteenth century.[13]

Service buildings

Few of the early domestic buildings survive. Wolsey's fish cellar, used
briefly as a prison for heretics in 1528, was still in use in the later sixteenth
century, and the early disbursement books mention a slaughterhouse, a

Detail from David Loggan's 1673 engraving showing the surviving medieval buildings from St Frideswide's priory, but also the new west window installed in the cathedral in 1584.

bakehouse (repaired in 1581), stables and ox-houses (with a new one built in 1601).[14] Sampson Strong's painting of Wolsey from 1610 and David Loggan's engraving from 1673 show many outbuildings to the south – stables and animal pens, and other ancillary structures such as storehouses, cold rooms, garden sheds and barns. None of these remains.[15]

Two brewhouses provided the residents with all the liquid refreshment that was needed. The northern brewhouse is the earlier of the two, but the southern one was definitely functioning by the mid-seventeenth century, when it was called the malthouse.[16] Nearly all the older colleges had their own brewhouses, some of which have detailed accounts of the building and maintenance of the building with all its equipment, but there is no evidence in the archive at Christ Church for the construction of either or of

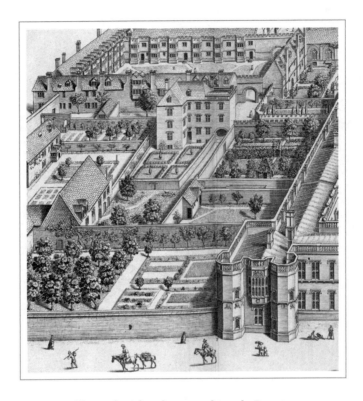

The northern brewhouse, as drawn by Loggan.

the process of brewing. Neither is there any payment to a brewer. It is not impossible that the beer was supplied from Christ Church's own brewhouses under contract; all through its history, the college purchased vast quantities of ale. Certainly the north brewhouse could well have been run by the Bull Inn on St Aldate's, which had been a possession of St Frideswide's Priory.

The northern brewhouse, now within the curtilage of Blue Boar Quad, has more the appearance of a barn than a brewhouse, with its through cart passage, and was perhaps used for other purposes in its earliest history. As a brewery, it remained in use until the early twentieth century. In 1923 plans were drawn up for its conversion into a house for a member of the Chapter, at a cost not exceeding £7,000. The architects John and Paul Coleridge proposed a vernacular design that was almost out of date and certainly not in keeping with its surroundings, harking back to houses such as Lutyens's

Brasenose College, in particular, has detailed accounts from the 1690s of the construction of its brewhouse, with all its fixtures and fittings. Other colleges have records of excise duty being paid, and of wages to brewers, often from around the same period. The date may be related to the creation of the Boards of Excise and Customs in 1671 and 1683 respectively.

Deanery Garden in Sonning, with its Gertrude Jekyll garden, built between 1899 and 1901. Much extended, the residence would have included a day and night nursery, a servants' hall and four servants' bedrooms. The kitchen and associated services would have been housed in a wing at a slight angle and pushed back from the main elevations, matching far grander houses. The stables at the gate would have become garages.[17] The big plan was evidently never implemented, although it may have been at this time that additional dormers were incorporated in the roof and new windows, including the three-light mullioned window in the east end, added to the ground floor.

Between the 1920s and 1965 the brewhouse remained almost redundant except as a rather large garden shed, so when construction began on Blue Boar Quad, two coppers were still in place on either side of the fireplace and a spiral staircase led to the malt loft above. The coppers were sold and the staircase was found a fresh use elsewhere. The original red-tiled floors were removed and replaced by a concrete slab as the central portion of the ground floor was to become an electrical sub-station, leased to the local generating company. The Governing Body decided very early on in the discussions about the old coal yard that the brewhouse would be retained intact and incorporated into the Blue Boar scheme.[18] The west end was intended as a flat for a porter – originally the Blue Boar development was to have its own gate onto the street; later the remainder of the upper floor became a residence for a senior member. It was not until 2007 that any further changes were made. With the refurbishment of Blue Boar Quad, and the decision to provide a new lecture theatre in staircase 4, it was necessary to find a new home for the archive, previously housed – very unsatisfactorily – in the Blue Boar basement. Head Chef Roland Dépit, the last resident of the west end,

Also in 1923 a plan was drawn up for a new Junior Common Room and Lecture Room to be constructed between the east end of the brewhouse and the canon's lodging to the south, using the War Memorial Fund. A rather late 'Queen Anne'-ish design, the JCR would have been on the ground floor with the lecture room on the first floor reached by a grand double-balustraded exterior staircase. Its appearance could reflect a galleried medieval inn, or a first-floor hall house, or even sixteenth- or seventeenth-century West-Country church houses. In the event, neither this nor a further idea to convert the dean's and canons' garages into servants' cottages was implemented.

CCA GB i.b.5, 201; Maps ChCh 30

was about to retire, and so it was decided to convert most of the building into a new archive facility. The sub-station was moved into the space previously occupied by the canons' garages behind, and the vacated space was fitted with rolling shelves. The old 'garden shed' occupying the east end is now the archivist's office, and the whole of the upper floor, with its lovely vernacular arch-braced timber roof opened up, is fitted out with storage and facilities for researchers. Only the lower floor of the residence at the west end remains residential, as accommodation for a junior research fellow.[19]

The southern brewhouse, within the garden of the south-west canonry, has even less history than its northern counterpart. Chapter minutes suggest that everyday repairs were carried out to walls and roofs, but again there is no reference to brewing or any other use.[20] In 1972 the building was converted into a residence for a lonely and sick W. H. Auden, who had dropped heavily weighted hints that he would like to return from America to his alma mater.[21] The cottage, now known as Auden Cottage, is currently occupied by the sub-organist.

* * * * *

The first fifty years of Christ Church's existence were almost a period of retrenchment. The dean and canons of both King Henry VIII's College and Christ Church had been left with a large and unfinished home in which to begin running the new diocese and educating young men. They ensured that the existing buildings were habitable and that all services were up and running, and then began, cautiously, to develop the site to suit the needs of the new and unique foundation. Come the seventeenth century, however, caution was thrown to the wind, and expansion and development became all-important.

5

Expansion: the seventeenth century

Sampson Strong's portrait of Thomas Wolsey was painted a considerable time after the cardinal's death, in the early years of the seventeenth
century. In the top corner is a vignette of Wolsey's college, showing the
dining hall and the kitchen, both with elaborate louvres, the cathedral, the
hall stair tower with a crenellated roofline, the Priory House, the old library,
possibly Chaplains' Quad and numerous ancillary buildings to the south.

While the late sixteenth century had been a period of consolidation,
bringing the buildings into a state of good repair after several years of neglect,
the seventeenth century saw new things beginning to happen. This was not
unique to Christ Church; colleges across the University were beginning to
revamp, and Wadham College was built from scratch. St John's built the first
side of a new quadrangle, which included its library with chambers below,
and Merton reconstructed some of its street frontage.[1] At Christ Church the
first project was the early adaptation of Peckwater Inn into more suitable
accommodation for Students and gentlemen commoners of the House, and
to cope with the influx of students after the matriculation statute of 1581.[2]

The Old Library

The arrival of ever more students required better facilities, and one large
project of the early seventeenth century was the refurbishment of the

The matriculation statute of 1581 required all new students to subscribe both to the new religious settlement and to the statutes of the University. Matriculation had to take place within a week of admission to a hall or college. The new statute, along with the 1579 decree requiring all students to move into colleges and halls from lodgings in town, brought many more students officially under the banner of the University and into the colleges. There was a marked leap in the admissions of commoners, from 21 in the decade 1571–80 to 166 in the following ten years.

McConica (1986), 50–51

Library. Once again, this was something that was happening in several colleges: at Merton, in particular, the substantial Library saw its medieval lecterns removed, to be replaced by the more modern and practical stall system, which allowed for the shelving of many more volumes. New stalls were incorporated right from the start at St John's, and All Souls, Queen's, New and Corpus Christi colleges, as well as the Bodleian, soon followed suit.[3] Magdalen College and Christ Church were not far behind.

The Dean and Chapter must have made provision for a Library almost as soon as the new college was founded, although little is known except that an appeal seems to have gone out around 1562 for donations.[4] The Library was housed in the medieval refectory: a handsome Gothic room, according to Anthony Wood, of good proportions, with three lancet windows at the back and a slightly raised dais at the east end. At the opposite end, through a portico, was the main entrance.[5] The inside of the north wall, at least, was decorated with beautiful blind arcading dating from around 1500.[6] Originally, there were six traceried windows on each side and six buttresses on the south side, one of which supported a richly decorated projecting pulpit.

Once Wolsey had built the Hall, the old refectory was connected to the new by an 'annexe' filling in the south-west corner of the cloister.[7] Today the frame of a blocked doorway is visible at the west end of the south cloister walk which could easily have accessed both buildings.

The Library was originally fitted out with old lecterns purchased

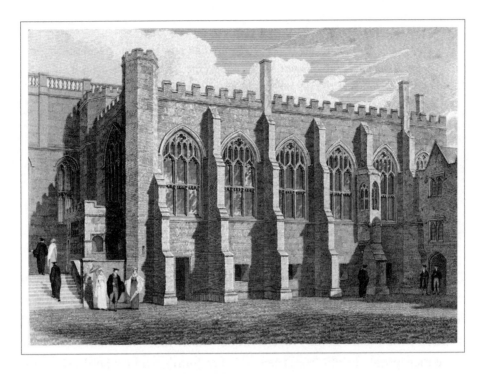

*The Old Library before its conversion into student rooms in 1776, drawn by
John Gooch, who was an undergraduate at the college from 1769. The engraving,
by Skelton, shows the large west window, the pulpit and the west porch. Both
the west window and the porch were probably blocked when the building was
converted and the traceried windows on the south side converted into sashes.*

second-hand from the then derelict University Library. Once Christ Church
Library was reasonably well stocked with books, a Bachelor was regularly
elected as Library Keeper and paid 10s. per quarter. Books were bound and
chained, and protected from harm as far as possible. Chains were certainly
being made in the 1580s, and the first record of a Library Keeper receiving a wage was in 1600, when Richard Etkins was paid 3s. 4d. During the
1580s and 1590s three men in particular were paid regularly for chains and
for book-binding: Norris, the college smith, Richard Garbrand and Richard
Cakebread. Occasionally, however, damage did occur; in 1592 a payment
was made to Norris for mending a copy of Hermogenes' *Rhetoric* which had
been torn out of the Library safe.[8]

By the early years of the seventeenth century the Library was beginning

*The Old Library and doorway into the cloister. The door was
converted into a window with unusual angular tracery.*

to outgrow the refectory, and its fixtures and fittings needed updating.
Various odd jobs had been done, including repairs to the huge west window
in 1597 and the creation of new casements in 1604.[9] The rooms over the
east cloister walk were probably built at this time, partly to accommodate
the growing Chapter Archive, and the chamber over the south cloister walk,
later to become the Allestree Library, was built in 1612 by the college mason
Thomas Wetherall.[10] Around the same time, late in 1611 or early 1612, the
undercroft was converted into two rooms.[11] Samuel Fell, soon to be dean,
appears to have had some care for the Library at this time: numerous odd
jobs, such as the cleaning of the Library, the mending of the key and even
the binding of new books, were paid for from his pocket and reimbursed
later.

Not only was the Library filling up, but it was also beginning to look

*The reconstruction of Hereford Cathedral library, built to the
same specifications as Christ Church's Old Library.*

distinctly old-fashioned beside those of the neighbours, and Christ Church
decided on a major overhaul funded, at least in part, by Otho Nicholson,
Examiner of the Court of Chancery, who gave £800 for its renovation and
a further £100 for the purchase of new books. On his death in 1622 he
bequeathed some of his own library to Christ Church.[12] Why Nicholson was
so beneficent to Christ Church is unknown; he gave the city the Hinksey and
Carfax conduits, but there is no apparent connection with the House. But
generous he was, and new rules were drawn up to ensure that the benefaction was protected.

The roof was altered to allow for new highly decorated panels and
carved mouldings and spandrels. The doorways at the western end were
blocked and a new one pierced through and given a stone porch.[13] Internally, the shelving style was changed from the outdated lecterns to new
presses, following the new fashion already adopted by Merton, Queen's,
Corpus Christi and New colleges, as well as the Bodleian, to take all the new

Most college libraries were stocked by gift, or by the required graduate donations, for which several students often clubbed together. The disbursement
books for the late sixteenth century record not only the costs of rebind-
ing and chaining books but also the costs of transporting donations from
London. For example, the 'nine great books given by Lady Burghley' were
carried up from town at a cost of 4s. 8d., and Mr Simberbe was paid 7s. for
chaining the books given by the dean.

books that were to arrive.[14] The contract with the joiners William Bennett
and Thomas Key specifies the sizes and quality of the new desks and closets
to hold both chained and unchained books.[15] And administration was tight-
ened up, with new statutes issued in 1614, as soon as the alterations and
improvements were completed.[16] All graduates had to give either a book or
money towards a book. For a BA or MA the sum was 13s. 4d., while doctors
and gentlemen commoners had to contribute 20s. or a book of a similar
value, scholars 10s., canons £2 and deans £5. One of the most significant
was a copy of the first edition of Robert Burton's *Anatomy of Melancholy*,
given by its author on publication in 1621.[17] Theft from the Library incurred
automatic sending down. The post of Library Keeper was formally established. All those who were entitled to use the Library were given a key and
could use the Library during the summer from 6 a.m. to 5 p.m., with a closed
period for lunch, and then from dawn to dusk in the winter. The oath that
had to be sworn on receipt of a key included a promise not to steal, barter,
erase, disfigure, lacerate, split up, annotate, write between the lines, deface,
obliterate, contaminate or in any other way destroy any book belonging to
the Library.[18] In gratitude, the Dean and Chapter presented Nicholson with
a pair of gloves and set up a marble monument (which cost £6 and an additional 20s. to erect) above the old refectory pulpit on the south side of the
Library. It did not survive very long there: a further entry in the disbursement books records its removal in 1615 at a cost of 26s. 8d. It is now in the
cloister.[19]

By the early eighteenth century the Library was bursting at the seams

The Old Library after its conversion to rooms, taken by Henry Taunt
(1842–1922), a prolific local photographer and publisher, c.1870.

– a gallery, or cabinet, had been built around 1713 to help ease the strain caused by the arrival of Dean Aldrich's bequest of books. The work was not cheap (around £100), considering that it was to prove relatively temporary.[20] As the new shelves were filled, so in 1717 the Dean and Chapter signed the contract with William Townesend to begin the construction of a new library on the south side of Peckwater Quad.[21]

For a short time after the books were removed to the new library, the old library was used for lectures, having been converted for that purpose in 1775, using a legacy of £100 from Daniel Burton. Only a year later, though, the Dean and Chapter came to an agreement with the brother of Richard Nash that the annuity Richard had left to Christ Church in 1754 – for the annual Commemoration speech – be commuted to a lump sum of £300, which would be used to turn the old library into twelve sets for Westminster Students.[22] The task of conversion fell to James Wyatt. Two new floors were inserted and a staircase built with passages to all the rooms separated from

Daniel Burton was the son of a local man, and came up to Christ Church at, allegedly, the age of twelve in 1717. He was appointed rector of Slapton in Buckinghamshire and then of St Peter le Poer in the City of London. Soon after Burton's death in 1775 his church was considered to be in such a dilapidated state that it was demolished.

Richard Nash was a Westminster Student. He entered Christ Church in 1730. Nash inherited a substantial estate in Worcestershire He was appointed a prebendary of Winchester Cathedral in 1742, a position he held until his death in 1757.

the preserved north windows by balusters. The windows on the south side were altered to sashes; semicircular windows were inserted on the north; and new small windows took the place of the great west window, which would originally have thrown light into the refectory. Two lecture rooms took the place of the undergraduate rooms on the ground floor.[23]

In 1829, once the new lecture room was built over the kitchen lobby, the lecture rooms on the ground floor of the old library were converted back into three sets of chambers, and another undergraduate room was created in 1883 with a rearrangement of the 'milk room', presumably a cold room for the storage of dairy produce.

At some point between the seventeenth century and the mid-twentieth – probably during the eighteenth-century alterations – the ceiling must have been covered, for in 1954 the decorated panels were rediscovered after the chance remark of an electrician doing rewiring. Only a hundred complete panels out of the original 192 had survived, and the roof was in a dire condition. Thirty-two panels were saved to create one complete bay, and most of the remainder were given to the Bodleian Library, to be placed in the Selden End of Duke Humfrey's Library.[24]

The Allestree Library

Alongside the Old Library, over the south cloister, was the small room created in 1612. Possibly it was always intended as an annexe to the main Library, but no record of its early use survives. In 1680, however, it was made ready to receive the library of Richard Allestree, regius professor of divinity. The collection was bequeathed to the University, but, as the professorship was based at Christ Church, it was felt sensible for the books to be housed there. The long and narrow room (42½ feet × 11) was adapted, with the installation of shelving over a floor that had been laid previously with thirteenth- and fourteenth-century tiles, probably from the cathedral, perhaps removed in the 1630s, when Dean Duppa made his alterations to the interior, although two of the designs are the same as those purchased in 1623 for the floor of Merton College Library.[25]

The north-side canonries

The Civil War and Commonwealth of the 1640s and 1650s had put a stop to building and beautifying, but very soon after the Restoration and the appointment of John Fell as dean the 'Great Rebuilding' of Christ Church commenced. It was to last for well over a century. In the cathedral, apart from the reinstatement of the organ and the generous gift of new communion plate, Fell only undertook necessary repairs on the cathedral spire; masons and smiths were constantly at work there throughout the 1660s, and finished in the spring of 1669. John Bartlett received his final payment of £45 on 1 April, the smith received £23 15s. and an unnamed expert was given £1 for regilding the weather-vane.[26] But other, far more significant, projects were initiated almost immediately.

Fell's three aims were to bring order to the 'squallore' into which he felt Christ Church had sunk during the Commonwealth (although records suggest it was less than beautiful even before the war, in spite of the efforts of his father, Samuel Fell), to finish Wolsey's quad and then to embellish everything that was already there. Fell described the dire state of Christ Church's buildings:

the fabrick itselfe partly demolisht, and the timber of the whole north side of the Great Quadrangle sawed down from the walls and roofe, and applied to firewood; and the remaining buildings wholely let goe to ruine, insomuch that within a few moneths after our returne we were enforc'd to repair the timber and lead of the whole south side of the Hall, as also all the Cloysters, and a great part of the Church and Great Quadrangle; as also to rip up and secure from weather the slatted parts of the Colledge, the whole Chaplains' Quadrangle, Peckwater's Inne, Canterbury Colledge and the Almeshouse.[27]

Samuel Fell had made an effort to complete the north side in 1641, when his mason, possibly Thomas Robinson, had floors laid and timbers prepared for roofs, but the war intervened and all the materials were used elsewhere on the site, for firewood or for the defences that were built across the Meadow.[28] William Cartwright began a poem describing Christ Church as a 'sacred heap' and urged that something be done to render the buildings as 'glorious as thy name'.[29] But it was not until things had returned to normal and George Morley – evicted from his canonry in 1647 and made dean, to great acclamation, in July 1660 – had been replaced by John Fell that work was recommenced.[30] First among the indefatigable Fell's tasks was the completion of the Great Quadrangle. He began gathering subscriptions, which were encouraged by the patent for a £1,000 earldom given by the king to be sold and the proceeds put to the building costs – no doubt to compensate Christ Church for the expenses it had suffered during the residence of Charles I between 1642 and 1646.[31] By the middle of the 1660s Fell had raised around £9,400, but work had begun long before. In March 1661 payments were already being made to carpenters and sawyers, working with deal boards brought up by river from London, or with elm and oak. Masons and plumbers were also working on site.[32] The traditional 'gift' of plate from every new gentleman commoner was commuted to cash, and placed in the new building fund, and many old members, particularly the restored Anglican clergy, were generous.[33] The money was to be entered in a 'vellome booke (which Mr Treasurer Dolben is desired forthwith to provide for the purpose) together with the names of such persons which gave the said summes'.[34]

At the other end of the west front, a few years later, in 1693, three tenements abutting the south-west bastion beside Cutler's Gate (the gate into
the stable yard) were also demolished, and another new wall built between
the bastion and the gate to enclose an enlarged garden.

CCA D&C i.b.4, fols 28ᵛ, 29ᵛ

On 11 March 1661 Richard Allestree, a canon and friend of Fell, had
been promised a residence on this new north side, and he only had to wait
until 1665 for all the work on the lodgings to be finished. Only the sprucing
up of the quadrangle itself remained to be completed during the summer
of 1666.[35] The two new residences must have instantly relieved pressure of
space and turned the quad into, in practice, a cathedral close, finished in the
same style in which it was begun, even down to the re-creation of the unfinished cloister and a bastion at the corner of the north and west sides matching that at the south end.[36] At the other end, one room extended over the
passage towards Peckwater to join with the deanery and probably formed
part of the dean's accommodation right from the start. For the first time the
main frontage was complete, and all the odd buildings that had accumulated
there over the previous 150 years – including a wash-house, a coach-house
and a kitchen – were demolished. A new wall was built between the north
side of the bastion and the Bull Inn.[37]

Only the new balustrade, replacing Wolsey's original battlements
around the whole of the quadrangle, showed any compliance with the
more classical fashion.[38] A description from Torevin (or Jorevin) de Rocheford, who saw Christ Church soon after the completion of the quadrangle,
gives the real effect of Fell's work: 'it is more like some fine castle, or great
palace than a College; it is built with great hewn stone, and has a large court,
surrounded by great buildings, with a terrace on the top, and a fine walk
encompassed with balustrades.'[39]

The two residences remained relatively untouched until 1848, when,
during the occupation of Archdeacon Clerke, floors were replaced, new

partitions added and an extension added to the rear of the premises to the westerly canonry (which has traditionally been the home of the archdeacon). A century later, in 1933, more drastic changes were undertaken. When Canon Kirk refused to move into the dilapidated canonry next to the deanery (to be taken by Claude Jenkins, who was completely unfazed by its state), it was proposed that Killcanon be surrendered to the college and that part of the money paid by the college be used to split the archdeaconry into two unequal portions. The old storerooms at the back were altered to create a kitchen and sitting room, and a tunnel was dug to allow access to a garden.[40] The architects were Christ Church's favourite practice in the 1920s and 1930s: Coleridge, Jennings and Soimenow.[41]

The whole of this side of the quad was re-leaded in the early 1950s, but otherwise the more easterly lodging remained unaltered (apart from some modernisation) until 1972, when Peter Walker, canon and bishop of Dorchester, was installed.[42] It was at this time that Canon Jenkins's lodgings were permanently alienated to the college.[43] Part of the agreement between college and cathedral was for the eastern lodgings on the north side to be converted, at college expense, into two.[44] One of the windows was converted into a door to match the rest of the elevation, but otherwise, from the outside, no change was visible.[45]

Just around the corner from the archdeaconry, the west side of the quad was completed at the same time as the north. For much of its time, staircase 7 was occupied by undergraduates and Students, until 1887. A Junior Common Room was first set up in 1886 and was given the use of Great Quad 6:1.[46] Within a year the undergraduates had moved to room 3 in staircase 7, and in February 1890 they were asking to extend into neighbouring rooms. There were objections from Edward Sampson, the Senior Censor, to giving up more space, and he proposed a rearrangement of the existing rooms, including a new door in the corner by Archdeacon Dr Palmer's residence. A new pantry for the staircase scout was also suggested, so that the existing scout's room could be added to the JCR's accommodation. Plans were drawn up by Harry Wilkinson Moore, putting on paper Sampson's proposals.[47] Everything was approved except the new door, and the work went ahead with the JCR meeting part of the cost.[48] By 1895 the Common Room had expanded into room 2, although this does not seem to have been formalised until 1911, when the members of the JCR were granted indemnity for having proceeded with the 'reconstruction of the Junior Common Room' in the long vacation without the sanction of the Governing Body. In 1923 the Governing Body proposed using some of the War Memorial Fund to construct a new Junior Common Room, but the fund never reached the necessary level and was used instead, and perhaps more appropriately, for the creation of the Memorial Garden. Mr Edward Warren was asked to look at the existing facilities and to draw up plans and estimates for alterations, including the appropriation of the Tom 7:1 set.[49] How much of this work was done, if any, is impossible to say; the annual reports of the time are more concerned with the Memorial Garden and the construction of new school rooms for the choir in Brewer Street, and the room rent books show the Junior Common Room remaining in just rooms 2 and 3 well into the 1940s. It was not until 1963 that the first major refurbishment took place. This was prompted by the foundation in 1960 of the Graduate Common Room, which was accommodated on the ground floor of Tom 7, in room 1, next door to the JCR. Within a couple of years the GCR had outgrown its tiny premises, and the censors made available the rooms still in use on the first floor of the same staircase (Tom 7:6): rooms that had been the set of Charles Dodgson in the late nineteenth century and of Robert Dundas until his death in October 1960. Albert Einstein had been given use of the same rooms while he was resident in Oxford in 1931 and 1932.[50]

In 1963 the Junior Common Room saw structural work, new electrical and gas fittings, kitchen fittings and new plumbing, but changing needs and the arrival of women at Christ Church prompted large-scale improvements as proposed in 1980.[51] The principal work was to create one large room out of the three small ones overlooking St Aldate's, but new lavatories (for both men and women) were installed, the turret rooms were refurbished, the entrance was improved, and a new bar and shop (with access from Tom 6) were added. The plumbing and heating were renewed too. Bosanquet was the architect and A. E. Hobley the contractor for the work, which cost

A room in Tom 7 that was to be occupied by Charles Dodgson and then by Robert Dundas (Student and Tutor in History, 1909–55) before it became part of the Graduate Common Room. The picture was taken during Dundas's residence.

£175,000.[52] During the 1990s the Graduate Common Room was redecorated and refurbished, with additional study spaces provided for increasing numbers of graduate students.[53]

*　*　*　*　*

Williams's plan of 1733 is annotated with the allocation of the canons' lodgings, and it is evident that those sixteenth-century canonries which had been the least desirable fell out of favour and were abandoned as soon as the north side of the Great Quadrangle was ready, particularly the one in old and dilapidated Canterbury Quads but also the one right on the street next to the main gateway. The eight canonries were now the lodgings next to the deanery, in front of the cathedral, in the south-west corner of the Great

Quad, in Chaplains' Quad, in the south-west corner of Peckwater Quad, the Priory House in the oldest part of the site and the two new ones on the north side of the Great Quadrangle.

Chaplains' Quad and Fell's Buildings

But one of these lodgings was about to be lost. On 19 November 1669 a fire broke out in the medieval Chaplains' Quad. Robert Cholmondeley, one of the gentlemen-commoners, had lit a fire in his room which ran out of control and caught the joists under the chimney. Cholmondeley had to scramble over the roof to save himself. To prevent the fire spreading to the cathedral and the Library, £5 worth of gunpowder was brought in, and, according to Anthony Wood, Canon Sebastian Smith's lodgings were blown up to act as a firebreak, a technique employed during the Great Fire of London just three years earlier.[54] Wood may, however, have had the talents of a tabloid journalist: the disbursement books after the event refer just to the mending of Mr Smith's windows, rather than a complete rebuild. Richard Gardiner's canonry was, however, destroyed by the blaze along with several student rooms.[55] Whether or not Wood exaggerated the effect of the explosives, much of the old quad was damaged or lost altogether.

Chaplains' Quad was a remnant of the old priory buildings, possibly including the old infirmary and the infirmary chapel, which may have been adapted for use as the Audit House.[56] The Library was on its north side, and the kitchen on the west. A passageway continued the east cloister walk towards the Meadow. The Audit House appears throughout the archive, principally in the accounts for the provision of beer for the auditors, but we know that a new Audit House was fitted out between 1603 and 1605.[57] On 13 September 1605 Mr Sampson was paid 2s. 7d. for 'laying a culer upon the new audit house door' and Matthew Atkins 5s. 9d. for work on the pentice to the back door of the new Audit House. Other work included iron-mongery by Mr Corbett, wainscoting by Mr Keys and the repair of a press in the treasurer's lodgings, which was to be moved to the Audit House.[58] Part of Chaplains' Quad was apparently rebuilt in 1638 at the expense of the then auditor, Philip King, and it was King's lodgings – with a portion

The south-west corner of Chaplains' Quad with the kitchen to the right. Probably part of the accommodation, or even the infirmary, of St Frideswide's Priory, Chaplains' Quad was renovated after the 1669 fire but demolished in 1863 to make way for Meadow Buildings.

of Richard Washbourne's set – that were offered as temporary accommodation to Richard Gardiner after the fire.[59] General maintenance works took place in the Audit House, including whitewashing, picture cleaning,

Richard Gardiner had been a Student at Christ Church from 1607 and was installed in a canonry in 1629, before being evicted in 1648 by Parliament for his outspoken Royalism. He was reinstated in 1660 and remained at Christ Church until his death on 20 December 1670, the day that William of Orange made his tour of Oxford.

ODNB

Chaplains' Quad from the Meadow in 1863, by J. H. Le Keux.

slatting, repointing and even the construction of a new 'necessary house', until 1737, when a second room was fitted up for the purpose underneath the Old Library.[60]

After the fire Fell set about rebuilding Chaplains' Quad, in a domestic style, and constructing a new eponymous accommodation block. The appearance of Chaplains' Quad may have changed little, and the work was probably more repair than complete reconstruction.[61] A small archway through the east side led to Fell's Buildings (apparently also called the Garden Staircase on occasions), which fronted the Meadow. Work began in the autumn of 1669 and continued for ten years. This new block was rather square and dull; it had twenty-four chambers, each with two windows, over three storeys.[62] A bill submitted in January 1678 was for work done by seven labourers: John, Frances and Thomas Robinson, with James Hollten, William Curtis, Daniel Sparrow and Simon Cross, who worked for about eleven days with thirty-six feet of ashlar, three loads of walling, one load of

A sketch made in 1792 showing Fell's Buildings from the Meadow.

flanking stone and thirteen loads of gravel. A carpenter billed Christ Church for labour and for boards in a variety of shapes and sizes: 14 half-inch, 77 quarter-inch, 4 'slitt and salle', 3 one-inch, 2 deal and 29 feet of elm boards, along with 42 feet of oak timber and 35 feet of 5 by 5 inch oak.[63] These may well be invoices for a portion of the work on Fell's Buildings; the new accommodation does not appear on Loggan's 1673 engraving, which suggests that it was one of the final parts of the post-fire reconstruction. By the end of the eighteenth century both Fell's and Chaplains' Quad were deemed to be ready for demolition, but both survived until 1863 and the construction of Meadow Buildings.

Killcanon

There were two further consequences of the 1669 fire. The Killcanon lodgings were built close to the canonry in Peckwater to replace Gardiner's destroyed house; and the reservoir was dug in the centre of the Great

Killcanon is also the name of the passageway that runs from the Great, or Tom, Quad into Peckwater. The wind that whistles through, funnelled by the tall walls that separate the canon's and dean's gardens from the rest of college, is said to be cold enough to 'kill the canons'.

The coldness of Christ Church was evidently a problem from the earliest days: Anthony Wood wrote in the seventeenth century about a 1259 petition by the canons to Pope Alexander IV requesting that they be allowed to wear their caps during services in winter.

Clark (1889–90), vol. ii, 157

Quadrangle, funded by Gardiner, who determined that Christ Church would never again suffer such a disaster.[64]

Killcanon was a substantial house, possibly another commission for Thomas Robinson.[65] Loggan's engraving of Christ Church shows the house newly built: an L-shaped house with four storeys, including attic rooms and a basement, except over the open passage, which has rooms over at second- and third-floor levels and a balustrade surrounding a flat roof. The front door was then in the second bay, and the first bay was an open, arched passage-way with a classical broken pediment, giving access to the garden.[66] A fine staircase ascends from the ground floor over a basement with kitchen, stores and a well.

Killcanon is another of Christ Church's buildings that is barely mentioned in the records. Williams's plan shows the same building, perhaps slightly diminished after the intrusion of the Peckwater canonry in 1707.[67] It is possible that the east elevation, at least, was refaced and refenestrated when Peck was built, so that it fitted in with the Palladian finish.[68] A model of Christ Church dated to 1860 shows the carriageway closed in and a small wing built around it, turning Killcanon into an uneven U-shape. The new accommodation was given a mansard roof – retaining the balustrade – providing additional attic rooms.[69] Another small extension was constructed on the north side too. At some point a raised terrace was built between the two wings, and one doorway from the rear of the premises blocked. Nowhere in the archive is there an account of these changes.[70]

The residence remained the abode of the canon of the third stall into the nineteenth century but in 1859 was found to be too small for Canon Arthur Stanley, who needed extra room to accommodate his eight daughters. Frederick Barnes, one of the longest-serving members of the Chapter who occupied the lodgings of the seventh canonical stall in Peck 9, died in 1859, so it was relatively easily to alter the boundaries between the two properties. Much of the remainder of Canon Barnes's residence became a suite for a censor.[71]

Stanley moved from Oxford to Westminster Abbey just a few years later, by which time the constitution of Christ Church was undergoing tremendous change. The new statutes separated, to a large extent, the functions of college and cathedral. Parts of the site were held by the cathedral as Chapter property, and the remainder was managed by the college. From this time on, the increasing demands of the college – for student rooms, tutorial rooms and offices – have meant that Chapter property has, on occasions, been taken over, notably the residences vacated when two of the canonries were suppressed after the changes to the constitution.[72] The Chapter has been protective of its property since the division of buildings between college and cathedral. During the twentieth century this may have been the only major area of dissent between the two bodies.

Killcanon never really made it back into the hands of the Chapter; in 1899 the drawing room of Killcanon was being used as a temporary lecture room, and it was one of the first buildings to be acquired and to be altered for college use, in 1934.[73] Once in the hands of the Governing Body, the changes were made more permanent, with a party wall erected through the middle of Peck 9 and new entrances into Blue Boar Street created.[74] The house now belonged to the Governing Body, and the garden to the Chapter.[75]

In the 1950s stone repairs, using Box Ground Bath stone from near Corsham in Wiltshire, were made to the west and north elevations, and the roofs were repaired.[76] Further masonry repairs, this time to the south elevation, were made in the 1980s, with the sundial (which probably dates from the early nineteenth century) being repainted in 2008. In 2014 alterations were made to make the top-floor rooms safe for use under current fire regulations. Today the house is used principally as tutorial rooms, with accommodation on the ground floor for the college nurse and the seamstress.[77]

Mercury

The other lasting memorial to the 1669 fire is the pond in the centre of the Great Quadrangle. The quad may have been dug out and given a sunken centre very early in Christ Church's history; the disbursement book for 1599 shows a certain John Taylor, who was employed regularly at this period, working 'at the steppes in the great quadrant next Mr Deane's lodging', but Fell had it dug deeper still, beginning in 1666; in 1668 a John Browne (presumably *not* the college's third cook of the same name) was paid £110 for 'sinking the quadrangle', with the spoil used to raise and improve the Broad Walk.[78] In 1670 the centre was excavated still further, and the 40-foot pond connected up to the water supply from Carfax.[79] Canon Gardiner had been determined that fire would never cause as much devastation to Christ Church again, but the pond was not merely a reservoir: it was also to be beautiful. A fountain created by master carpenter Richard Frogley was sur-mounted by a globe 'gilded and beautified with the celestial planets', carved by William Bird, and a statue.[80] Bird was no mean sculptor; he had worked on the Sheldonian Theatre and had carved the elaborate and character-ful memorial to Sir Edmund Fettiplace and his predecessors in Swinbrook church in west Oxfordshire, but his globe did not last long, in spite of the Chapter decree which promised to keep Gardiner's bequest in good repair in perpetuity.[81] In 1695 Anthony Radcliffe gave the first Mercury to replace the neglected globe; its pedestal was painted in the autumn of that year, and the statue itself was brought to Oxford late the following year.[82] The pond was always in use as a water supply for the scouts and as a reserve for use in emergencies, most notably during the 1809 fire, which struck the south-west canonry. The statue, however, was treated with less respect: in 1773 the figure was pulled down and hung by the neck on one of the canonry doors, and in 1819 Edward Stanley, later to be Prime Minister and Earl of Derby, tore the statue from its plinth. The bronze head of the original is kept

Foggintor quarry operated from 1820 to 1938. It was one of the three great granite quarries on Dartmoor, and stone from here was used to build Princetown, Dartmoor prison, Nelson's Column and London Bridge.

in the Library, but it was not until 1928 that a new lead Mercury, given by Herbert Bompas, was erected in the centre of the pond. In 1934 a new plinth, one of only two Lutyens designs in Oxford (the other, a touch larger, is Campion Hall), replaced the temporary one, which had been found in the corner of a local builder's yard.

Over the years the arrangement of the steps and pathways through the quad has been changed. Loggan and Williams show semicircular steps on the north, east and south, with paths in a diagonal pattern, but in the nineteenth century this was changed. In 1841 a new wall and steps up to the terrace were built, at a cost of around £2,000; the steps were supplied by William Johnson of Grosvenor Wharf, Westminster, in Dartmoor granite from Foggintor quarry. They were loaded on to a barge in London on 9 September and arrived with a week.[83] The old wall and steps were reused as foundations for the new. The quad always needed maintenance, but Dean Liddell, along with all his other building works, took its restoration and care to greater heights. So, thirty years later, the Belfry Committee – which later became known as the Quadrangle Committee – turned its attentions to the quad more generally.[84] The level of the terrace was lowered by about 15 inches, revealing the bases of the cloister shafts. In doing this, the foundations for the external buttresses were uncovered. These were protected within the stone 'cases' that stick out from the raised terrace.

The Great Quadrangle as we see it today is largely the creation of two of Christ Church's great builder deans: John Fell and Henry Liddell. Under Fell, for the first time since Wolsey began his great project in 1525, the site began to show some cohesion, developing to accommodate a settled foundation that had been functioning within a multitude of construction sites for well over a century. Fell's letter to Gilbert Sheldon, archbishop of Canterbury, in which he had described the condition of Christ Church's buildings as he had inherited them in 1660, concluded that through the generosity of friends he had managed to build the north side of the Great Quadrangle, finish the west front and rebuild one side of Chaplains' Quad.[85]

Tom Tower

Fell was not one to rest on his laurels, however. Next on his 'to do' list was the completion of the tower over the great gate, left largely open to the elements since Wolsey's builders left. What it was that Wolsey had intended for the tower above the gate is uncertain; but it would probably have been similar to contemporary colleges such as Corpus Christi or Brasenose – albeit more elaborate – with a two-storey tower perhaps providing part of the residence for the dean or maybe the college archive. But fate had dictated otherwise. Bereblock's 1566 illustration clearly shows the turrets, part of Wolsey's original design, but no tower over the gate. There was, though, a small timber-framed bridging construction – a sort of roofed corridor with an oriel window – on the west front, still shown in Loggan's engraving of a century later.

In 1663, presumably hoping to get all the work on the Great Quadrangle finished in one go, Fell commissioned John Jackson, a local mason, to design a tower. Jackson had been employed in 1655 by Brasenose College as overseer of their project for a new chapel and Library, designed in seventeenth-century Gothic style using materials from other college properties, and by St John's College, so his credentials were good.[86] A model was prepared, but Jackson died before he was paid for the model and before his designs could be approved.[87] It was not until 1680, when Great Tom, the principal bell of the Christ Church peal, had to be recast for the third time in just a few years, that Fell first conceived the idea of a bell-tower.[88]

The following winter the dean met Christopher Wren to discuss plans. Wren was still heavily involved with the rebuilding of churches in London after the Great Fire, including St Paul's Cathedral, and with other commissions, such as the Greenwich Observatory, the library of Trinity College in Cambridge and Kilmainham Hospital in Dublin. He was also President of the

David Loggan's 1670s engraving of Christ Church. Tom Tower has still to be built, but otherwise this is Christ Church in its modern form.

Royal Society. In spite of this, he submitted a design to Fell in the spring of 1681. Letters passed backwards and forwards between the two men discussing all the details of the construction, and Wren's estimate of £1,512 9s. 6d., based on Fell's own research into the cost of Headington and Burford stone and all necessaries, was accepted.[89] The design followed Fell's desire to fit in with the original Tudor appearance of the college, and Wren agreed, with one small reservation: 'I resolvd it ought to be Gothick to agree with the Founders worke, yet I have not continued soe busy as he began', wrote Wren in his letter to Fell dated 26 May 1681.[90] The idea of a bell-tower meant that Wren had to fit a square tower on to the rectangular gateway, which he achieved by constructing piers in each corner of the gateway, with those against the inside walls slightly larger than those on the outside. Once a square had been created, allowing a decorative vault, he could continue the Gothic upward thrust past the square ringing chamber to an octagonal

A sketch of Tom Tower, possibly by David Loggan, dated 1681.

bell-chamber, surmounted with the ogee cupola to produce a construction that has become almost synonymous with Oxford.[91]

Christopher Kempster, from Burford, was appointed as principal mason, to work with Thomas Robinson.[92] Kempster, who owned a quarry at Upton, had worked on Wren's designs in London, including St Paul's Cathedral, and, more locally, had been responsible for the County Hall in Abingdon. Along with two sets of neighbours – the Strongs, who held the Taynton and Little Barrington quarries, and the Beauchamps, who worked with the Strongs – the Kempster family provided top-quality building stone and skills for the great architects of the seventeenth century, including Hawksmoor, Vanbrugh and Wren.[93] Wren visited Kempster's quarry in person, following in the footsteps of Wolsey's masons nearly two centuries earlier, to select the materials he needed. About a third of the stone for Tom Tower came from

Tom had originally hung in the central tower of Oseney Abbey, and was moved with the other abbey bells to Christ Church to ring from the cathedral tower. Originally dedicated to St Thomas of Canterbury, Tom was renamed after the queen during the reign of Mary I.

Burford, with the cheaper ashlar from Headington being used for the main construction. It was Wren who recommended Kempster to Fell, describing him in a letter as 'a very able man, modest, honest, and treatable [and] very carefull to worke trew to his designe'.[94] Frogley, the master carpenter who had created the globe for the reservoir, was responsible for selecting all the timber that was used to build Tom Tower, including that for the bell frame for Tom itself.

It would seem that Fell was impatient, galloping ahead with scant regard for Wren's instructions and before Kempster's arrival on site.[95] Wren wrote to Fell reminding him that the building was planned to last five hundred years and should not be rushed. Adding new to old, he explained, was a tricky business and required considerable preparation. He recommended ramming the ground thoroughly, laying the earth bed as evenly as possible and then laying large, flat stones over the top. The foundation should be built on top of this, using square stones and with bedding joints 'as trew as for a good building in sight'. The mortar was to be thin, and the whole tamped down with heavy beetles. After a winter to allow everything to settle, the walls could then be constructed. New stonework must not be within a finger's breadth of the old to prevent cracking, so the bonding stones needed to have thicker mortar beds.[96] 'I trouble your Lordship with scrupulosities', said Wren, 'but a thing well settled at first prevents more trouble, and errors in building are often incorrigible.' Even so, the contract stipulated completion in record time – by Michaelmas 1682 – and in September of that year Wren was arranging for the casting of the weather-vane and investigating the possibility of obtaining a bronze statue of the king to adorn the front niche of the tower.[97] This came to nothing, and Wren

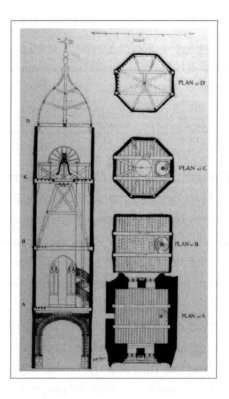

*A section of Tom Tower, drawn for Caröe's 1923 volume
on the correspondence between John Fell and Christopher
Wren concerning the construction of the tower.*

recommended Grinling Gibbons to produce two larger-than-life statues in Portland stone, one of Henry VIII and the other of Charles II, for which he was to be paid £110, but these did not materialise either, and the two niches on either side of the tower remained empty for some time.[98] It was another twenty years before Robert Harley donated the imposing figure of Queen Anne, attributed to Francis Bird, for the inside niche. She was unveiled on 25 January 1706, the day before the foundation stones were laid for the new Peckwater Quad, when, no doubt, Christ Church was full of dignitaries.[99] The outside niche was only occupied in 1872, when the marble image of Cardinal Wolsey, which had been sculpted by Bird in 1719 and was the gift of Jonathan Trelawney (Christ Church Student and bishop of Winchester), was moved from the archway over the Hall stairs to fill the space.[100]

The original completion date of Michaelmas 1682, stipulated in the agreement between Fell and Wren, was evidently a bit optimistic. Lead for the roof was delivered throughout 1683. In 1684 the troublesome Great Tom, recast four times before it was considered satisfactory, was hoisted into the tower. The bill for the manufacture of the bell frame and all the pulley system for getting the bell into place was substantial, totalling £105 16s. 7d., of which £47 15s. 6d. was for the ironwork to hang the bell.[101] Tom's clapper was brought by river in March. The staircase and bell wheels were painted, and all the moving parts oiled. Once the bell was in place, the coats of arms and the rose over the bell hole carved by Daniel Hook could be installed in the vault, and Tom was rung for the first time on 29 May, Restoration Day. The bill for the frame and the labour involved was not settled until December of that year. From this time on, the Great Quad was also known, on occasions, as Tom Quad (although the name was not used regularly in official papers until the 1970s).[102]

Along with the bell-tower, Fell had harboured a pet idea of having an observatory right at the top of the tower, but this was successfully countered by Wren, who argued, very diplomatically, that a bell-tower and observatory would not be practical partners. The masons and labourers had received over a shilling a day.[103] One odd feature of the tower is the rather lovely spiral staircase which leads from the ringing chamber up to the bell itself. Its turned balusters seem elaborate for such a little-seen space. Perhaps it is one example of Fell and Kempster's enthusiasm, and the staircase was installed when the notion of an observatory was still unquashed in Fell's mind.[104]

Tom Tower has been under repair for much of its existence.[105] The first recorded repairs are to the stairs, which needed attention in 1730, but it was in the late nineteenth and early twentieth centuries that the masonry saw a major overhaul. In 1876 George Bodley replaced the pinnacles on the interior face of the tower, using local Burford stone, but this was soft and barely survived thirty years. In 1901 the pinnacles – 'so far perished as to need for its restoration the intervention of an Architect' – were repaired again, with Doulting stone.[106]

By 1908 the urgent need of masonry repair to the entire tower and to

*Tom's clapper, photographed during the restoration
and rebuilding of the bell frame in 1952.*

the whole of the west front could no longer be ignored. For a couple of years Tom was shrouded in a bird's nest of scaffolding which alone cost £300. It was said to have included 27 miles of poles and was immortalised as the illustration on the 1910 University Almanack.[107] Under the watchful eye of W. D. Caröe, Symm repaired the entire tower using Clipsham, another oolitic limestone from further afield in Rutland, but less prone to deterioration and made popular in Oxford by Thomas Jackson, the architect of the Examination Schools.[108]

Further work was done, again by Symm, on the body of the tower from the top of the gate arches to the base of the dome in the 1960s using Clipsham stone. The lead of the dome was replaced completely in medium-grade 7lb. lead by Collett Brothers.[109] The whole bell frame was replaced to commemorate the coronation of Elizabeth II. Tom had not swung on its frame for some years as the gear had become damaged, so the bell had been 'clocked' instead, which involved tying a rope to the clapper and pulling the clapper against the bell. This method could easily have cracked the bell, so a new cast-iron headstock was installed, designed to counterbalance the weight of the bell. Tom can be swung on occasions, but most of the time it is struck with a new tolling gear to regulate the force of the hammer.[110]

*　*　*　*　*

But it was not just the great projects that occupied the Dean and Chapter. Work of all sorts continued all the time: the records are full of payments to masons, smiths, carpenters, plasterers, pargeters and slaters. John Showell's bill of January 1678 is divided into ten separate parts, beginning with work done for the dean, 'My Lord Bishop'.[111] This included spicks for the kitchen, hanging a door with new hinges, a lock for the gate into the little garden, a lock and new door for the cellar, mending a key for the door to the quad, and a lock for the gallery.[112] The bill continues with work in Dr Croyden's lodgings, including an essential new bolt for the 'boghouse dore'. Dr South wanted a new lock on his boghouse too; Dr Lockey needed keys for the garden gates; and Dr Smith asked for new window hooks. Once finished in the canons' lodgings, Showell made chains for 39 books in the Library, of which 23 were ell chains (45 inches) and 16 were yard chains. He then did some general work about the college buildings: a key for the timber yard, mending the pump irons over the road at the almshouse and repairing the hinge on the gate near the new Fell's Buildings, as well as work in the kitchen.

And it wasn't just the hardware: contractors were also brought in to make life a bit more comfortable too. Thomas Miles charged Christ Church £2 for eight yards of mohair to make cushions, and a further 8s. 8d. for fringes. The silk to sew the cushions, with Miles's labour, came to 2s. 6d.[113]

Perhaps the last act in the seventeenth century was the installation of new glass in the great east window of the cathedral. In 1699 Dr Birch, once a chaplain, funded new glass designed by James Thornhill and executed by John (or Isaac) Oliver, glass painter and master mason.[114] At the time Thornhill was almost an unknown quantity, but he was to become famous

117

The deanery may always have had a small gallery. There is an account in 1670 for the cost of the picture, frame and boards for the portrait of Henry VIII, which was then placed in the gallery. But it was not until Henry Liddell moved in to the deanery that the long gallery was created, with the Lexicon stairs at its north end.

Alternatively, there are hints that there was a gallery in the Audit House and that pictures were hung there.

CCA xii.b.113

for decorating the dome of St Paul's Cathedral. He also worked at All Souls and Queen's colleges, and at Blenheim Palace.[115] In spite of his eminence, this window, which may have shown the deliverance of St Paul from prison, was destined for only a relatively short life.

David Loggan's engraving shows a college changed almost beyond recognition. The tall tower over the Hall stairs has been removed, but the fourth side of the Great Quadrangle – now with its reservoir (not yet with Mercury) at its centre – has been completed, and with it the ends of the deanery and the St Aldate's frontage. A new building, Killcanon, has appeared. The whole aspect is one of order and more completeness than had been seen before. There was still a jumble of buildings and structures around the old Canterbury Quad and on the south side of Peckwater, but in the next century all this was to change.

6

The 'Great Rebuilding': Christ Church's eighteenth-century renaissance

The impetus generated by John Fell was continued in the early eighteenth century, when, after a mere twenty years of peace without the sound of building and builders, and under the supervision of the energetic polymath Henry Aldrich, Peckwater Quad was changed from its more homely Tudor into a grand edifice – 'a serious and academic essay in classicism'. This was a change occurring all over Oxford: under the influence of men of science, such as Christopher Wren, and antiquarian polymaths, such as Henry Aldrich and George Clarke, a city that had been predominantly medieval and Gothic in style was slowly introduced to classical architecture.[1]

Peckwater Quad

The medieval Peckwater Inn, probably both an actual inn and a residential hall for undergraduate students, had occupied much of the area between what is now Alfred Street to the west, King Edward Street to the east, the boundary of St Frideswide's Priory to the south and the present Bear Lane on the north, and was acquired by Wolsey as part of the site for Cardinal College.[2] Initially used to house the workmen and their workshops, the inn became an annexe for members soon after 1546. By the end of the sixteenth century the hundred Students on the foundation had been joined by an ever-increasing number of fee-paying commoners, and accommodation was needed for all of them. From the 1580s, there were around twelve fee-paying undergraduates each year, but the proportion of gentlemen commoners, who expected a better class of room, was rising.

Thomas Ravis, who was dean from 1596 to 1605, was unpopular – possibly because he was appointed at the request of the Chancellor over the heads of the canons, although probably because he attempted to reform and regularise payment for commons – but he was a born administrator and committee man. Revamping an old and rather tired medieval inn would have been a project right up his street. The Peckwater Quad shown on Agas's 1578 map – with buildings to the north, west and south – was soon under scaffolding, and accounts from 1600–1601 show gravel and clay being brought in for the new buildings, payments to a Mr Austin for making new cocklofts (or attic rooms) and other chambers over the old hall of the inn, the purchase of trees for the rafters, the settlement of bills from Atkins 'the slatter' for roofing the dormer windows and payments to a plasterer for all his work in the inn.[3] It was a quick job; by the end of the summer of 1601 everything seems to have been completed, and on 17 July it was announced that the new rooms were to be used primarily for gentlemen commoners.[4] But the number of gentlemen commoners continued to rise; between 1580 and 1600 there had been only two or three each year, but in the first decade of the seventeenth century there were fifty-seven new arrivals, followed by over forty in each of the next two decades. By 1616 more rooms were needed, and plans were drawn up for still more commodious accommodation on the vacant east side of Peckwater Quad.[5] Loggan's engraving from the 1670s shows the north side packed with south-facing dormer windows

Thomas Ravis was the first of the Westminster Students to be made dean. Another reason for his unpopularity may have been the intervention of Lord Burghley in Ravis's election as a Student back in 1575. The Chapter had originally refused him entry on the grounds that Westminster boys, though proficient in grammar, were less so in logic.

ODNB

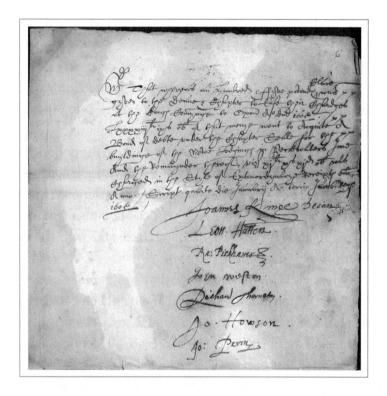

A Chapter decree of 1606 concerning the costs of rebuilding Peckwater Quad. The Dean and Chapter had been given £105 in recompense for moneys laid out during the visit of James I in 1605, and £93 9s. ½d. was put to the Peckwater fund.

to the cocklofts, a crenellated wing on the east with large, three-light windows, a free-standing building on the south (where the Library stands today), a wing to the west, which must have had student accommodation at its north end, and the canonry to the south. One upstairs room on this west side has an elegant oriel window which would have received the afternoon and evening sun. Arches separate the quad from both the old Canterbury College and Killcanon.

But within a century the domestic 'Jacobethan' style had fallen out of favour. Oxford had been considered a 'Gothic backwater', but Queen's and Trinity colleges soon adopted a classical style, and Aldrich, inspired by Palladio, and influential in the major rebuilding across Oxford in both the colleges and the University, evidently wanted to make his mark on his own college.[6]

In 1706 Christ Church received a bequest of nearly £3,000 from Canon Anthony Radcliffe, which Aldrich seized upon as his opportunity to do something grandiose to encourage the wealthy in to Christ Church.[7] Three foundation stones were laid on Saturday, 26 January 1706, one of them by the Earl of Salisbury, who had given £100 to the project.[8] All of the Chapter, and the noblemen in residence at the time, each added a stone to get the building off to a fine start.[9] The design was Aldrich's, and the construction began under his supervision.[10] Articles of agreement were signed with William Townesend, mason and architect, and with the carpenter George Smith.[11]

Out of step with the Baroque style that was popular and evident in new stately homes such as Castle Howard and Blenheim Palace, Peckwater Quad was ahead of its time with its stern and strict classicism, anticipating later Palladian architecture.[12] The wings are all identical, and give the appearance of an Italian palazzo. The ground floor was rusticated; then the first floor – the *piano nobile* – and the second floor were given Ionic engaged columns on the central five bays (which stand slightly forward of the rest of the wing) underneath a grand pediment, with square pilasters for the five bays either side. The first-floor windows were given alternating triangular and semicircular pediments, a feature perhaps copied from Inigo Jones's Banqueting House. A balustrade hides the low roof and the attics.[13] The design, however, is a peculiarly English adaption of Palladianism adopted by connoisseurs such as Inigo Jones, something very definitely Italian but also 'distinctly English'.[14]

Each side was built separately, apparently beginning with the north, so that the old accommodation in the other two sides could remain in use and to allow for funds to come in; Radcliffe's money paid only for the north side, which carries an inscription to that effect – 'Atrii Peckwateriensis quod spectas latus extruxit Antonius Radcliffe S.T.P. huiusce aedis primo alumnus deinde canonicus' – under the parapet.[15] The stone was supplied by two men – John Green and Robert Robinson, perhaps Townesend's quarry masters

The Townesend family, who owned the Headington quarries, had a significant impact on the building and rebuilding of Oxford. The family dominance
was begun by John, master mason, in the later seventeenth century and
continued by William and then John, who became not just masons but also
architects. The family's business papers show that William alone worked at
Brasenose, Queen's, Corpus Christi, All Souls, University, Oriel, Wadham,
Worcester, Lincoln, Trinity, St John's, New and Balliol colleges as well as for
the University Press and at the Schools and the Botanic Garden. Outside
Oxford, his commissions included work at Blenheim Palace, Cirencester
House and Rycote Park. During his busiest years, from *c*.1719 to 1723, he
was sometimes operating on as many as sixteen projects simultaneously.

– and the bricks by Henry North. Most of the stone was from Headington, but
accounts show that 'fine Barnsly stone' from Gloucestershire was purchased
for capitals and pilasters.[16] Cellars were dug, to be used as wine cellars for
the undergraduates, and as the old buildings were gradually demolished, so
the materials were reused elsewhere to rebuild, for example, Dr Stratford's
outhouses.[17]

Townesend's contract for the construction of the west side of the quadrangle is detailed. He was obliged, for a fee of £1,670, to supply stone, brick,
lime and sand and all other materials necessary within nine months of 1
January 1708 to construct the wing, 144 feet in length. The walls in the
cellars were to be of common walling stone 4 feet 3 inches thick, except
under the columns, where they were to be 5 feet 9 inches. The walls of the
first storey were to be of fitting stone, to match the north side, and 3 feet
thick. The second and third storeys were to be 2 feet 3 inches. Walls between
the bedchambers and general room were of brick, with a thickness of one
brick's length, and walls between bedchambers and studies one brick's
breadth. Everything was set out in the same detail, including the projection
of the pilasters (7 inches) and columns (1 foot 9 inches) and the numbers
and positions of chimneys. One chimney stack was to be large and fit for
use in the kitchen marked on the plan. George Smith's contract for all the

Dean Henry Aldrich was a real polymath. He was particularly fond of music, and left Christ Church one of the greatest collections of early church and popular scores in the country. But Aldrich was also a talented architect; he wrote a treatise on architecture – *Elementa architecturae civilis* – of which two parts were published in 1789. With George Clarke, of All Souls, he influenced many of the buildings that sprang up in Oxford at the end of the seventeenth century and beginning of the eighteenth, including All Saints church and, possibly, the Fellows Building at Corpus Christi College, which bears a remarkable resemblance to Peckwater Quad.

ODNB; Hiscock (1946); Hiscock (1960)

woodwork was equally precise. Everything was to be of oak, except for the three upper flights in each staircase, which would be of elm.[18] Most rooms, particularly those on the ground floor and *piano nobile*, were rather grand. On the first floor were large double sets suitable for gentlemen; the sharing of rooms had fallen out of favour, and sets were increasingly common. In the attics were smaller rooms for servants or for servitors (poorer undergraduates who were given light, but menial, duties in return for their tuition).[19]

Aldrich did not see Peckwater completed. Townesend, who was soon to manage the building of the New Library, had probably completed all his tasks, but whether the expensive wainscoting was finally nailed in before Aldrich's death at the end of 1710 seems unlikely. At least some of the work on Peckwater Quad was done on credit; £500 that had been left to the building fund by Charles Somerset, Lord Herbert, in his will was not released until the beginning of 1711, and so the final bill from the external contractors was settled only on 3 January 1712, but other tasks still remained to be done at college expense, including the glazing of the north-east corner and the numbering of all the rooms.[20] Internal finishes, such as the wainscoting, or panelling, were the responsibility of the residents of the rooms. This was funded by the 'thirds' system: the first resident of the room suffered the full cost but was reimbursed a third by his successor in the room. In turn, his successor paid a third and so on, until the figure reached just £5, when it was written off.[21]

Little happened to Peckwater Quad between the completion of its building and the twentieth century, except in 1728, when an omission by Aldrich was corrected and a door was opened from Peck 4 on to the roof to provide access for maintenance. In 1733 the window sashes were repaired.[22] In 1740 a door was made from Peck 6 (where the privies were) into Blue Boar Lane so that the removal of rubbish would be easier, and during the 1740s all the chimneys were rebuilt and the quadrangle was laid out once the structure of the New Library had been completed.[23] Stones were set up along the north side of Peck, in Blue Boar Lane, to protect the stonework from damage by carts and carriages.[24] In the 1770s new sashes were installed, and a general cleaning and whitewashing was undertaken, perhaps to bring the quad up to a state to match the New Library on its south side.[25] The theft of lead, thought of as a modern crime, was also taking place in the late eighteenth century; an Anthony Smith was prosecuted by the Dean and Chapter for stealing roofing from Peck in 1786.[26] The balustrade was renewed using Bath stone in 1829, and many of the windows were replaced in 1874, with a slightly different design; eighteenth-century windows did not have 'horns' on the lower edge of the top sash.[27]

By the 1920s, however, the stonework was beginning to look particularly dilapidated, so between 1926 and 1930 Symm & Co. completely refaced Peck in Clipsham stone.[28] A single stone bears witness to the previous sorry state of the masonry: just outside the door to Peck 3 is a block scratched with the name Vyner. Frederick Grantham Vyner was murdered

---

Clipsham stone, a type of limestone from Lincolnshire that was more resilient to pollution than the local limestones, rapidly became the stone of choice for repairs and for new Oxford buildings from the late nineteenth century into the 1960s. It was used by Thomas Jackson and George Gilbert Scott in the 1870s, and for essential repairs to the Houses of Parliament in the 1920s.

Howell, in Brock and Curthoys (2000), 749

*Peckwater under scaffolding in the 1920s. The stonework
was being renewed and repaired by Symm & Co.*

by Greek brigands in April 1870, and, although the inscription was nothing
more than undergraduate graffiti, it was protected in his memory. Like the
lost foundation stones, this has suffered from the elements and is now barely
legible.[29]

Staircase 9 in Peckwater Quad has always been separate from the rest.
Right from the beginning there was a canonry in this corner, and this tradition was continued with the eighteenth-century rebuilding (hence the odd
numbering of the staircases, with 9 before 1). When Arthur Stanley was
appointed regius professor of ecclesiastical history in 1858, and was allocated Killcanon as his lodgings, the new professor, who had eight daughters, was allowed to take over part of Peck 9 as an extension.

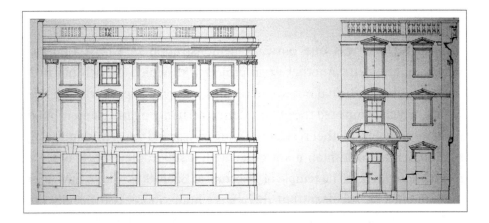

Elevation of the south face of Peckwater 9 in 1912, before the door was moved to the bay further west, and the east elevation of Killcanon.

Since then, Peck has been updated and modernised: in the 1950s hot and cold water was made available to all rooms where 'hitherto, running water has come only through the roof', and in the 1970s further repair of the stonework took place, as well as improvements to the heating and plumbing.[30] Kitchenettes were introduced on each staircase to meet changing student demands, and fireproof doors placed in the lobbies and on the stairs.[31]

In 1979 staircase 9 was refurbished, still for use by the Junior Censor and as additional student accommodation.[32] Some years later a student computer room was incorporated into the ground floor, and the first floor taken over by the Development and Alumni Relations Office.

In mid-2016 Peckwater Quad was shrouded in scaffolding again, undergoing the first phase of a major restoration and refurbishment, including repairs to the stonework, roof and windows, the provision of ensuite facilities in some rooms and additional bathrooms in the basement, and the renewal of all services, including data systems.[33]

The New Library

Peckwater Quad was one outward demonstration of Christ Church's increasing grandeur. Another great project with which Aldrich has been credited, although he did not live to see this one even begun, was the New Library, which completed the quad. Aldrich certainly planned a new building here, probably another residential wing on a grand scale, this time using a monumental Corinthian giant order with a subordinate Doric order at ground-floor level.[34] The temple of Bacchus at Baalbek is said to have been one influence on the dean, but there were many more, both locally and further afield, such as the Temple of Hadrian in Rome and the portico at Old St Paul's.[35]

Judging by the ground-floor plan, Aldrich's building would have had nine bays with an open, central entrance. Two staircases against the south walls would have risen at the east and west ends. The rooms would have been generous, and so were perhaps designed for the noblemen that Christ Church's early eighteenth-century canons wished to attract; the more composed and restrained Peckwater buildings were better suited to the gentlemen commoners. Aldrich's designs reflected status.[36] A tall cupola would have graced the roof. William Stratford wrote on 20 September 1716 that £500 from Dr South's bequest had arrived and was to be put to the new building on the south side of Peck. Work was to follow Aldrich's design for the exterior, but it would now be 'the finest library that belongs to any society in Europe'.[37]

A new library had become an essential, rather than a solely desirable, addition to Christ Church's buildings. Otho Nicholson, who had refurbished

---

Robert South came up to Christ Church from Westminster School in 1651. A Royalist, South eventually gained a canonry in 1670. He was one of Christ Church's greatest benefactors, leaving the college his estates in Caversham and Kentish Town.

ODNB

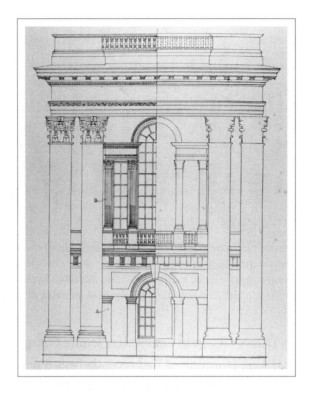

*An elevation, by the architectural historian A. S. G. Butler
(1888–1965), of the west end of the New Library with its
Venetian window and square Corinthian pilasters.*

the old library in the early years of the seventeenth century, bequeathed some
of his own books; and John Morris, the regius professor of Hebrew, had left his
collection of Hebrew, Syriac and other Middle Eastern texts in 1648. Robert
Burton, author of *The Anatomy of Melancholy*, bequeathed five hundred books
in 1640.[38] On his death Aldrich left to Christ Church his own large collection
of books, pamphlets and music, all of which had to be accommodated and for
which a new gallery was installed, at a cost of nearly £40.[39] While still magnificent, if a bit dilapidated, the library's old-fashioned presses and cupboards
were unable to cope, and a new building was becoming even more urgent.

The New Library was planned not just as a repository for books but
also, like Peckwater Quad, as a means to entice wealthy aristocrats to Christ
Church. There may well have been an element of competition too; other

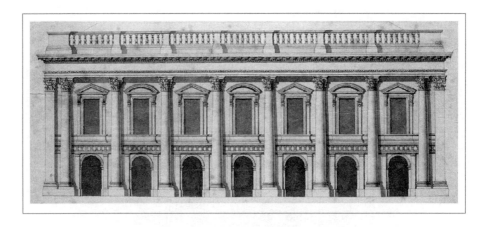

*Townesend's alterations to Aldrich's design. The building that was
to become the library was originally planned as further student
accommodation. After Aldrich's death, a decision was taken by the Chapter
to use the site, still following Aldrich's drawing, for a new library.*

colleges (such as Trinity College in Cambridge, Trinity College in Dublin and
All Souls, Oxford) were planning or had recently begun new and magnifi-
cent libraries. Under the supervisory eyes of George Clarke, who succeeded
Aldrich as an influence on Oxford architecture and who had collaborated
with Nicholas Hawksmoor and James Thornhill, and of William Townesend
the building began in 1716.[40] Townesend (1668–1739) was the son of
John, master mason and twice mayor of Oxford. Like his father before him,
William Townesend's skills were employed on numerous buildings around
Oxford, including All Saints Church and the cloister and Fellows' Building
at Corpus Christi College.[41]

The hands of both men are seen in the adaptation of Aldrich's drawings to provide a grand new Library building, some of which show Townesend's alterations and design features and are signed by him.[42] The bold
design was a deliberate contrast with the severity of Peckwater, based on
Michelangelo's Capitoline palaces, borrowing features such as the open
ground-floor loggia from earlier libraries such as the Wren Library at Trinity
College, Cambridge, and St Mark's Library in Venice.[43] Headington hard and
free stones were used for the main constructional elements, with the more
decorative features, such as the capitals and the window embellishments,

in the differently coloured Burford stone, which arrived by river, delivered at Hythe Bridge.[44] Townesend's proposals show how widely the costs of the different stone varied, depending on their type and the extent of their elaborate designs: the simple, plain freestone work would cost 8d. per foot, but the highly decorative capitals on the great pilasters cost £8 apiece.[45] The change of use from residential to library meant that Aldrich's planned attics could be abandoned, and the number of bays was reduced from nine to seven. The ground floor would be a loggia, open to the elements on three sides, as the library at The Queen's College was originally, and the upper floor would house the library and other collections.[46] The façade of Christ Church's building would be a giant order rather than the plainer Doric and Ionic orders of Trinity's. The beautiful stone staircase was *à la mode*; although not a newly fashionable cantilever, it reflects the growing fashion for stone staircases with iron balustrades and mahogany handrails.[47]

Construction was funded by gifts from old members, and the account book records the incoming benefactions on the left of each opening, and the expenditure on the right. It was a long, slow process – members had, after all, only just been asked to contribute to the rebuilding of Peckwater Quad. There were five years (1722–5 and 1746) when no money came in at all.[48] The trickle of gifts was supplemented by graduates redirecting their caution money refunds into the building fund and the transfer of balances from other funds.[49] Dean Boulter even bought a couple of lottery tickets, but he was not on a winning streak.[50]

Another anticipated source of income for the building project was the profits from John Urry's edition of Chaucer.[51] Dean Atterbury had commissioned the new edition in 1711, but it was incomplete when Urry died in 1715. His executor, Browne Willis, entered into an agreement with the Dean and Chapter, and with Barnaby Lintot, a bookseller, to complete the work. The college and Willis were to prepare the text, and Lintot was to pay for the paper and printing. All three contractors were to receive an equal number of the printed books. All new students would be obliged to purchase a copy and to sell as many as they could to their friends and families. Browne Willis felt that he received the rough end of the deal: the Dean and Chapter had a captive audience for their copies, and Lintot was in the business of selling

Browne Willis (1682–1760) came up to Christ Church in 1700. He left without taking a degree but developed antiquarian interests after visits to Westminster Abbey as a boy. He was a high-church Tory, devoted to his native Buckinghamshire, an eccentric and an architectural patron and church builder.

ODNB

books, but Willis, having done the lion's share of the work, found that he was stuck with most of his third of the stock. The plan was not a success, not helped by the early death, in 1719, of Thomas Ainsworth, who had been chosen to continuing the editing. The book was finally published in 1721 but, in spite of all the efforts by so many, did not sell well.[52] In February 1734 Willis commented that he had not sold a copy for several years. He handed over what little money he had made to the building fund.

The first task, early in 1717, was the demolition of old chambers and outhouses that had occupied the site.[53] Three Students ousted from their rooms – presumably in the western wing of Canterbury College – were given new ones in the cloister.[54] By Townesend's death in 1739 most of the masonry work had been done, and the roof was just about complete; articles of agreement had been signed with Townesend and Charles Cole, the plumber, for the roofing two years earlier.[55] Townesend was employed in 1733 to clear out the rubbish – presumably the inevitable mess left after construction – from underneath the Library.[56] Elizabeth, the daughter of William Sheppard of Hart Hall, reported in 1738 that the Library was a 'fine shell', with beautiful Venetian windows at each end.[57] After September 1742, by which time the roof had been leaded and the windows sashed and glazed, work ground to a halt with only £1 17s. 3d. left in the kitty. Four years went by before the coffers were sufficiently replenished to allow the college carpenters to begin on the timberwork; the English oak floor was laid by Jeremiah Franklin, who had worked with Townesend at Queen's, and, according to the accounts, Jeremiah's wife, Catherine.[58]

But even before the shell of the building was completed, the original designs for the interior of the Upper Library were thrown into confusion. The upper room is 142 feet long, 30 feet wide and 37 feet high, and the original plan was to have shelves at right angles to the long walls, much as they were in medieval libraries and in the more contemporary library at The Queen's College. But gifts of books had continued to arrive: Lewis Atterbury, the dean's brother, had given 3,000 pamphlets in 1722; Canon William Stratford bequeathed 5,000 books in 1729, for which new shelves were built in the old library; and in 1731, 2,500 books and all the scientific instruments belonging to Charles Boyle, the fourth Earl of Orrery, were given to Christ Church.[59] In 1737 the enormous bequest of the archbishop of Canterbury, William Wake, was delivered.[60] Along with Aldrich's collection, which had already caused a major upheaval in the old library, space had to be found for all of these. Once a rent had been agreed, two Students were evicted from their chambers – Great Quad 1:2 (now part of the Senior Common Room) and 4:2 – which were then used as temporary storage for Orrery's and Wake's collections.[61] The collections remained in packing cases while designs and ideas were debated in Chapter.

These huge bequests prompted a rethink; the shelves were now to be placed against the walls, rather than at right angles, as they were in the Arts End of the Bodleian Library and at the Codrington Library at All Souls College; in consequence, four of the seven windows were blocked up on the inside. This seems an odd thing to do, and it has been suggested that it provided additional space for the new books, but this is unlikely. A second idea is that the new bequests were so grand, and with so many artefacts as well as volumes, that the medieval shelving style was abandoned to create instead a space for display and to turn the Library into more of a 'cabinet of curiosities'.[62] After George Clarke's death in 1736, James Gibbs was asked to come up with suggestions for the shelving. He proposed first that the Library be shelved using the whole building, with a single room covering the entire length and height, and with a gallery on either side. This did not meet with approval, so Gibbs adapted his idea and retained the two levels but enclosing the ground floor to create a two-storey Library space. Gibbs's design for

Jeremiah Franklin was also employed at All Souls, on the building of the Codrington Library, and at the Radcliffe Camera. He served as Oxford's mayor twice. Several women worked on the Library project. In addition to Catherine Franklin, there were Mary Borton, who took away rubbish and brought in gravel, Jane Fifield, a slater and plasterer, and Mary Witherington, a painter.

Cook and Mason (1988)

upstairs seems to have been the one adopted, by and large, by Dean Gregory, and the proposed use of the ground floor was only too prophetic.[63]

Funds for the decoration of the Upper Library were pulled in by David Gregory, first treasurer and then dean, and the work was done by two London carpenters, George Shakespeare and John Phillips, who worked with the rich and unvarnished Norwegian oak to produce the pedimented bookcases, in the Ionic order, and the gallery. A local craftsman, Thomas Roberts, who beautified the Senior Common Room at St John's College and the Radcliffe Camera, was responsible for the elaborate plasterwork, including the staircase ceiling, the decoration under the gallery and the remarkable 'trophies' – the drops of scientific and musical instruments, celebrating and complementing the collections of music and the Earl of Orrery's scientific and astronomical instruments.[64] The three men together produced a design of Rococo exuberance, with overtones of Grinling Gibbons, in sharp contrast to the restrained classical exterior.[65] Roberts's work on the ceiling alone cost £663. In 1762 and 1763 the finishing touches were added: the engraving of the Christ Church arms for bookplates had been commissioned and inkstands purchased ready to stand on the five new mahogany desks. Thomas Chippendale's stools and George James's matching steps had been brought from London, matting had been laid, locks were installed, the painter had finished – even in the little south-facing rooms – and the mahogany rail on the stairs had been fitted by George Shakespeare.[66] The statue of John Locke by Rysbrack was already standing on the Library stairs.[67] And finally the whole Library was cleaned and dusted ready to receive the books.[68]

The positioning of shelves in the library was rethought several times. This was one idea, which included ceiling-height shelves upstairs and down.

But even at this late stage events prompted another redesign. General Sir John Guise, who had left Christ Church in 1702 and become a professional soldier serving with the Duke of Marlborough in Flanders and then in Spain, the Caribbean and Scotland, was an avid collector of Renaissance art. A visitor to Guise's house in London commented on the famous artists who were represented and made particular comment on Carracci's *Butcher's Shop*, a painting so vivid 'where you may take a slice whenever your Appitite serves of either mutton veal or lamb'.[69] Just as the Library project was nearing completion, Guise's extraordinary collection, consisting of 258 pictures and over 900 drawings, was given to Christ Church.[70] A brave decision was made to close in the fashionable open loggia and create a gallery, and it was Henry Keene, surveyor to the Dean and Chapter of Westminster Abbey, who was given the challenge of executing this plan.[71] Keene was a Gothic revivalist,

After the arrival of the Guise collection of Old Master paintings and drawings,
the lower library was converted from its open loggia into a gallery. The west
end continued to house pictures until the middle of the twentieth century.

influenced by the architecture of the abbey, and he implemented the style in
several places, not least the chapel at Hartlebury Castle, which he remodelled
for the bishops of Worcester, and the interiors at Arbury Hall in Warwick-
shire. In spite of this and of the patronage of Roger Newdigate, the MP for
Oxford and a fan of Gothic, most of Keene's works in Oxford were classical in
style.[72] At Christ Church he had little choice in his adaptation of the Library.

All of a sudden there was upheaval. The archways leading into the
loggia had to be converted into windows and doors; floorboards had to be
laid where there would have been stone flags; plasterers and glaziers had to
be called back. What would have been just tidying up and finishing touches
in 1765 became work that took at least another five years.[73] The Lower
Library was far more restrained in its decoration than the Upper, with each
side divided into three compartments separated by short walls and Ionic

The aptly named Mrs Showwell, who showed the art collection to visitors in
the eighteenth century. An artisan called Mr Showell undertook repairs and
maintenance across the site at this period; the chances are that the two were
related (irregular spellings were commonplace, even for surnames, at this period).

columns. Bookcases decorated with simple Grecian designs were placed
around parts of the walls with space left for the pictures. The ceilings were
the embodiment of simplicity compared with that on the upper floor.

Keene's bill was settled in 1771, but craftsmen, including the gilders,
Abaudio Campioni and William Rought, and the picture-framer, Masken,
did not see all their invoices cleared until 1779.[74] But the Library was in
use before then: during the summer of 1771 the porter, another Thomas
Roberts, and his assistant, William Pound, were paid 5s. apiece to move the
books from the old library to the new, and a Mr Neale supplied charcoal to
warm the hands of the studious members who were permitted to use the
beautiful space.[75]

All the bequests meant that the Library was almost full from the day it opened. Wake's manuscripts and coins, Orrery's scientific instruments – including the model of the solar system named after him – and Aldrich's music were all located in the side rooms off the main library. Edward Smallwell was entrusted with the thankless task of producing a new catalogue.[76] His reward was the rich rectory of Batsford in Gloucestershire, which he was permitted, against the usual rules, to hold in conjunction with both his Studentship and his Librarianship.[77]

The New Library remained part-library, part-gallery until the mid-twentieth century. Increasing demands for a working undergraduate library coincided with the development of Blue Boar Quad and the provision of a dedicated place for the display of Christ Church's superlative collection of paintings and drawings. Generous donations allowed a new gallery to be constructed, and as the pictures moved out, so the Library was made more useful for undergraduates.

All sorts of odd jobs had been done on the building since its completion in the mid-eighteenth century. In 1799, not long after the Library had been completed, guttering and drains were installed at the east and west ends.[78] At the same time the practice, which had evidently grown up very quickly, of using the East Library as a lecture room was stopped; visitors who had to buy threepenny tickets to be shown the collections by Mrs Showwell and her successors had found the lectures a terrible inconvenience.[79] A century later Thomas Vere Bayne fought tooth and nail to stop lectures returning to the

Only a few years later Wake's coin collection was supplemented by a gift of oriental coins that had belonged to Canon Richard Browne, the regius professor of Hebrew, one of English coins from Canon Barton and one of Classical coins bequeathed by Robert Welborne. The Christ Church coins now form a large part of the collections in the Ashmolean Museum. It is difficult to be certain how the rooms, or closets, off the Upper Library were used. As late as 1804, shelving was being installed in the Orrery Closet and the Upperbrake Closet.

The Lower Wake Archive Room is usually known as Wake Arch. Inf. It is one of the six small rooms off the main Upper Library that contain specialist collections and provide access to the Orrery gallery. The others are Arch. Inf., Arch. Sup. (or the Music Room), Wake Arch. Sup., Hyp. and Z.

Library when the Lecture Room Committee proposed that the west end be used for lectures in the morning, and that the Lower Wake Archive Room be converted into a reading room.[80] 'The library is a place of study', said Bayne, 'too much dirt and dust is caused by visitors who regard the Library as a showplace, without adding scores of undergraduates'. He proposed that the Library could continue to be used for special lectures, something that could no longer happen if it were in regular use as a reading room, and that two of the rooms in the old Library building could be thrown together and made into a convenient facility for classes.[81] But he lost, and the west end of the Library was used for lectures from 1894.[82]

During the nineteenth century the granite paving around the building and the new steps were laid (in 1845), and new gutters and tiles added to the roof (in 1837).[83] Heating was first introduced in 1866; it was thought antiquated in 1931 but not replaced until 1963.[84] The gallery was inserted into the East Library in 1869 to provide additional shelving in a rather functional Gothic style, and books from the Undergraduate Reading Room, which had been established in 1884, were reabsorbed into the Library's main collections in 1929.[85] In 1921 the floors were found to have dry rot and beetles, and the joists were replaced with steel girders.[86] The cleaner was provided with a cupboard with a tap, conveniently hidden by the bust of George IV, in 1908, and electric light was introduced in 1928. Until then the Library had only been open during daylight hours. Also in 1928 a proposal was made that the Library begin to expand into the basement under the west side of Peckwater.[87]

But the major works that were to take place were the refacing of the exterior and the redecoration of the interior. The hallway and staircase were

The Undergraduate Reading Room in Tom 4, photographed c.1900.

redecorated in burnt orange under the guidance of the renowned interior designer John Fowler in 1957, and the busts of royalty and distinguished old members placed in the hall. The vast statue of Dean Jackson by Francis Chantrey, which had stood in the centre of the lobby, moved to the ante-hall, to be replaced soon after by Jacob Epstein's bronze of Dean Lowe.[88]

Attention was then turned to the outside. The appalling state of the stonework was first noted in 1893; William Gates, of the Institute of Chartered Engineers, described it as 'very badly scaled and weathered'. The Headington freestone was suffering from exfoliation, the hardstone from cavernous decay and the Burford stone from blistering and warts.[89] Immediate repairs were made to the cornice then, and again in 1908, but not the major work that was evidently needed.[90] Peckwater Quad was refaced in the late 1920s, leaving the Library looking particularly shabby, and by the 1950s the crumbling stonework – which Sir John Summerson described

The soft local stone used to build the library in the eighteenth century was in a parlous state by the late nineteenth. It was not until 1960, however, that real work began to restore and repair it. This photograph was taken in 1947 as part of a survey of the condition of all Christ Church's stonework. At one point a barricade had to be placed around the building to ensure passers-by were not injured by falling masonry.

as having 'about as much artistic meaning as a painting might which had been run over by a fleet of lorries' – was being removed for the safety of those walking below. The development of the Blue Boar site was put on hold for a decade, partly because of the urgent need for conservation work on the Library frontage, but it was still not until 1960 that the real work began, when three sides of the building – north, east and west – were refaced. There had been some concern a few years earlier that the use of the by now ubiquitous Clipsham would render the quadrangle dull, but the worries were needless; the restoration was completed in a dramatic combination of Portland Shelly Whitbed and Clipsham stone, replacing the old Headington and

In 1928 the Library only occupied the space under Peck 9:2. In 1964 the tentacles began their spread under Peck 9:1. Slowly over the next thirty years the Library took over the whole of the west-side basement. The Librarian, Dr John Mason, declared in the mid-1970s that there was sufficient storage space to see the Library through to the twenty-first century. Dr Mason's intention was that the Library should be able to resist what he called 'the modern idea of self-renewal': i.e., the development of a policy of disposal as well as of acquisition. He was just about right in his predictions for modern books but did not anticipate the concerns of the surveyors who conducted the 1992 decennial survey. New metal shelving had been inserted into the side rooms of the main Library, and the volumes placed on them were exerting parlous strain on the eighteenth-century floors. The shelves had to be removed, and, as a consequence, the Library basement expanded under part of Killcanon between 1992 and 1994, and further still in 2001.

In 2016 the Governing Body requested the return of the space under Peckwater 1 and 2 for other uses. Dr Mason's jealously guarded overflow and little-used stock must be drastically reduced and a policy of disposal – no bad thing – introduced.

Burford stones, which allowed the re-creation of the original contrasting colours.[91] The effect was to draw the quadrangle together as a 'historically and architecturally' cohesive whole.[92]

Whether the same work would have been done today is debatable. In 1957, when the Historic Buildings Appeal was launched in Oxford, architectural and aesthetic considerations carried more weight than archaeological ideals. However, the condition of the Library was such that it could well have been the only option.

Then back to the inside. In 1963 the pictures that remained in the Library were moved into temporary storage, allowing more space for books and, for the first time, turning the whole of the ground floor over for Library use.[93] Symm & Co. were commissioned to build bookcases in the West Library to match those in the east, and the downstairs rooms were lined with a hessian, painted off-white. It was then that the daunting task of redecorating the Upper Library was tackled. Once again John Fowler was called in to advise and, after problems determining what the original scheme by Roberts might have been, it was decided to start from scratch. The basic plan was agreed, including the gilding of Roberts's ceiling plasterwork, but choosing the colour was to cause many hours of heartache, not least for the Librarian, John Mason. Neapolitan pink or white were the favourite options, with pink being the Librarian's choice. Fowler was less than amused at the proposal of a bolder pink, suggesting that 'if Christ Church wants a scheme in knicker pink, it must find another consultant'.[94] Part of the problem was the size of the committee, swelled by many advisers. The vote was taken in Michaelmas term 1964, influenced by the prearranged intervention of Lord Robert Blake, and pink won the day by twenty-one votes to nine.[95]

There have always been debates about making more use of the Library building, particularly the Upper Library. Redecoration, fire precautions and updated lighting and heating systems prompted the proposal in 1962 that it be used as a reading room for senior members and graduate students. Grilles would have been needed to protect the antiquarian books. The chance for a general clear-out of 'bric-à-brac and unsightly showcases and cupboards' could have been seized. But neither this scheme nor the proposal to remove the Victorian gallery in the East Library downstairs was carried forward.[96] The gallery survived because the Library was full to bursting, but the editor of the Annual Report remarked ruefully, 'I suspect also that the 1869 improvements, being Victorian and also ugly, would find eager champions inside and outside Christ Church, as soon as they were seriously threatened.'[97]

In the 1990s the increasing demands of conferences and an ever-growing body of students prompted a renewal of the arguments for an upper reading room, this time scuppered by far stricter fire regulations, which demanded a second escape route.[98] No plan could meet with the approval of the heritage bodies, and a survey showed that 'bums on seats' in the Library were actually dropping, so the Upper Library remained as it was designed. However, there were other problems that needed remedying.

One remaining challenge is the provision of office space for the librarians. In 1962, when the post of Librarian was made full-time, one of the small rooms off the Upper Library was adapted as an office 'temporarily' while other possibilities were researched. One plan, which involved breaking a door through the Library into one of the deanery orangeries at the back, was revisited in the 1990s but rejected for a second time. At the time of writing, the librarians in the working Library occupy the entrance hall and potential desk space for students.

There were increasing concerns about the state of the Library's electrical system and fire safety from the early 1990s, but it was not until 2009 that work began on the wiring, on the roof – the lead of which was perishing – and on the stonework of the south face, which had not been tackled when the other three sides were renovated forty years earlier. Generous donations from old members allowed Donald Insall, conservation architects, to be called in to oversee the project.[99]

Over the summer of 2009 the whole Library was shrouded in scaffolding. Surprisingly few horrors were waiting to be discovered: just one roof timber needed attention after a limited attack by beetle, and there was the inevitable asbestos found around the old heating pipes. The south side was repaired, partly in Clipsham to match the few repairs that had been done in the 1960s, but predominantly (for the large panels and the tympanum of the central pediment) in Stoke Ground Bath stone, which was a better match for the Headington of the original construction. The roof was re-leaded and re-slated, and the attic space insulated with sheep's wool. The electrics were completely renewed, and the opportunity was taken to upgrade the lighting both in the Upper Library and in the working Lower Library. Downstairs, huge modern light fittings with an almost 1930s look were installed in each bay to replace the inadequate fluorescent tubes which had been hidden on the tops of the bookcases. Environmentally friendly, the new lights were designed to dim when there was no movement in the rooms.[100]

Cardinal Wolsey, by an unknown artist, late sixteenth or early seventeenth century. Wolsey is shown holding the document from the Pope granting him the titular church of Santa Cecilia in Trastevere.

This decorative moulding beneath the oriel window at the south end of St Aldate's front is the only indication that Wolsey may have intended this to be the grandest residence of Cardinal College.

Examples of Wolsey's emblems, which decorate the Hall. These were repainted in 1979–80 and cleaned during the repair work of 2014–15.

The Hall after the major repairs and restoration of the roof in 2014–15. All the portraits (except Sampson Strong's painting of Wolsey, which was removed for conservation) were covered, rather than removed, during the work.

The noblemen's oriel window in the Hall. The central boss of the fan vault carries Wolsey's arms, with putti as supporters.

Tom 4 staircase.
Tom 3 and 4 are the only staircases that are essentially in their original state, with Wolsey's emblems in the spandrels over the internal doors, the timber frame still exposed, and wooden stairs.

Peter Lely's portrait of John Fell (the first of the great 'builder deans'), John Dolben and Richard Allestree. Dean Fell commissioned the completion of the Great Quadrangle in the 1660s and then the construction of Tom Tower. John Dolben, as Treasurer, was responsible for the financial management of Fell's projects. Richard Allestree was the first resident of one of the new canonries on the north side of the quadrangle.

The south-east corner of Tom Quad as it is today, showing the Hall, George Gilbert Scott's double-arched entrance to the cathedral, Thomas Bodley's Wolsey Tower, and Mercury on his plinth in the centre of Richard Gardiner's seventeenth-century reservoir.

A classic view of Tom Tower flanked by (at left) the west end of the New Library and (at right) staircase 9 of Peckwater Quad.

The Upper Library, facing west. In 1716, the Dean and Chapter set out to build 'the finest library of any society in Europe'. It took fifty years to complete.

A detail from the St Cecilia window, designed by Edward Burne-Jones and made by William Morris & Co. in 1874.

Detail of a pew in the cathedral, executed in elm and depicting Jesus calling Peter from the boat in the storm.

The Bishop King window, executed by the van Linge brothers in the 1630s, along with a series of painted glass for at least twelve other windows in the cathedral. Only this window (removed by King's descendants for safe-keeping) and the 'Jonah' window survived the Commonwealth. Robert King was the last abbot of Oseney and the first bishop of Oxford.

The George Bodley/William Brindley reredos at the west end of the cathedral. This twentieth-century photograph clearly shows Gilbert Scott's more Romanesque reconstruction of the east end and the new paving by Clayton and Bell. The reredos (installed in 1882) was designed by Bodley and carved by Brindley, who also sculpted the decorative stonework on the Albert Memorial and at Westminster Cathedral.

One of Patrick Reyntiens's designs for the Hall windows. The 'Alice' window shows Charles Dodgson ('Lewis Carroll') and Alice Liddell, Dean Liddell's daughter, for whom Alice's Adventures in Wonderland was written. Also represented, by their coats of arms, are Deans Gaisford, Liddell, Paget and Strong. Throughout the window are John Tenniel's characters from the 'Alice' stories.

One of a series of cartoons by Thomas Rowlandson illustrating 'The tour of Dr Syntax in search of the Picturesque', a poem by William Combe published in 1812. This drawing shows the landing on the Hall stairs before alterations by James Wyatt in c.1800.

The 'lexicon staircase' in the Deanery, funded by the profits from Liddell and Scott's Greek dictionary.

Meadow Buildings in 2013, soon after the restoration and refurbishment of the tower and staircase 3.

The back of the deanery and canonries on the east side of Tom Quad, showing the masonry conservation undertaken by Wells Cathedral Stonemasons in 2012.

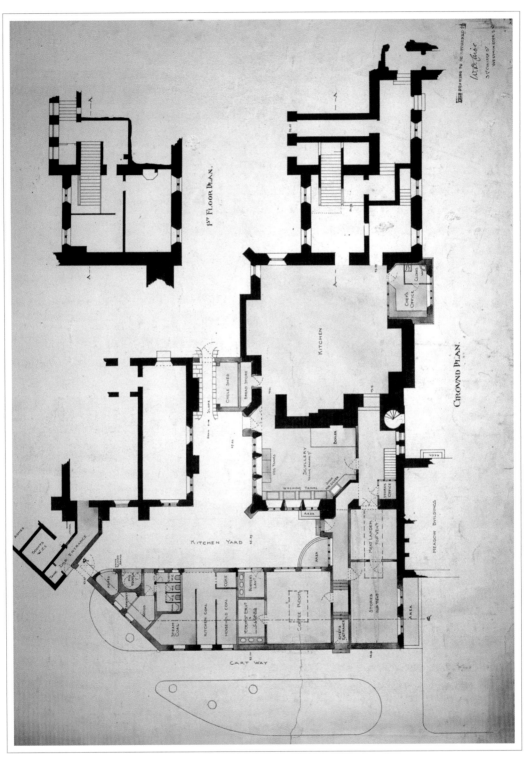

W. D. Caröe's 1910/11 plan for the extension to the kitchen providing staff rooms, store rooms and offices to the south.

Bosanquet and Diplock's 1974 impression of the Porter's Lodge at Tom Gate.

St Aldate's Quad, built in the 1980s behind the medieval houses fronting St Aldate's.
The quadrangle won a RIBA award for its sensitive conversion.

The basement of the old Anatomy School, now the Undercroft, was turned into a college refectory
and bar just after the Second World War. It was completely refurbished in 2014 by Purcell as the
architects, and Knowles as the contractors.

The Jubilee Bridge was installed in 2014, allowing much easier access to the sportsground. It replaced a long-defunct punt which had to be pulled across the Cherwell by a chain.

The sports pavilion, built in the 1970s, has been altered and refurbished several times, most recently in 2014 when changing and catering facilities were updated for the twenty-first century.

The stairs from Tom Quad to the Hall. The beautiful fan vaulting was installed in the 1640s, probably at the behest of Samuel Fell. It was executed by an otherwise unidentified mason called Smith. The staircase itself was altered by James Wyatt in the early years of the nineteenth century, when the steps were pushed slightly further east to allow better appreciation of the slender pillar holding the vault.

The second year of work required scaffolding inside rather than out. The Upper Library plasterwork was completely cleaned by skilled conservators; repainting, except in one or two tiny corners, was unnecessary. The burnt orange of the entrance hall and staircase was renewed using the same paint as had been used in 1960.[101] In the Lower Library the hessian wall covering was removed, with some trepidation. No one was entirely sure whether the condition of the walls beneath would be suitable for exposure. After skilled repair the panels were painted a grey putty colour, and the pillars and woodwork a matt white. Plasterwork on the ceiling was picked out in grey. Finally, new furniture was designed and fitted for the Library staff. The rooms probably looked fresher and brighter than they had ever done, but the continuously changing needs of an academic library and its students mean that adaptation will always need to be managed within the confines of a listed eighteenth-century building. Already plans are afoot to provide more varied and versatile study areas, and to secure the building to allow access twenty-four hours a day.

* * * * *

The ground plan of the whole of Christ Church as the Library was going up was recorded by William Williams in the early 1730s, as one of a series illustrating the Oxford colleges, and published as *Oxonia depicta*. The plan shows the canons' lodgings, annotated with the stall number and the name of the current incumbent, as well as buildings such as Fell's Buildings, Chaplains' Quad and domestic accommodation. Formal gardens and the layout of quadrangles show just how much styles and tastes have changed, although the otherwise undocumented pond in Peckwater Quad may have been aspirational rather than actual.[102] The plan shows how the rooms on the ground floor were arranged, and what remained of the old Canterbury College, including a range of sheds that remained between the incomplete New Library and the deanery garden.[103]

While the major building work of the eighteenth century was taking place in Peckwater Quad, smaller works were taking place elsewhere, sometimes by design, sometimes through necessity. The fire in the Hall in 1720

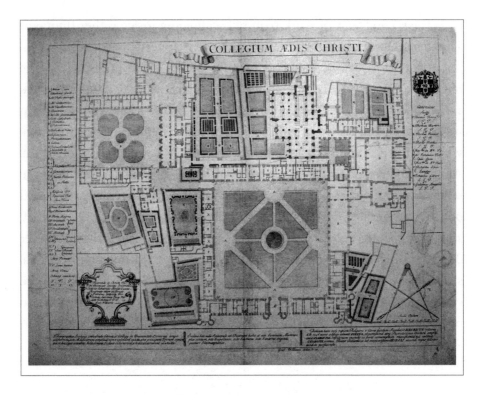

*William Williams's 1733 ground-plan of Christ Church shows the
Library shell completed, although it would be another thirty years
before members could actually use the building for study.*

occupied Townesend during a lull in income for the Library project, and
some of the rooms under the Hall were altered to make a new Treasury.

The buttery

The buttery, alongside the Hall, also received attention after the fire. From the
earliest times this was the place from which the butler issued bread, butter
and beer for meals. Strict rules were set down from early on for the control
of stock and concerning those who were and were not allowed to enter the
room, but in 1722 John Hammond, one of the canons, paid for its refurbishment so that it could be used as a place for relaxation.[104] In 1949, when
the kitchen acquired its new servery, C. C. Handisyde ingeniously copied the

1722 buttery west front to minimise the impact of the alterations behind and towards the kitchen.[105]

Canterbury Quad

Little is known of the appearance of Canterbury College except for the representation on Loggan's engraving and a drawing by John Malchair of the old gate. There was a small quadrangle, with a hall on the west, a chapel on the south and chambers on the other two sides. Somewhere on the western side there had been a library, and the kitchen with other domestic buildings probably lay in the range of buildings that ran along the lane between Christ Church and Corpus Christi College, or in the north-west corner.[106] In 1546 the canonry here was considered the meanest.

Soon after the Library was completed, attention was turned to this medieval survivor. An academic college for the monks of Christ Church, Canterbury, attended by great men such as Thomas More and John Wycliffe, the site had remained untouched until the commencement of the construction of the New Library, apart from some repairs during Brian Duppa's deanery.[107] The old refectory had been used by Dean Massey as a chapel for Catholic services during his brief tenure under James II, and the north-east corner was used as a canonry until the Great Quad was finished.[108] After Massey the deans retained a private apartment in the ancient buildings; Lewis Bagot received £300 compensation for its loss in 1783, and to allow new 'offices' to be built in a 'more commodious place and manner'.[109] The remainder of the rooms must have been used as chambers by Students or commoners. They would hardly have been up to a standard suitable for gentlemen commoners or noblemen, and would have looked terribly tatty and old-fashioned alongside Peckwater Quad and the New Library.

The west side of Canterbury College was lost in the early eighteenth century, under the east end of the New Library. Recent archaeology suggests that it had been well built in good stone.[110] The complete rebuilding, to bring Canterbury Quad to the same level of grandeur as Peckwater and the Library, was begun in 1773, thanks to a gift of £1,000 from Richard Robinson, the archbishop of Armagh. Robinson, first Baron Rokeby, had been

Canterbury Quad in the 1670s, showing its hall, chapel, kitchen and lodgings.

an undergraduate at Christ Church from 1726 and, on leaving Oxford, had risen rapidly through the church. According to his memoirist he was 'publickly ambitious of great deeds and privately capable of good ones', and he certainly demonstrated this in his projects in the town of Armagh, including a public library, an infirmary and a hospital. On his death he left £12,000 for charitable purposes.[111] The architect chosen by the Chapter was James Wyatt. Wyatt, whose buildings combined refined decoration – if not particularly original ideas – with new constructional techniques, exactly in accord with the industrial and aesthetic mood of the time, had designed the Radcliffe Observatory in 1772, which had marked the beginning of nearly forty years' predominance over Oxford's architecture.[112] The Observatory trustees included William Bagot, personally known to Wyatt and the brother of Lewis, soon to be dean of Christ Church. Two years later, Robinson gave another £1,000; the two gifts funded the construction of most of the north side and part of the south.[113] Much of this work was completed by 1775.[114] Other moneys came from a surplus in the South Trust, the proceeds of a benefaction in India Stock (probably shares in the East India Company) and a loan from Thomas Walley Partington.[115] The dean and the treasurer borrowed money on the college's behalf too. Interest

The old Canterbury Gate in 1775, by John Baptist Malchair.
Malchair was a musician and artist who recorded many
buildings in Oxford that no longer survive.

on the loans was to be paid from the Treasury, and the principal to be paid off as soon as the buildings were complete.[116] A quit rent of 3s. 10d. had to be paid to Oriel College for part of this land, and the old iron gates were sold, with the money arising from the sale put towards the enclosure of land between Canterbury Gate and Oriel College stables.[117] The design of most of the small quadrangle is simply elegant, astylar, designed almost to frame the grand Library occupying its west side.[118] It was built of Burford stone.

The old gate into Oriel Square, illustrated by Malchair, was not replaced by the magnificent triumphal arch, in uncompromising Doric, until 1778. It is, possibly, too grand for its location, with its southern end – even in the eighteenth century – tucked away behind Corpus Christi, now ignominiously in that college's car park. Greening Lamborn described the gate – one

*Canterbury Quad in the early years of the twentieth century, showing
sunblinds with decorative wooden 'pelmets' covering the rollers. Neither
screens nor blinds survive. The deterioration of the local stone is also evident.*

of the last classical constructions in Oxford before the revival of Gothicism
– as a 'pompous absurdity'.[119] Its design was, however, a first: fluted base-
less Doric columns had been used for interiors, but not on the outside of an
English building before this.[120]

Canterbury's south-west corner, abutting the gate to the deanery
garden, which matches Peckwater exactly in its exterior design, was not
begun until early in 1783, soon after the dean and treasurer had been
exhorted by the Chapter to start with 'all convenient expedition'. There
must have been great excitement on 31 March 1783, when a skeleton 'of
very large dimensions', wearing boots and buried with coins of Edward I,
was uncovered about three feet below the ground during the digging for
the foundations of the south side.[121] This corner alone cost £4,000, funded

entirely by the munificent archbishop, on the condition that it was used only by undergraduates of the highest social standing.[122] The dean was constantly requested by the Chapter to write thank-you letters.

The quadrangle must have been remarkably well built, for it appears little in the archive. The window frames were repainted in 1808, and new windows were opened in the basement in the mid-nineteenth century, but otherwise it was not until the twentieth century that major work was done. In 1926 new wrought-iron gates were added under the arch, although the old wooden ones remained in place to be closed at night to 'prevent ingress'.[123] In 1930 the electric lighting in all four staircases was reinstalled, and the stonework was treated with a preservative. The following year bathrooms were created out of basement rooms.[124] By 1958, as in Peckwater, all rooms had hot and cold water.[125] From the end of the 1950s through to the early 1970s work was constant on Christ Church's stonework, and Canterbury Quad was no exception: all the inward elevations were renovated, and all of the south and west external elevations. Much of the east side too was repaired, and the pediment over the arch completely renewed. The roofs were re-tiled using Welsh slate while the stonework was again repaired with Clipsham.[126]

It was not until the 1980s that serious work began on the modernisation of the interiors: in 1987 the basements of staircases 1 and 2 (on the north and north-east sides) were damp-proofed and five new undergraduate rooms created. By the end of 1989 the whole of the quad had been brought up to date and twenty new rooms provided on the south side alone, in the basements and by dividing larger rooms. The plumbing was improved too.[127]

The Anatomy School

Peckwater and Canterbury quadrangles were now grand enough to draw young men from wealthy and influential circles, and the New Library was a major boost to Christ Church's academic facilities, but there was another attraction for those with enquiring minds. As the Library was finished, so the construction of the Anatomy School in 1766–7 put Christ Church head and shoulders above other colleges in its science teaching. Dean David Gregory

The organist's house had to be demolished to allow the construction of the Anatomy School. The college mason and carpenter were ordered to erect 'a proper convenience' in compensation. This seems to have stood immediately behind the kitchen and was incorporated into Meadow Buildings in the 1860s as staircase 7.

CCA D&C i.b.6, f.148

had drastically overhauled the curriculum in mathematics and science, and John Freind had made a bequest of £1,000 for the creation of the school and the foundation of a readership in anatomy.[128] Freind's gift alone was insufficient, but it was supplemented by Matthew Lee, a graduate in medicine from Christ Church who became a royal physician and who in his will left over £20,000 specifically for the advancement of Westminster Students and to assist with the construction of the School.[129] Public human dissections were to take place twice a year, for which most spectators had to pay a fee.[130] The project was supervised by the dean, the sub-dean and the treasurer, and a decision was soon made to put this new detached building in School Yard, just to the south of the Great Quadrangle, near the kitchen.[131]

Keene, who had already created the picture gallery on the ground floor of the Library, quoted £2,289 for the entire project. His estimate was accepted, and only a year later the first Anatomical Lecturer, John Parsons, was elected. Working alongside Parsons, as Assistant Dissecting Surgeon, was John Grosvenor.[132] The Anatomy School is a simple, astylar box with unembellished sash windows and a plain parapet. Only the staircase to the 'ground' floor has any decoration, in the form of a small portico.

The school rapidly became known as 'skeleton corner', with cadavers from the prison used for anatomy teaching, and almost as soon as the theatre opened for use, the Anatomy Reader complained that he needed more south light in the dissecting room. A new window was installed to match the others, and a chimney removed.[133] The *Oxford Journal* of 24 July 1790 records that 'In the afternoon of Monday the bodies [of Shury and

The kitchen and the Anatomy School in 1827, drawn by Thomas Fisher.
The chimney stacks on the kitchen were taken down in 1981.

Castle, executed for the murder of David Charteris] were conveyed in a cart to the Anatomy School at Christ Church, where Dr Thomson, the Reader in Anatomy, next day gave a publick lecture on the two bodies.' A plan of about 1840 shows the school as it was before alterations were made after

John Parsons (1742–85), the son of an army major, came up to Christ Church in 1759. He studied medicine in London and Edinburgh, as well as in Oxford, winning the Hope prize medal in 1766. His first course of clinical lectures in the new Anatomy School was delivered in 1781. Parsons died in 1785. His widow, after a respectable period of six years, married John Grosvenor.

ODNB

The interior of the Anatomy School, showing all the anatomical
specimens before they were moved to the new University Museum in the
1860s. Many, if not all, are still stored in the museum's basement.

the building of the University Museum, with tiered seating around a central arena and a gallery for more spectators.[134] A skylight was inserted in 1789 to improve the lighting to the lecture room.[135]

As the curriculum changed, alterations were made to the Anatomy School. In 1841 the surveyor Henry Underwood noted that the School was suffering from subsidence. Although efforts had been made to prop up the building with buttresses on the south and west sides around a decade earlier, followed by some underpinning and strengthening, there were still cracks and evidence of settlement.[136] Underwood was concerned that nothing had been done to address the state of the ground beneath and surrounding the building, 'which is now continually absorbing the surface rains, and causing the soil on which the Building stands always to be in a soft and swampy state'. He proposed digging out the soft ground and back-filling with dry rubble or concrete, then covering the surface with a course of paving.[137] Work must have been done to put the building into a state of decent repair, as by 1854 a reading room had been incorporated and a gallery installed for the better exhibition of the collections of anatomical and zoological specimens that had been collected over the years. In 1861 Edward Bruton reported on the state of the School and decided that Underwood's work of underpinning and strengthening the shallow foundations had in general succeeded, although the staircase had settled differently from the rest of the building and would need pinning in its own right.[138]

Although Henry Acland, Reader in Anatomy, hankered after a new dissection room, his wishes were not to be granted. By the mid-1850s the new University Museum was already well advanced, and the proposal that the Christ Church collections be transferred there was made in 1856.[139] In the early stages of the discussions Dean Liddell argued that the Christ Church Anatomy School was open to any who wished to attend and that its collection served as a university museum. He drew attention to the fact that Acland had added two thousand physiological specimens and had created the pathological collection.[140] By 1860, however, the University, under the Evangelical Francis Jeune as Vice-Chancellor, had come to an agreement with Christ Church. The specimens would be moved to the new museum, but Christ Church men were to retain the same rights and privileges to lectures and access to the collections as when they were on college premises.[141] After 1860 the Anatomy School was converted into a chemistry laboratory in the charge of the Lee's Reader in Chemistry, and Christ Church continued to be at the forefront of the teaching of natural science in the university.[142] In 1903 Symm's quoted for an additional storey to be added, which was to be covered, in part, with 'Hope's Patent Glazing'.[143] At the same time alterations to the laboratory furnishings were made, and the ground-floor room, originally both a lecture room and laboratory facilities, was converted for lectures solely.[144] The extra floor was short-lived, however. By 1929 the needs of the scientists had changed, and two schemes were designed by Coleridge, Jennings and Soimenow for consideration. Scheme A – the chosen (and cheaper) option – consisted of a large, double-height laboratory with circular skylights in the roof, with a smaller laboratory on the ground floor and a library above. Scheme B proposed a lecture room and library on the ground floor, and two laboratories on the first with circular skylights over the small lab and an almost

The short-lived extra storey on the Anatomy School was clearly visible when the buildings on St Aldate's were cleared to allow the creation of the Memorial Garden in the early 1920s.

full-length skylight over the larger. Neither scheme allowed for the 1903 storey, which was removed.[145]

It was not until after the Second World War that the Anatomy School ceased to be associated with the teaching of science. In 1949 the basement was turned into a refectory. Upstairs the big room was turned into a picture gallery and the smaller rooms were to accommodate the books and manuscripts of the diarist John Evelyn, deposited by his descendant C. J. A. Evelyn.[146] In 1959, just before the Library was renovated and as proposals were made to reorganise accommodation across the site – proposals that included the construction of Blue Boar Quad – it was suggested that the School could be used to house the whole art collection, but the Accommodation Committee's report to the Governing Body included the first hint

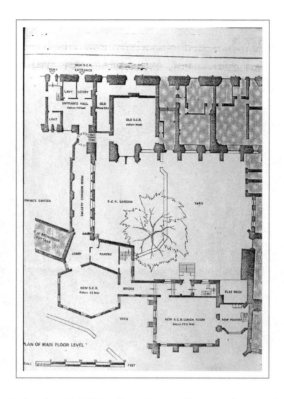

A sketch plan dated 1965 by the architects Playne and Lacey, showing
the new building proposed for the Senior Common Room.

that the premises were being eyed by the Senior Common Room from across
School Quad.[147]

Originally, the suggestions were for the Common Room to expand
further into Tom 1 staircase, with a couple of rooms in the Lee Building as
a mere possibility. Soon, though, the acquisition of the old Anatomy School
was seen as essential.[148] Several ideas were put forward: one design by Playne
and Lacey proposed using the Lee Building and constructing a new hexagonal building between the Lee Building and Auden Cottage, with a long
gallery – with cloakrooms at ground-floor level – linking both to the present
Common Room.[149] Another plan involved converting the rooms under the
Hall with a direct link to the kitchen. On 9 November 1966 the Committee
on Senior Common Room Accommodation voted in favour of the second by
four to two with one abstention. At the end of the month the committee's

A photograph of the site in 1965 with hand-drawn additions showing
how the hexagonal building would appear from the Memorial Garden.

recommendations were laid before the Governing Body, which promptly voted the other way: the committee's proposal was rejected by sixteen votes to twenty. The final decision, by twenty-one votes to twelve, was to proceed with part of the first proposal – to go ahead with the conversion of the Lee Building, but to put on hold the construction of an entirely new building.[150]

The plans were not universally popular: one senior member, Carl Collie, stated in a paper to the Governing Body that 'It will be difficult to defend a scheme which increases the amenities of the Students, at the expense of undergraduates, and takes out of the academic field a building which has been used for college teaching for two centuries. The defence will not be helped by the admitted need for more lecture and seminar rooms.'[151] His was a minority report, however, and the conversion of the Anatomy School into a Senior Common Room facility went ahead. The original estimate, in

1965, was £34,500. By 1968, when the work was about to begin, the architects advised that this had risen to £70,000. This was partly due to inflation, but also because of additional items requested by the Governing Body, such as a passenger lift, wall panelling, a terrace to the south of the building over the kitchen yard, modernisation of the kitchen buildings below and the kitting out of a pantry. In the end, the wall panelling and the lift were dropped, reducing the costs to £50,000. Unusually, the treasurer had advised the Governing Body not to base its decision on financial grounds; there was enough in the Building Fund, he said, to cope with the building of Blue Boar, the construction of the Picture Gallery, the restoration of the west front and the conversion of the Lee Building as parallel projects.[152] The lift was soon reinstated in the plans. As for the new terrace, this occupied the Governing Body for several months, and in the end cost £3,000 more than the original £6,000 quoted, largely because of the cost of the stone surrounding walls. The first Governing Body meeting in the Lee Building was held on 27 January 1971.

Apart from the refectory, created in 1949 and known now as the Undercroft, little has changed since, except for occasional redecoration. The Undercroft, however, saw major refurbishment in 2014, which entailed opening the space out into a light and airy bar (almost at the expense of the rooms above when walls that were not meant to be supporting walls were found to be so) fit for use by undergraduates and conference guests alike.[153]

* * * * *

All the way through the eighteenth century alterations were made to modernise the buildings and to regularise their use. In 1716, soon after Peckwater Quad was completed, new rules were laid down for the use and maintenance of chambers and lodgings. A month later, at the annual meeting at which the election of Students and officers took place and business was sealed before Christmas, the Chapter required that a list be drawn up of rooms that could be made into doubles, and that all those rooms that had been doubles in the past should be returned to that state. The list was to be lodged in the great trunk in the Treasury.[154]

Accommodation at the end of the eighteenth century

On the Great Quadrangle
> The deanery and two canon's houses on the east side
> Hall, Treasury, School and Common Room on the south side
> Porter's Lodge, canon's house and fifteen chambers adjoining the Hall
> Eleven chambers on the north side of the tower
> Two canon's houses on the north side of the quad

Peckwater Quadrangle
> Canon's house
> Canon's houses and twenty chambers on the west side adjoining the
>> above
> Twenty-four chambers on the north side
> Twenty-eight chambers on the east side

Canterbury Quadrangle
> Gateway and three chambers on the east side
> Ten chambers on the north side
> Four chambers on the south side

Chaplains' Quadrangle
> Nine chambers and two lecture rooms on the north side
> Canon's house, audit rooms and five chambers on the east side
> Nine chambers on the south side

Fell's Buildings
> Seven chambers
> Kitchen separate
> Anatomy School
> Organist's house

In the Stable Yard
> Four coach houses and ten stables
> Coach house and stable
> Four coach houses and stable
> Wash-house and laundry belonging to the deanery
> Another building separate behind the canon's house behind Peckwater
> Another building

CCA D&C i.b.6, f.305

Towards the end of the eighteenth century an insurance valuation was made of the buildings which gives a sound indication of the architectural state of Christ Church after nearly two centuries of construction.[155] Interestingly, the concern seems to have been principally with residential buildings; neither the cathedral nor the Library, which might now be thought to be the greater insurance risks, is included. There were 145 chambers excluding the private lodgings of the dean, the canons and the organist. The entries in the battels book for May 1779, the date of the valuation, show a resident population of 153 Students and commoners.[156]

7

The Gothic revival

While the eighteenth century had seen grand additions to the medieval and sixteenth-century fabric of Christ Church, the nineteenth was a period of modernisation and adaptation to the changing University. Funding the work to be done never ceased to be a challenge. In the early years of the eighteenth century, when the Library project commenced, it had been decided that, on admission to their posts, new deans would pay £200 into the fund and new canons £100. Originally, half the sums donated were in lieu of a treat formerly given to the whole college, but over time they became an expected part of revenue. The other half was considered a voluntary donation to the end. The scheme was continued until the end of the Canterbury Quad project, but once those books were closed, the financing of building and maintenance was thought through afresh. In the spring of 1791, when the medieval Chaplains' Quad was declared to be in a parlous state and it was acknowledged that something needed to be done as a matter of some urgency, a Buildings and Repairs Fund was established to pay for the rebuilding of the medieval quad and of Fell's Buildings. The new fund was initially derived from caution money and a bequest of £100 from Richard Cust, dean of Lincoln; it was further increased by a benefaction from the canon and bishop of Oxford, Edward Smallwell.[1] The dean and canons were unanimous that the payments made all through the preceding century would continue 'on the footing of a voluntary but customary benefaction'.[2]

But no major works were initiated for many years. The interest from the fund, however, was used over the next half-century to pay for all sorts of projects and maintenance, including new stables for the canons, alterations to the Hall staircase, cleaning and whitewashing in both the Hall and the cathedral, new steps and paving in the Great Quadrangle and repairs to all the buildings. Before too long, the pot began to run dry.[3]

In order to pay for the repairs after the fire of 1809, which destroyed the south-west lodgings, the buildings fund was reorganised once more. Divided into two, there was to be a Fund for Extraordinary Repairs and a Fund for New Buildings. Added to the funds were the rents from some rooms, royalties from the coal-mines on Christ Church's manorial estate in Midsomer Norton and the surpluses from the Land Tax account.[4] Timber trees, when they were not needed for estate repairs, were to be sold.[5]

Just rearranging the building funds did not replenish them. An injection of cash was sorely needed. At the same time as the stable conversions were on the table, on 7 March 1832, the Chapter noted that 'It having been shown at the last Audit that the expenses of Domus have of late years been much greater than its receipts, and it having been referred to the dean and treasurer to prepare a scheme for the augmentation of that fund with the view more especially of providing for the sustentation of the fabrick, it was this day ordered' that entrance fees be raised, room rents increased and that the SIGA rents from some Peckwater chambers be transferred to the extraordinary repairs fund.[6]

Things were not looking much better in 1841, but still there was no cessation of work. In fact, the Chapter secretary recorded the many repairs that had been done recently: the cathedral had undergone stonework repairs, including some to the spire, and the installation of new stoves; the organ had been altered and the organ loft somehow fitted up to accommodate the choir; the Chapter House roof had been improved; John Hudson had installed new gutters and Westmorland slates on the Library;[7] a new lecture room had been built over the kitchen lobby in 1829;[8] the almshouse had been rebuilt and refitted; and both the cathedral and Tom Tower clocks had been repaired. A new wall had been constructed in the meadow, and further

SIGA rents were certain small rents from a few estates, mainly in Oxford-shire, Worcestershire and Cheshire, as well as capon, boar and wether rents, tithes from Binsey and later a few other places near Oxford and the rents of certain rooms in college. From 1715 the rooms are specified as those from Peckwater staircases 1 and 2 and 6 to 8.

SIGA stood for 'Sus, incrementum, gallusque, ariesque' ('Swine, interest or increments in land, cocks and rams').

expenditure was still required not only for ordinary repairs but also for the complete renovation of the terrace steps and of the balustrades in the Great Quadrangle.

It was also at this time that Christ Church, and Oxford more generally, began to look back to Gothic, and away from classical, influences for its architecture. In 1839 the Society for Promoting the Study of Gothic Architecture was founded at Christ Church, the aims of which were strengthened by the Oxford Movement. Pugin's influences were evident, but Ruskin, a Christ Church man, was less bound by the 'English' style and happier to embrace a more European outlook. Within thirty years Oxford saw: the construction of the Martyrs' Memorial and Exeter College chapel (both by George Gilbert Scott); the debating room of the Oxford Union Society (by Woodward); Keble College and the new chapel at Balliol (by Butterfield); and, of course, the restoration of Christ Church Cathedral (by Gilbert Scott).

Interestingly, while architecture was harking back to medievalism, reforms in the University pointed in the opposite direction. In 1871 religious 'tests' were abolished and the University was opened to those of any, or no, religion, and new subjects such as modern history were added to the examination syllabus. A career in the church was no longer the principal path for an undergraduate.

Christ Church had always been a centre for science, and although its architectural and theological leanings were back to the Gothic, the need and desire to press forward with new technologies and ideas were always present. In 1818, not long after the cataclysmic fire of 1809, the Dean and

Chapter sanctioned the installation of gas, particularly for the Great Quadrangle.[9] Everything was considered very carefully: a plan of Christ Church was drawn, showing where the gas supply was to go, and lists were made of lamps that were to be lit all the time. According to the estimates, if twelve lamps were lit all year round, and three more for nine months, it would cost £87 10s. each year. Hornley Ironworks in Birmingham estimated that installing gas in the quads and on the staircases would cost £595, provided the old candle lamps were used. Any new lamps would be 30s. each. Pipes were laid by the City Gas Light and Coke Company during the long vacation of 1819, and an agreement was drawn up for the supply of gas for lamps that would be lit at dusk and extinguished at 1 a.m. The lanthorns were designed by Francis Skidmore.[10] Clericalism and antiquarianism certainly did not stop the canons from driving a hard bargain: only one lamp in four was to be left burning all night, and at no extra cost to the Dean and Chapter. Full lighting would cease during the long vacation. This was definitely a step forward, but a hesitant one. Gas lighting was only for the outside for many years; the Hall was still lit by candles until its major refurbishment in the 1860s and 1870s.

The stables

Much of this late eighteenth- to early nineteenth-century work was undertaken by James Wyatt, a proponent of new ideas cased in beautiful garb. The new stables, erected immediately to the south of the lane to the Meadow, although not directly attributable to Wyatt, are very likely to have been his work and demonstrate the application of a simple but elegant classical style to a very functional building – the last of its kind at Christ Church. A plan of the road to the Meadow, dated 1797, shows the 'new stables and coachouses' [sic], while drawings from the 1830s, when it was proposed that the stables be converted for the almsmen, show an elegant and elaborate construction.[11] The only illustration of the stables is on Edmund New's early twentieth-century engraving shortly before they were demolished in 1925 to make way for the Memorial Garden, although the remains are shown on the University Almanack for 1927.[12]

Meadow Buildings

In the first quarter of the nineteenth century there was a steady rise in matriculations. For thirty years or so after that numbers remained pretty constant at about four hundred matriculations a year, but after 1855 matriculations in the University at large began to rise inexorably; within ten years they were at nearly six hundred, and still increasing year on year.[13] For a while there were waiting lists for the 'top' colleges, such as Balliol and Christ Church. The increasing number of grammar schools provided more eighteen-year-olds fit for university; when the University tests were abolished in 1871, the doors were opened to non-Anglicans, and the growing industrial and commercial aristocracies began to send their sons to Oxford.[14] New buildings were evidently the way forward.[15]

It was seven decades since the Dean and Chapter had acknowledged that Chaplains' Quad and Fell's Buildings were old and dilapidated; now they were also far too small and old-fashioned for the growing population. Basic maintenance had continued for two hundred years, including new sashes for Fell's Buildings as late as 1838, but the whole quad had long been destined for demolition. In 1859 the Dublin architect Thomas Deane and his partner Benjamin Woodward had suggested a French Gothic château-style remodelling of the St Aldate's front of Christ Church, which would have raised the roof into a high gable and increased accommodation but would probably have raised the odd eyebrow as well.[16] This idea was rejected, but in 1862 Deane's son Thomas Newenham Deane produced drawings for a large new accommodation block in high 'Rhenish Gothic'. Much influenced by Benjamin Woodward, Meadow Buildings bear considerable resemblance to the University Museum.[17] Fell's and Chaplains' at last met their fate.

Meadow Buildings are probably the worst documented of all the projects undertaken at Christ Church since 1525. Construction fell in the middle of all the negotiations surrounding the changes to Christ Church's constitution, when record-keeping appears to have been at an all-time low. In the Chapter minutes they are mentioned a mere five times, beginning with the acceptance of Deane's design, with no detail at all, and the signing of the

An elevation of Meadow Buildings, not exactly as built, as illustrated in the Builder *in 1862. This is one of only two drawings that survive from the original proposal.*

contract with Joshua Symm, the builder, whose firm was much patronised by Dean Liddell.[18]

The accepted design was, like the University Museum, tall with steep roofs, flat in the façade and in a muted constructional polychromy of Bath stone embellished with Hornton and Mansfield string courses. Both buildings followed the fashion for Gothic, and it was said of both that Ruskin might have been influential in the planning.[19] Even if Ruskin had no personal input, his ideas were embraced whole-heartedly: there are Italianate balconies and the beginnings of elaborate decoration, steep gables and lancet windows, and a certain asymmetry.[20] Both were decorated with carvings of plants and birds, the main gateway at Christ Church being embellished with vines and grapes, convolvulus and chestnut leaves. Curiously, the carvings on both the University Museum and Meadow Buildings were left unfinished, with only the gateway and the windows of just three staircases on Meadows showing what must have been intended for the whole frontage. The carving on the University Museum was undertaken by James and John O'Shea with

*Details of the decoration around the door and windows of Meadow
Buildings, probably created by the Irish craftsmen, James and John O'Shea
and Edward Whelan, who also worked on the University Museum.*

their nephew Edward Whelan, from Co. Cork, considered by Woodward the
best men for the task. But funds ran out, and the O'Sheas were asked to stop.
Legends have arisen over what happened next. One tale recounts that one
brother was so upset at the project being cut short that he offered to work
free of charge and began to carve parrots and owls around the main door
to parody Convocation; Henry Acland requested that the birds be removed
forthwith, and the doorway remains scarred to this day. Another, from
Ruskin, is that the carvers were sacked for introducing too many cats into
the scheme. How far the problems at the University Museum are reflected in
the unfinished decoration of Meadow Buildings is impossible to say, but it is
known that Deane employed Whelan on the project.

Constructed under the eye of Henry Liddell, the third of Christ Church's
great builder deans, by Joshua Robinson Symm, Meadow Buildings was to
provide fifty-seven sets of rooms.[21] On 15 August 1862 Henry Grant, the

168

A Romantic impression by Le Keux of Meadow Buildings under construction in 1864. Both Fell's Buildings and Chaplains' Quad have been demolished. A lone worker stands on the roof sorting out the scaffolding for the construction of the next staircase.

butler, reported that the interior of Fell's Buildings would be stripped by the following day, and that the cloisters had been closed off so that workmen were excluded from the rest of the college.[22] The new building went up quickly, beginning at the east end. John Henry Le Keux's engraving, executed for the 1864 University Almanack, rather fancifully shows workmen constructing the shell opposite the end of the Priory House, roughly halfway through the job.

By 4 October 1864 the first staircase was complete and ready to hand over to Grant. The tower roof was partly on, and the rest nearly finished. There was some discussion about the type of stone to be used for the staircases; Symm had been requested to finish the tower stairs in Portland stone, but the other staircases were to be reconsidered, principally for financial

A rare albumen photograph of Meadow Buildings taken by Hills and Saunders soon after its completion, probably c.1880, showing sun blinds above the balcony windows. The company of Hills and Saunders was founded in Oxford in 1856. They were a leading Victorian photographic studio and later had branches in London, Harrow, Eton, Cambridge, Rugby and Sandhurst, as well as elsewhere. The Oxford branch was taken over by Gillman and Soame in 1931.

reasons. The dean was certain that there had been some shady dealings – 'something behind the curtain' – as a decision had been made at some point that all the staircases were to be wooden rather than stone, except for the two already completed, but Symm had purchased still more Portland.[23] It would appear that Symm got away with it, for all the staircases in Meadow Buildings are of stone. The costs were high: in total, £30,486 2s. 11d. was laid out, of which Symm was paid £27,756 0s. 3d. and Deane, the architect, received £1,681 5s.[24] It was not a popular building, described by contemporary critics as 'joyless and dull' and 'a monument to Ruskin and his architectural doctrine'.[25] W. J. Arkell, writing in 1947, commented that 'Meadow

The interior of a room in Meadow, probably taken during the Edwardian period. Students usually resided in the same room for all three years of their degree and often decorated them to their own tastes until the 1970s, when the decoration of rooms began to managed by the college rather than by the resident of the rooms.

Buildings have the distinction of being almost the only major building [in Oxford] left shrouded in greenery (a dispensation for which, in this particular case, the public should be grateful)', which demonstrates just how far Victorian Gothic had fallen out of favour.[26] It did, however, do what it was designed to do, and accommodated the growing body of undergraduates. The completion of Meadow Buildings was marked, a few years later, by the planting of the Meadow walk with seventy-two elms, formally opened by Princess Louise in 1872.[27]

Like all the other residential facilities at Christ Church, Meadow Buildings served well for many years, until the expectations of greater comfort, the still increasing numbers of students (and of teaching fellows and

lecturers) and the beginnings of the conference trade began to make different demands. It was one of the very few Christ Church buildings not to
receive any attention from the Oxford Historic Buildings Fund. In 1959 hot
and cold water was laid on to every room in Meadows, leaving only Tom
Quad and the Old Library staircase lagging behind. And in 1973 the division
began of double-sets into singles. By 1975 thirty-seven new rooms had been
achieved.[28] In 1995 Meadows 2 had been completely 'ensuited' and the old-
fashioned bathrooms on Meadows 4 modernised. Over the following years
the other staircases followed, and more structural renovations – particularly
of the roofs – were undertaken. Only the refurbishment of Meadows 6 and 7
and the renovation of the tower of Meadows 3 remained to be tackled.

Meadows 3 was a major project – the first works under the guidance
of the new House Surveyor – and entailed the renewal of the stonework,
the refurbishment of all the rooms and the creation of two duplex rooms
in the attic which had previously been unusable owing to fire regulations.
The work took place in 2010 and in 2011, along with the new lift to the
ante-hall, the restoration of the 'watching loft' in the cathedral and the new
railings at 3 Brewer Street, and won an award from the Oxford Preservation
Trust.[29]

* * * * *

After the restoration of the Great Quadrangle in 1809 there were minor
repairs and changes, including repairs to the cathedral organ by James C.
Bishop and alterations to the loft under the tower so that the choir could
sing from there.[30] Early in the century, repairs were made to the battlements
on the east side of the cathedral and to the spouts on the north side of the
Chapter House.[31]

These changes, which undoubtedly caused their own debates and ruc-
tions, were small. One proposal, however, hinted at the great changes that
would occur in later years. This was made in 1842 by an H. Coddington,
who suggested that a portion of the Great Quadrangle be demolished so that
a great west end to the cathedral could be erected. Dr Bull, the treasurer,
called it an 'extraordinary scheme', but it may have sown seeds in the minds

Thomas Vere Bayne came up to Christ Church in 1848, matriculating in June. He took a second class in Classics in 1852. Bayne was elected proctor in 1867, and was Keeper of the University Archives from 1885. At Christ Church he was indefatigable, active in the reforms to the constitution and practically running the college while Dean Liddell was occupied with his building projects. He was Censor, Tutor, Librarian, Secretary to the Governing Body and Curator of Common Room. He sat on innumerable committees, notably the Belfry Committee, the Cathedral Restoration Committee and the Staff Salaries Board. When he died, in 1908, Bayne left over £100,000 to Christ Church.

CCA xlix.a.1; lv.c.48

of the Chapter that just needed germination by one extraordinary man.[32]

This man was Henry George Liddell, a Christ Church Student in the 1820s and 1830s, then headmaster of Westminster School from 1846 and appointed dean of Christ Church in 1855. Liddell was a doer, but his ambitions lay in directions other than the day-to-day administration of college and cathedral, which fell to the capable hands of Thomas Vere Bayne, Student and executive *extraordinaire*. Instead, as well as fulfilling his roles as vice-chancellor and a dedicated commissioner on the body appointed to reform the University, Liddell built and rebuilt. The Meadow Buildings had been his first great project, but he soon turned his attention to the cathedral, a building that had not been touched in any major way since the seventeenth century, except for some small-scale work in 1856 by John Billing of Westminster.

The cathedral as college chapel

Brian Duppa (dean 1628–38) was the first to make changes or alterations to the cathedral beyond daily maintenance.[33] He went through the cathedral like a dose of salts. In the first instance old grave slabs, some of which were said by Anthony Wood to date from the Saxon period (although he

*The interior of the cathedral, with Cyril Jackson's statue, by Chantrey, in the
north transept, drawn with the organ screen and seating removed. Dean Duppa's
screens are just visible behind Jackson, filling the arches to the north chapels.*

probably meant Norman), were moved from the nave and chancel to make
way for a new black-and-white pavement, laid by Nicholas Stone and his
cousin Gabriel Stacy.[34] Wood was horrified by what he saw as nothing less
than vandalism; the memorials, he said, were 'looked upon by the dean
and canons as old superfluous stuff and unhandsome'.[35] Old stalls (possibly those that are now in the Latin Chapel) were removed from the nave or
sanctuary.[36] New screens were installed to make worship more seemly and
to separate one chapel from the next, the church was plastered and whitewashed throughout, and fashionable painted windows were commissioned
from the van Linge brothers.

In his future positions, notably in Chichester and Winchester, Duppa
showed no great zeal towards his buildings; his work at Oxford was probably

prompted by the appointment of the Arminian William Laud as Chancellor of the University in 1630. Duppa was also tutor and spiritual adviser to the future Charles II.[37] There is nothing in the usual expenditure accounts on Duppa's work, but disbursements for the period December 1632 to August 1633 are entered in the back of the 1631 receipt book.[38] Samuel Fell, the treasurer, set aside £300 for the changes. Marble steps were fitted, presumably up to the sanctuary, new 'columns and rails' were provided for some windows by William Edwards, and new oak wainscoting by Thomas Wells and Thomas Gardiner. The new nave floor included a step sent up from London, and the whole church was plastered and whitewashed by Thomas Maylard. The rest of the church was relaid with freestone. John Burdges re-slated the north chapel. The choir was wainscoted, and the pulpit was probably also installed at this time.[39] The cloister was altered too, with a new doorway opened opposite the Chapter House, and the Gothic tracery removed.

Perhaps the most significant piece of work undertaken by Duppa was the commissioning of new painted windows by the van Linge brothers, who were also commissioned by Balliol, Lincoln and University colleges. Abraham and Bernard van Linge, from Frisia, did much of their work in Oxford, creating painted, rather than stained, windows.[40] A long poem published in Abraham Wright's collection *Parnassus biceps* (1656) describes their Christ Church designs and defends their use in teaching, as well as

---

Parnassus biceps is a nostalgic royalist publication designed to demonstrate, during the perceived cultural dearth of the Interregnum, what an 'Ocean of Wit' flowed from 'those brests of this Nation, the two Universities' before the disruptions of the Civil War. The ninety-four poems date mainly from the period 1610–40. Most were written by Oxford men, including pieces by Donne, Corbett, Strode, King, Carew, Jonson, Herrick, Waller and Shirley. The 1656 edition includes facsimiles of Wright's extracts from Shakespeare in his manuscript commonplace book (British Library, Add. MS 22608).

Wright and Beal (1990)

praising them as beautiful artefacts. Among others, there were illustrations of the Nativity, the Fall of Man, possibly one of the Last Supper, the Crucifixion and the burial of Christ's body, Moses parting the Red Sea, and Abraham and the sacrifice of Isaac. Pentecost, Noah's Ark, Jonah, and Elijah's ascent into heaven in his chariot were also represented.[41] Paid for by the Dean and Chapter, or by individual canons, the windows – the installation of which had required not only the removal of medieval glass but also changes to the tracery of the windows – were, however, short-lived. On June 1651 it was ordered 'that all Pictures representing god, good and bad Angells or Saints shall be forthwith taken down out of our Church windows, & shall be disposed for the mending of the Glasse that is out of repair in any part of the Colledg'.[42] The only complete survivor is the one showing Jonah contemplating Nineveh – Jonah was no saint or angel, and his story was one that probably appealed to the strict Puritanism of the Commonwealth period.

By 1856, almost nothing having been done after Duppa, the condition of the cathedral was a disgrace according to ecclesiologists and architects alike.[43] Both services and the church itself were arranged purely for college consumption, with hardly a sermon or communion given for the diocese at large, and the stalls were set out in such a way that any member of the public bothering to turn up would be unable to participate or even see the service.

The seventeenth-century stalls in the choir for senior members, noblemen and gentlemen commoners resembled, according to one commentator, 'third-class railway carriages'. The organ screen, inconveniently placed right at the centre of the cathedral under the tower, effectively excluded anyone seated further west. The undergraduates were squashed on to benches, east of the organ, facing west, and jammed up tightly against the altar rail. The choir were perched aloft in a gallery above the organ, and the bell-ringers above them.[44] The cathedral barely functioned as a college chapel, and certainly not as the centre of the diocese.

Plans to make the interior better for everyone involved the removal or alteration of much of the seventeenth-century woodwork, but no one wanted to destroy it completely just for the sake of convenience. So the changes were made using just the old timber, with no new added. John Billing gave very

The choir in the early nineteenth century, clearly showing the seventeenth-century box pews described as 'third-class railway carriages'.

specific instructions that the carpenters should 'carefully take down, clean, mark and stack the whole of the wood work in the choir, including the wood flooring and the joists and sleepers, attention being given to the mode in which the same is to be refixed'.[45] The marble floor was to be protected throughout the works under a wooden casing. To open up the crossing, the organ was moved to the floor in the south transept and the stalls of the canons were moved westwards to allow the whole length of the church to be used for services. The view of the choir aisles was opened up. Undergraduates and censors now sat in the choir, and everyone else (tutors, graduates, noblemen and gentlemen commoners) west of the transepts. The choristers stood more safely on the floor at the crossing, and seating was installed in the north transept for the general public.[46] Other tasks overseen by Billing included repairs to fittings and the floors by John and William Fisher, repairs

Edward George Bruton was a Gothic Revivalist architect practising in the mid-nineteenth century in Oxfordshire. He worked mainly on churches but also on private houses. As Surveyor to the Dean and Chapter, he was also responsible for the Christ Church Old Buildings in the Hamel, a tenement block built around the time when the almsmen were removed from their lodgings in St Aldate's.

Tyack (1998), 235, 238

using Bath stone to the piers in the choir and tower, new candle-holders and the modernisation of the heating by warm-air flues under the paving.[47] The work under the floor involved the lifting of memorial slabs and protecting and fixing coffins, but the excavations met with great excitement among antiquaries when a reliquary chamber was discovered under the west end of the choir. Billing's sketch drawings show a chamber seven feet wide and nearly nine feet deep.[48]

It took another decade for Liddell to put his mind to more major work. A few further changes had been made during the 1860s – these included the installation of the St Frideswide window, by Burne-Jones, in the Latin Chapel and another in the south nave aisle, and Edward Bruton had removed eighteenth-century balustrades from the clerestory and cleaned the roof – but the dean's ill health, the construction of Meadow Buildings and the major constitutional overhaul of Christ Church had taken priority.

In 1866 Liddell received two estimates from George Gilbert Scott for fitting out the cathedral, but in spite of much discussion things were put on hold, perhaps in anticipation of the Christ Church Oxford Act, passed in 1867, which laid down a statutory requirement for a decennial survey of the fabric to ensure its maintenance and 'sustentation'. Almost immediately after the creation of the new Governing Body, John West Hugall, a Gothic Revivalist architect who had begun his career in Yorkshire but who had moved south to Cheltenham and Oxford in the 1850s, was appointed surveyor. His report, submitted within six weeks, evidently recommended works on the cathedral, for early the following year the Chapter and the Governing Body put their heads together for the first time.[49]

A Committee for the Restoration of the Cathedral was established on 11 March 1868.[50] The members were an interesting group: representing the Chapter were Thomas Chamberlain, Archdeacon Charles Clerke, Edward Bouverie Pusey and Richard Jelf. William Bright would soon join. On the college side were the treasurer, Robert Faussett, Charles Sandford, the ubiquitous Thomas Vere Bayne and Henry Thompson. The dean chaired. Several of the committee, including Liddell, belonged to the Oxford Architectural Society. The society aimed to moderate the 'restoration' zeal of many Victorians, which had often resulted in the destruction of architectural or decorative features either considered not valuable or thought to interfere with the re-creation of the medieval.[51]

Of the Chapter, only Bright showed any real interest in proceedings. Pusey resigned because of ill health in 1872, and Jelf died in 1871. Chamberlain was a high-churchman, rector of St Thomas's Church in Oxford and an active member of the Oxford Movement. But he was busy with St Edward's, his newly founded school, and his parish commitments. Clerke seems to have been prepared to follow Liddell.

On the college side were Thomas Vere Bayne and Robert Faussett. Together they must have been a formidable administrative team; the former was a committee man and record-keeper of tremendous diligence, and the latter showed real skill in negotiating Christ Church through treacherous financial waters in the last quarter of the nineteenth century. Vere Bayne's overriding interest was to return Christ Church to its condition in Wolsey's time, even to the point of creating what Wolsey had been unable to finish; Faussett had a knowledge and love of Jacobean work in particular – unusual at the time – and rescued pieces from all over the county, including some of Duppa's stalls, which he removed to his parish church in Cassington. The third college member, Thompson, later biographer of Liddell and historian of Christ Church, was a moderate who cared deeply for the fabric of his college. His tolerance and even gentleness are revealed in his books, which show a light touch and self-deprecating humour. Sandford was busy with commitments elsewhere.

The newly created Governing Body agreed to spend vast sums on the new scheme and made an initial donation from the House of £1,000, which was matched by the Chapter.[52] Another appeal to old members, probably the first rigorously organised fund-raising campaign, was proposed.[53] The canons were not entirely in favour of more fund-raising, so Vere Bayne sensibly suggested that before any letters were sent to old members the Restoration Committee should obtain plans and firm estimates. Separate quotations were to be obtained for the different parts of the work, and these were to be laid before the Governing Body so that it could be decided whether a competition should be launched or whether an architect could be chosen. The committee came up with five projects: the renewal of the woodwork of the choir, nave and transepts, and the removal of the organ from the south transept; the repair of the east end; work on the north transept window and the thirteen aisle windows; the restoration of the south transept, with or without a new south aisle, and the removal of the Muniment Room from the north cloister walk and the south porch; and the re-extension of the nave to the west with a new west window.

George Gilbert Scott, evidently already in communication with the dean, objected to a competition for work on a sacred building, so architects, including Thomas Deane, were approached privately.[54] But Liddell was evidently determined to have Scott, one of the most fashionable architects of the day. Only three days after Scott had raised his objection to a competition, the dean wrote asking him to draw up a report on the condition of the cathedral and to quote for the specific works.[55] Liddell's list was slightly different from that of the committee, adding to the proposals the possibility of building the cloisters and the restoration of the medieval pitched roofs, the lines of which are still evident on the faces of the tower.

Scott's plans, building on the earlier changes of 1856, were outlined in a detailed document covering the refurbishment and modernisation of the cathedral. He dealt first with the history of the architecture of the building and then turned to the condition of the fabric, which was, on the whole, pretty sound. His ideal would seem to have been a return to the 'superior interest' of the twelfth-century building, but he obviously understood that this was impossible. He tentatively suggested the replacement of the fourteenth-century east window with something more Norman, but he anticipated 'that it would be negatived'. His wish was to render the interior suitable as both a cathedral and a college chapel, at a cost of over £37,000.[56] The two most expensive items, at £12,000 apiece, were the general repairs to all the stonework, including the restoration of the south transept and windows, and the extension of the nave. By Scott's standards, however, this was a small project.[57]

All through June 1869, and then again in November, once term had begun, discussion took place between Scott, Liddell, the committee and the Governing Body. In spite of Chapter's misgivings, an appeal and draft letter to old members were approved by the Governing Body on 17 November 1869.[58] In the first instance, the proposal to extensively remodel the east end was left out. Most members responded positively, with donations of £5 or £10; others were less enthusiastic, commenting that their own churches – most of the membership were in holy orders and were incumbents of parishes the length and breadth of the country – were falling into ruins around their ears, and Christ Church should be contributing to the repair of these rather than beautifying and altering their own chapel. These comments were, if understandable, a little unjust; the Dean and Chapter had always helped out their incumbents, and their churches, since the foundation. In June 1872 John Barclay Thompson, new Student and later Lee's Reader in Anatomy, subscribed to pay £20, at £5 per term, provided that he remained alive, sane and solvent. By June 1874 the treasurer had received nothing, and so deducted the money from Thompson's stipend. Thompson complained immediately that his conditions had not been fulfilled – although which of the possible conditions was unmet was not mentioned. The treasurer thought better than to argue and returned the £20 with a copy of Thompson's letter of donation.[59]

Some members objected to the employment of Scott; one thought that he was involved with too many cathedrals and that it was not good that one man should have so much influence; another feared that he would make the cathedral look like a new building. Granville Leveson Gower was against

*Sketch by the artist and architect John Buckler (1793–1894) showing
the evidence uncovered by George Gilbert Scott for the original design
of the east end of the cathedral. A is the core of the Norman arch;
B is the edge of the later medieval east window; C is the Norman
discharging arch; D is the spiral staircase in the south-east corner
turret; and E is a pillar of the Norman clerestory found in situ.*

the destruction of part of the quad to create a west end: 'what we know of
Ch.Ch. is Wolsey, and to destroy part of his Quad to extend the cathedral into
it thereby marring his design would in my opinion be a great mistake, and I
fervently hope you will run short of money for that part of the work.' Ruskin
expressed his regret.

In spite of these hiccups – and after the appeal was extended to the
diocese (this time with an abbreviated west-end extension and the pitched
roofs included) – the money came in, and the work finally began. Symm was
appointed again, aided by Thomas Leigh as clerk of works.[60] Scott's original plan for the east end was actually to restore the old Decorated window,

already altered in the seventeenth century, but during his surveys in 1869 he apparently found traces of a round one and sketched the beginnings of his idea, based on the east end of Laon Cathedral. Scott reconstructed the whole of the east end, removing the medieval traceried window. The fourteenth-century glass had been removed in 1696, when James Thornhill's depiction of the Nativity was funded by Peter Birch. This, in its turn, was removed in 1846, when 'gaudy French glass' by the Gérente brothers was installed in commemoration of the tercentenary of the foundation only seven years earlier.[61] This very short-lived gift had replaced a depiction of the Nativity by James Thornhill, installed in 1696 and funded by Peter Birch.[62] Scott's replacement gave a more Romanesque look, with a rose window and round-headed windows, a scheme that Geoffrey Bill called 'pious archaeology' rather than architectural imagination.[63]

The verger's 'cottage' within the transept was removed and replaced by the present sacristy and gallery room over the slype (the covered passage between the cathedral and the Chapter House).[64] Duppa's screens went the way of his earlier stalls, which opened up all of the interior, apart from the nave, choir and sanctuary, which were to a certain extent retained as seating dedicated to members of Christ Church.[65] The new stalls were made, in Symm's yard in Little Clarendon Street, of walnut.[66] The wrought-iron work atop those screens, which allowed separation without destroying all sense of participation by the congregation, was designed and executed by

James Thornhill (1675/6–1734) was a decorative painter, perhaps best known for his work at the Royal Naval Hospital at Greenwich and on the dome of St Paul's cathedral.

Peter Birch (1651/2–1710) was born a nonconformist but was admitted to Christ Church in 1673 through the efforts of Dean John Fell and by showing his conformity by taking communion. He took his BA and MA, and was appointed a chaplain at Christ Church before enjoying a successful career in the church.

ODNB

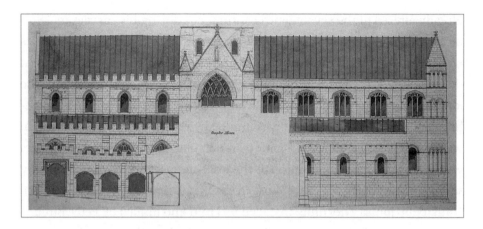

*Drawing of 1870 by George Gilbert Scott showing the south
elevation of the cathedral with the proposed restored gable roofs.*

Francis Skidmore of Coventry, who had worked with Scott on several cathedrals and on public buildings such as St Pancras Station and the Foreign Office, and at Exeter College in Oxford. The new paving, by the firm of Clayton and Bell, was laid, its images of the virtues matching those in the church of the Knights of St John on Malta, and similar to the floor of Siena Cathedral.[67]

Bright and Liddell fell out over the design of both altar and reredos. Bright wanted something with ornament, dignity and character, whereas Liddell's preference was for a simple altar table. Again the solution was a compromise; the altar table (now in the north choir aisle) was given elaborately carved legs but was inlaid with a simple cross, rather than Bright's preferred marble slab. George Bodley's reredos, carved by William Brindley and funded by Liddon and Bright, was not installed until 1882.[68]

One of the last items to go into the restored cathedral was the bishop's throne. In December 1875, £85 of the estimated £1,000 cost of the throne was still outstanding, and the cathedral committee proposed that £50 be donated from the Restoration Fund. Liddell, Bayne, Thompson and Sampson voted against the proposal, with the sub-dean, Bright and Faussett in favour.[69] Apart from a short note the following June that the bishop's throne was well advanced, its installation is not mentioned again.

The bishop was most definitely not considered a factor in the life of Christ Church.

Perhaps the most important part of Scott's work was the connection of the cathedral to Tom Quad by its extraordinary 'tunnel'.[70] From 1525 until the 1870s the only public entrance into the cathedral had been the south door in the cloister, the inconvenience of which was noted as far back as 1617. It was evident that the £12,000 that Scott had estimated for the full renewal of the west end was never going to be forthcoming. A complete reconstruction would be wonderful for the cathedral, he thought, but far less so for the college. A compromise solution was reached, and Scott constructed a new bay between the existing west end and the lodgings of the regius professor of divinity in a very plain Romanesque style to echo but not copy the original Norman design, and then broke through to the quad, splitting the residence in two.[71] Lecture rooms and offices were created in the portion nearest the Hall archway, with a Jacobean fireplace, purchased by Faussett, introduced into one.[72] The other side, between the tunnel and the deanery, was turned into a smaller residence.[73] Charles Dodgson thought that the new entrance, when it was first revealed in May 1873, 'almost rivals the Belfry in ugliness'.[74] Others were equally dismayed, including the local papers the *Oxford Journal* and the *Oxford Chronicle*. More plans for the west end, including a tower or gable over the new entrance, were abandoned for lack of money.[75]

After such efforts to put the cathedral in order, little more was done for some considerable time, except for the installation of new windows, including designs by Burne-Jones, for the memorial window in the Lady Chapel (1872–3) commemorating the death of Vyner in Greece, the St Cecilia window in the north choir aisle (1874–5) and the St Catherine window (1878) in the military chapel erected in memory of Edith Liddell.[76] Other windows erected at this time include the Jesse window in the south transept (in memory of Henry Parry Liddon) and the St Michael window in the north transept, given in 1872 to commemorate the 8th and 9th Earls of March. Both windows are by Clayton and Bell.

In 1926 electric lighting was installed for the first time, including floodlighting in the choir.[77] The Becket window was cleaned and re-leaded in 1952, and then restored completely in the 1980s. The spire saw yet more restoration work in 1960 and then again in 2005, once again by Symm.[78] The Latin Chapel was restored in 1965, and then again when St Frideswide's shrine was rebuilt and moved to the centre of the chapel in front of Burne-Jones's narrative window telling the story of the patron saint. The arrangement of the cathedral was examined by Martin Stancliffe between 1985 and 1990, when some reorganisation and conservation took place, including the restoration of the delicate painted ceiling above the Montacute tomb.[79] In 1991 English Heritage carried out its first Cathedrals Fabric Survey, with Stancliffe as the consultant architect and John Blair of The Queen's College as the consultant archaeologist. The cathedral was, on the whole, considered to be well maintained, although work on the pendants in the choir 'seems desirable'.[80] As a consequence, in the 1990s, the pinnacles at the east end and on the north transept were conserved, and attention was turned to the interior and the choir roof in 2014, when the beautiful stone lanterns were restored and their attachment to the rest of the ceiling ensured after concerns were raised in the 2009 decennial survey.[81]

The lighting was modernised in the 1990s by Robin Wade. The settings were designed to emphasise the particular part of the building in use at any time, and were tailored to suit the needs of a service or event. The seasons and hours were also taken into account. The crossing was lit in such a way that the eye would be drawn forward. Delicate light fittings for the choir stalls were designed by Saraj Guha. The design's flexibility was a success, for 'any church lighting project would be a complete failure if the architecture was lit with great care and attention whilst the congregation are left unable to read their hymn books and vice-versa'.[82]

Small projects make big differences. In 2005 new glass doors were added to the cathedral entrance to give a more welcoming appearance than did the heavy wooden doors at the end of the dark tunnel, and an extensive new project – 'Use of Space' – aims to extend this further.[83] The provision of a new kitchen and a new area for the cathedral flower arrangers to work – the first stage of a more extensive 'Use of Space' project – has meant that the

The watching loft or, perhaps more accurately, the chantry chapel of Sir Robert Danvers, stands at the east end of the cathedral, between the Latin and Lady chapels, and dates from the late fifteenth century. The stone tomb is topped with an elaborate but tiny wooden chapel. The stone steps to the upper level are heavily worn, perhaps by pilgrims visiting St Frideswide's shrine, and in 2008 the fan vault above the tomb was found to be cracking rather alarmingly. The chapel was conserved in 2012, and small finds including what may be the remains of leather purses, were deposited in the archive.

Kennedy (2012), 18–22

Bethel, an odd little shed-like building outside the east end, can be prepared for adaptation as an education centre. Much more is planned, not least the opening out of the nave to make the cathedral a place that embraces not just the members of Christ Church but the diocese and all its visitors too.[84]

The Wolsey Tower

After his success in the cathedral, it was to the bells that George Gilbert Scott next turned his attention. John Hudson had commented, back in 1835, that the 'spire wanted a great deal of repairing beyond cement'.[85] He had made good all the ribs, repointed any open joints and put up a lightning conductor and a new weather-vane.[86] But Hudson's repairs had evidently been short-lived or too modest. Towards the end of the work, in March 1871, Scott pointed out to Liddell the parlous state of the cathedral tower, no longer strong enough to carry the complete peal: 'its external decay progresses with such rapidity as not only to threaten the loss of much of the design but to increase the weakness of the structure.'[87] By June he was even more emphatic: 'There seems to be a constant movement going on and new cracks forming. The stair-turret is in dangerous condition having three fissures from bottom to top.' In spite of the fact that, as recently as 1851, Francis Boswell had estimated that the bells and bell frame needed only £17 worth of repairs, Scott proposed the urgent removal of the bells from the cathedral, and at the next Governing Body meeting this, the penultimate item on the agenda, received approval.[88] The bells were rehung in a shed-like structure over the Hall staircase, at a cost approaching £1,000, but the notion that something would have to be constructed to house the bells more elegantly does not appear to have crossed the minds of the Governing Body, particularly when financial constraints had limited, perhaps to the relief of many, the cathedral restoration. The structure was unflatteringly labelled the 'tintinnabulatory tea-chest' by Charles Dodgson, whose other epithets for it included 'the meat-safe', 'Early Debased', 'monstrous pile' and 'foulest blot on fairest face'. He proposed, with tongue firmly in cheek, that guests at the approaching gaudy should be presented with 'a portable model of the new Belfry, tastefully executed in cheese'.[89] More helpfully, the Christ Church land agent, Robert Castle, said that it would be cheaper to build a new belfry than to attempt to rebuild the spire.[90]

In May 1873 the Governing Body took the decision to complete the belfry, setting up the inevitable committee to obtain plans. The committee was headed by the driving forces of Dean Liddell and Vere Bayne. Gilbert Scott furnished the Governing Body with designs, evidently expecting that the job would be his. Vere Bayne, however, had other ideas and was deter-mined that there should be a proper competition this time. On 18 December 1873 he proposed that there should be a committee established 'with full power to choose a plan for the completion of the Belfry and to report the esti-mate to the Governing Body'.[91] This new committee met early in 1874 and agreed that several architects should be approached. Scott received a letter from the committee expressing its 'dissatisfaction with all the suggestions hitherto made for completing the Belfry and feeling the great importance of having a larger choice of designs in a matter of so much consequence, have resolved to apply to a limited number of Architects to furnish Sketch Plans'. Offended, Scott declined to be part of the competition. He soon changed his mind, possibly after G. E. Street, the diocesan architect, having decided not to take part himself, recommended to the committee that Scott be employed.

Invitations to compete were sent to: Arthur Blomfield, a Gothic Revivalist

George Gilbert Scott's suggestion for the belfry tower, as seen from the cathedral cloister. Scott's rather dull design was short-listed, perhaps out of a sense of loyalty to the architect, who had done so much in the cathedral, rather than because of any genuine liking of his drawing.

who had designed many churches and chapels worldwide; William Burges, one of the first Gothic Revivalist architects, who had designed St Fin Barre's Cathedral in Cork; Basil Champneys, a rising star whose great success was to be the John Rylands Library in Manchester; Thomas Deane, the tried and tested contender who had been responsible for Meadow Buildings only a decade earlier; John West Hugall, the local man who had undertaken Christ Church's first decennial survey, and who was working on two churches in Christ Church's patronage; G. E. (George Edmund) Street, the Oxford diocesan architect and designer of the Royal Courts of Justice, who embraced architectural history and the 'development' of buildings through time; and Alfred Waterhouse, whose great works were to include the Natural History

*George Bodley's proposal for the belfry, with its elaborate wood
and lead 'pepperpot'. In the end the Governing Body pleaded
poverty and decided not to go ahead with the lantern, and instead
to retain only the stone tower from Bodley's design.*

Museum and Manchester Town Hall.[92] Of this first group only Champneys,
Deane and Hugall expressed a desired to take the competition further, so
more letters were sent to George Bodley, who saw the belfry as an 'opportunity for good work in purely English late Gothic', Thomas Graham Jackson
and John Loughborough Pearson.[93] Pearson, already well established as
a restorer of cathedrals, was not interested, but Bodley, renowned as an
architect with a particular talent for beautiful churches, and Jackson,
whose name would become synonymous with late Victorian Oxford, both
said yes.[94]

Things moved quickly. Champneys came to visit on Ash Wednesday
(18 February 1874), and it was at this point that the committee decided

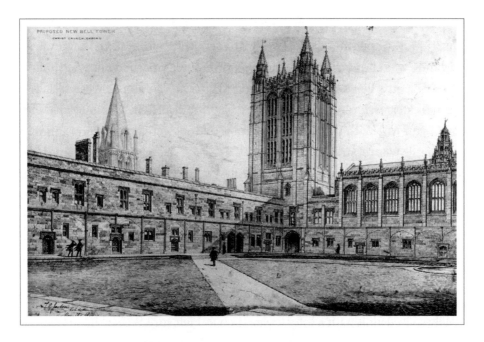

T. G. Jackson's towering design for the belfry, dated 15 May 1874.

it needed two sketches: one of the proposed belfry from Tom Quad looking directly towards the tower, and one from the south-west so that the relative proportions of the cathedral spire and the new design could be established. Tom Tower had to be considered too. A closing date of 17 May was set.[95]

It was not just a matter of appearance that had to be taken into account. Evidence for Wolsey's intentions for this corner of the quad was found in the foundations. The sheer bulk of the existing structure suggested something immense, but the Governing Body called in a civil engineer, John Wolfe-Barry, to make essential checks before any decision was made on the submitted designs.[96] He made exploratory excavations on the south, east and north sides, and found that the tower rested on a bed of sand and gravel. The north and south sides both stood on substantial bases, with the foundation walls more than eleven feet deep. On the east side, however, the foundation extended no more than eighteen inches below the cloister paving. Barry's reasonable conclusion was that Wolsey's intention was not a tall tower in this corner.[97]

Designs came in on time, and the committee sat down to inspect them on 20 May. Champneys's design, dismissed by Vere Bayne as a 'May Day garland', was eliminated immediately, and Hugall's merited not a comment. Two of Scott's five designs were disliked, but the remainder were reserved for more discussion. Two of Bodley's designs, one of which made the tower into a gateway with a 'leaden pepperpot' on top, were kept; Deane's Italian campanile was retained as a possibility, as was Jackson's overpowering 170-foot tower.[98] Two days later came the first vote. The dean abstained but let it be known that he preferred Jackson's design, with Bodley's 'pepperpot' in second place. Edward King, regius professor of pastoral theology, was unable to attend the meeting because he had hurt his leg, but he sent in a postal vote against Jackson.

In the end the decision lay between Jackson and Bodley, but there was still some prevarication. Jackson had decided that tall was the way to go: 'I boldly soared aloft with a lofty tower such as I felt sure Wolsey had prepared for with his massive substructure. None of the others ventured on so ambitious a scheme.'[99] Wolfe-Barry tentatively agreed that Wolsey's foundations could stand the weight of such an immense structure. Bodley, on the other hand, opted for a lighter touch, providing 'more of a gateway, rather than of a tower' with a lower stone stage, topped with a timber and lead, or even copper, octagonal confection that almost defeats description. Everyone was certain that they wanted a stone structure, rather than a wood and lead building, and Bodley's design needed iron girders. He was sent away to make amendments. After such a fast beginning, the final vote in committee eventually took place on 2 February 1875. Bodley's stone tower, topped with the octagonal lantern, with the amendments, was accepted unanimously. It was to be simple and low, so as not to interfere with the line of the cathedral spire, and was not to cost more than £7,000.[100] Symm was contracted for the stonework element of the design, which was completed by late 1877. The new statues, of Wolsey and two angels, funded by Henry Parry Liddon and sculpted by the firm of Farmer and Brindley, were erected just before the scaffolding was struck in 1878. Liddell had wanted scholars in academic dress flanking the cardinal, but Bodley supported Liddon, and, as is so often

*Henry Taunt's photograph of work in progress in Tom Quad, dating from the
early 1880s. Gilbert Scott's double archway into the cathedral has already been
constructed; the 'meat-safe' holding the cathedral bells is very evident, soon to
be encased within Bodley's design for the Wolsey Tower. The timber structure
over the cathedral was to show how the roofs would look if the gables were to be
reinstated. Over the Hall, the first portion of the crenellation and the first pinnacle
have been erected. The stepladders are evidently those of workmen restoring the
cloister shafts, and, on the far left, the steps are in the process of reconstruction.*

the way, the money won the day.[101] Castle advised raising a mortgage loan
to cover the costs of the new tower, as well as other repairs that needed to
be done, to the tune of £21,500.[102] As it turned out, the octagonal 'pepperpot' was never added, although the stone structure was to be finished with
sufficient strength to carry it, should funds ever permit.[103] Gothicisation
and medieval restorations were falling out of favour, and it is possible that
the failure to complete the tower was caused by a loss of nerve rather than
reduced finances.[104] Older members of college, such as Henry Thompson,
still held out a hope in 1899, but in vain.[105] The tower as it is just hides the
'tea-chest' behind an elaborate screen, but the corner turrets give an impression of height without overtopping the cathedral spire or Tom Tower.[106]

The 1970s saw a major restoration of the Wolsey Tower. This was the culmination of a major refurbishment project to façades and interiors throughout Christ Church, funded, at least in part, by the Oxford Historic Buildings Fund.[107] The tower's poor state was brought to light in the decennial survey of 1971, when it was proposed that Bodley's nineteenth-century addition be taken down and the tower returned to its earlier low level.[108] Although more expensive to restore the tower as it was, complete with the bell chamber and the turrets, the Governing Body decided that it was really the only way forward, if only the funds could be met. The Royal Fine Art Commission, whose advice had been sought, 'appreciated the financial problems involved and agreed that they would not oppose the idea of replacing it by something simpler and less expensive'. A conical or ogee-shaped lead-covered roof – to echo Tom Tower – was suggested, but the Commissioners also wondered whether this was an opportunity to explore 'an entirely new concept', perhaps 'a simple framework with the bells exposed in the continental manner [to be] a stimulating architectural incident in the Oxford townscape'.[109] Conservation won the day, and the tower was restored as it then stood.[110] Mr Biscoe-Taylor, the quantity surveyor, struggled to find suitable stone; the local stones originally used for Christ Church's buildings were long unavailable, and even Clipsham was becoming harder to source. He found four English quarries that could match the colour, but none that could reliably supply the quantities needed. In the end, he went to France and found an oolitic limestone of the right colour from Savonnières in the Meuse region of France, related to Headington and Wheatley stone, and of better weathering quality than Clipsham.[111] All the new carving for the grotesques was done by Percy Quick, using Briantville; blocks and tracery were made using Besace. English stone was only used on the east face: Portland for the plinth and Clipsham where repairs were needed on the main cornice. Phase I was completed in the spring of 1977, and the project was finished in March 1980, at a total cost of £607,235.[112]

Liddell always wanted to effect alterations, and the belfry scheme became just a part of his efforts to make the Great Quadrangle, still usually known as such in spite of the presence of the iconic Tom Tower, more of a cohesive whole. Charles Dodgson's *Vision of the Three Ts*, published in 1873, was a protest against the Gothicisation of Christ Church advocated by the dean and Vere Bayne, evident in the restoration of the cathedral and other designs. His targets were the 'tunnel' to the cathedral and the 'tea-chest' belfry, along with the 'trench'. This last was created, possibly as a preliminary to the belfry tower project, when the seventeenth-century curtain wall between the Hall and the staircase tower was removed, leaving a significant gap, or 'trench', between the east end of the Hall and the tower, over the ante-hall.

While discussions were taking place over the new belfry, there was much activity elsewhere. There were plans afoot in 1874 to actually build the cloister intended by the cardinal. In fact, the double-arch design of Scott's cathedral entrance may have been deliberately chosen to allow the central column to accommodate a springer. Dodgson objected publicly and received a reprimand from Vere Bayne for disloyalty, for the notion of interfering with Wolsey's work, of which, as we have seen, Bayne was a staunch defender even in its incomplete state.[113] Symm had gone as far as preparing an estimate for the work, but it proved too expensive and too controversial. Instead, between 1873 and 1878 Liddell contented himself with the repair and enhancement of the cloister pillars and springers.[114] He also replaced the parapet around the whole of the quadrangle, changing the balustrade to crenellation (thus restoring Wolsey's design), lowered the terrace so that the bases of the cloister shafts could be seen and protected the quad side foundations of the cloister within stone 'cases'. Further projects included the commissioning of the building of Fell Tower to Bodley's design, raising the roof between the cathedral and the belfry tower, adding the pinnacles and the little bell-cot to the Hall, restoring the inner pinnacles on Tom Tower with Doulting stone and generally refacing the upper level of the Great Quadrangle, above the string course, also with Doulting stone, which turned out to be a not particularly happy choice.[115]

At the same time Vere Bayne and the Quadrangle Committee were overseeing work on the other side of Christ Church. Oriel College had constructed King Edward Street in 1872 and in December 1875 proposed that the 'open space' between Peckwater and Oriel College be improved.[116] The idea met with general approval from the Governing Body, and plans were drawn up.[117] The Provost's orchard, between Canterbury Gate and the yard at the back of staircase 6 of Peckwater Quad, was to be closed in with a wall and fence; and the wall around the yard was to be built with a concave line to follow Oriel's proposed convex corner, considerably widening the access into Oriel Square from the new street.[118] The Oxford Local Board objected to the two colleges carving up the street between them, and requested that the designs be altered. After much to-ing and fro-ing, during which Dean Liddell protested that Christ Church had given up much to the city already – presumably referring to alterations to the street line on St Aldate's – the wall around the north-east corner of Peckwater Quad and into Oriel Square was built, altering the shape of the privy yard, cutting off the end of Blue Boar Lane and opening the entrance into Oriel Square.[119]

The cloister and the Chapter House

Towards the end of the cathedral restoration attention had been turned to the remains of the monastic cloister and to the Chapter House. When Wolsey imposed the Hall and the east side of the Great Quadrangle, he destroyed the west side completely, leaving a lopsided courtyard with openings on each remaining side into the cloister walk, much of which was almost new in 1525.[120] In the early seventeenth century alterations were made to the cloister, including the construction of new rooms above the south and east walks. Those over the east side may have been created to accommodate the growing Chapter archive; that on the south side, built in 1612 by the college mason, Thomas Wetherall, would later become the Allestree Library.[121]

At the end of the eighteenth century the alterations to the Old Library may have dislodged some of the Chapter's archive. Some may have been kept in the small room off the Chapter House (probably created by William Tresham soon after the foundation, and accessed originally from the Priory House rather than the Chapter House) and over the south cloister, but the college's burgeoning estates correspondence and all the associated documents, such as leases, court rolls, registers, cash books, bailiffs' books and

The cloister in 1837, showing the open arch into the cloister walk towards the Chapter House, closed by Gilbert Scott.

tenancy records, were expanding beyond the available space. A decree issued on 27 July 1712 that 'all book writings & paper belonging to the treasury to be brought in, or account given of them in writing, under the hand of the person, in whose possession they are' suggests that some papers were in private lodgings.[122] That same year saw Townesend infilling two of the windows in the Old Library, possibly to allow for an increase in shelving and the construction of the gallery at the east end to house Aldrich's collections. But in 1772, just as he was finishing the New Library, Henry Keene was charged with converting the north cloister walk, closest to the cathedral door, into a muniment room, the first space to be defined specifically for archives.[123] The work cost £154 4s. 2d. and involved building a wall to the south of the cathedral door and another across the end of the east cloister, making a room of about 44 feet by 10 feet 10 inches. In 1800 the Dean and

*Plan and design of sash window for the Muniment Room created
in the north cloister walk in 1772. This lasted for about a century,
until George Gilbert Scott restored the cathedral and cloister.*

Chapter told the House of Commons Records Committee that the cathedral's
documents were 'carefully preserved in dry places in the Chapter House and
a Muniment Room fitted up for the purpose'.[124]

George Gilbert Scott was to sweep this away. As his restoration project
continued, he offered the Governing Body two options: either to rebuild or
restore the cloister as far as was feasible or to build an additional west aisle
onto the south cloister. The evidence, Scott felt, was lacking for a medieval
aisle, and so he preferred the cloister option. Winning the day, if there was
ever much argument, he evicted the archives from their home in the north
cloister walk, returned the windows to their original Perpendicular from
eighteenth-century sashes and restored the vaulting. The decoration of the
new vault took place over several years. Thomas Vere Bayne funded the new

*Photograph of the cloister, taken before 1870, with the
sashes for the Muniment Room still in place.*

bosses in the north side, carved by John McCulloch in 1885, which show
angels as well as the arms of Dean Liddell and the seven canons in office
at the time. McCulloch also carved the entrance bay to the cathedral and,
possibly, the new archway just beyond the Old Library and Priory House
doors.[125] The east cloister walk was restored and altered, incorporating a
new and higher wooden vault, to allow the full beauty of the Chapter House
door to be appreciated. [126] The opening on the east, opposite the Chapter
House door, possibly inserted by Dean Duppa, was closed during Scott's
restoration.[127] Scott also cleared out the centre of the cloister, revealing
once more the substantial foundations of Wolsey's bell-tower, at the time
thought to be the priory lavatorium.[128] These remained exposed, an antiquarian oddity, until 1985, when, while alterations were being made to
the Priory House, a new garden was laid out in the cloister. Its design, by

*The east end of the Chapter House, showing its early pointed
architecture with elegant detached columns. Drawn by
Thomas Uwins and engraved by Samuel Rawle.*

Mavis Batey, included all twenty-four plants shown in the borders of Wolsey's lectionary.[129]

The Chapter House had been rather abused architecturally over the years. At some point in its history, certainly before Williams drew his ground plan in the 1730s, it had been divided into two with folding doors. These doors were only opened for the ceremony of the installation of each new president of St John's College.[130] The floor in the inner portion had been raised, destroying the beautiful proportions of the room, merely to create a store for the Chapter's wine beneath.[131] The work to restore the Chapter House was done by Bodley, definitely Christ Church's architect of the moment. Bodley quoted £989 for all the work, except for decorative painting and stained glass. In the end it cost almost twice that amount (excluding

The Chapter House as it was in 1976, with the new display cases designed
by Alan Irvine in place, and before the space was developed as a shop.

the architect's fee), but the Chapter were evidently pleased and threw an evening's entertainment for the Senior Students on 19 October 1880 to celebrate the completion of the project.[132] A small spiral staircase was added for access to the small sixteenth-century room which was used first as a Chapter meeting room and later as a practice room for the choir.[133] The foundation stone from Ipswich School (the only one of Wolsey's 'feeder' schools for Cardinal College to be founded), which had been discovered in 1750, when work was being done on a malthouse in the town, was bequeathed to Christ Church by the Revd Canning of Ipswich in 1789. Originally it had been inserted into the wall on the right of the main door but was moved during the renovations to its current location at the east end.[134]

The Chapter House remained the traditional meeting place of the dean and canons until the Anatomy School was adapted for Common Room use.[135] Soon after the Governing Body began to hold its meetings in the new facility in 1971, the Chapter House began to be used as an exhibition space and was later converted into a treasury for a permanent exhibition of cathedral and diocesan plate. The dean reported that financial support was available: £17,500 had been received by Christmas the following year, including £6,500 from the Worshipful Company of Goldsmiths, given as part of their Cathedral Treasuries Scheme.[136] The design, by Alan Irvine – a free-standing central display case supported on two hexagonal columns, framed in bronze and glass set in silver bronze sections designed to eliminate any dust – was starkly modern and yet fitted discreetly within the ancient space. Special foundations to overcome the natural gravel and high water table were installed by Arup Associates.[137] Around the walls, drawings and engravings from the gallery's collections were mounted in cases.[138]

In 1980 the room also became the cathedral shop, much to the disgruntlement of many. Even *Private Eye*, in 1989, bemoaned the surrounding of the elegant display cases with shelves and shop-fittings for commercial use, and only a decade later the Governing Body welcomed a proposal to return the room to its original purpose, for meetings and lectures, if space could be found elsewhere for a shop and to rehouse the diocesan plate.[139] This may be on the cards for the near future.

8

Regeneration and new responsibilities

The early twentieth century saw Christ Church taking a deep breath after the upheavals – financial, architectural and constitutional – of the nineteenth. There were no major building projects for some decades, but modernisation and restoration continued apace. The first item on the agenda was the installation of electricity. Nearly eighty years after gas illuminated Tom Quad, discussions began about the next step. The Steward was asked to draw up a report in 1891, and he took advice and quotations from the Oxford Electric Company. There were some concerns about undergraduates tampering with the fittings, but the contractor dismissed these swiftly: 'supposing an undergraduate should contrive to give himself a shock from the wires, it would hardly be violent enough even to deter him from repeating the experiment.' In spite of reassurances on safety and on cost, proposals were rejected and discussions deferred until 1900, when approval was given for lighting in all residential rooms, except those on the top floor of Peckwater Quad. The consulting engineer was Morgan Williams, and the work was undertaken by Hill Upton & Co.[1] A loan of £2,000 was received from the Board of Agriculture, and shortly afterwards the annual report for 1901–2 announced, with some ceremony, that 'The Electric Light has been installed in The Deanery, in the rooms of Students and Undergraduates, and in the Common Rooms and Lecture Rooms.'[2] However exciting and trumpeted this innovation was, undergraduate rooms were probably not much warmer or

College improvement loans were granted by the Board of Agriculture. The capital was held by the Board under the Universities and Colleges Estates Acts (1858–98). The loans were used to tide Christ Church over the problems of beneficial leases running out and for the improvement of the agricultural estate, but also for many of the repairs to buildings that took place in the late nineteenth and early twentieth centuries. These included improvements to the drainage system, the installation of electricity, new bathrooms and lavatories, the restoration of the west front and alterations to the old Anatomy School.

CCA MS Estates 130 and 131

brighter than they had been in the 1550s, as the permitted strength of light bulbs was tiny, about 8 cd (about the strength of eight ordinary candles). Hall was lit in 1903, after Bodley had proposed that there should be lights on the tables and on the west jambs of the windows, standard lights on the mantelpieces and brackets on the east and west walls. Morgan Williams quoted £800 for the work, and another loan was raised for £1,000.[3]

Restoration of much of the stonework was becoming crucial by the early years of the twentieth century. In 1908 William Douglas Caröe drew up plans for alterations and improvements all over college, including major refurbishment of the stonework of Tom Tower and the St Aldate's frontage. But Caröe's work was not restricted to repair; he also planned the improvements and extensions to the kitchen and designed the stone spiral staircase between the Senior Common Room and the Hall.[4] The construction of the staircase was ingenious. This spiral stair has often been cited as the inspiration for the well in *Alice's Adventures in Wonderland*, by Charles Dodgson (alias Lewis Carroll). Its construction, however, did not take place until 1908, a decade after Dodgson's death and more than forty years after the publication of the book. All Caröe's designs – plus the new timber case around the organ, and the installation of bathrooms in Peckwater and the Great Quads – were executed by Symm.

Sporting facilities

Off-site, but of some significance to the sporting men of Christ Church, were the changes by the river. Albert Gladstone, the President of the Christ Church Boat Club and grandson of William Gladstone, the great Liberal prime minister, proposed in June 1907 that a boathouse should replace the college barge, but sentiment and aesthetics won the day for many years to come; barges were considered part of the Oxford scene.[5] Houseboats on the river were nothing new; J. M. W. Turner incorporated them into his painting that was engraved for the 1799 Almanack. But the club barges had come from the great livery companies in the City and were adopted with delight by the college boat clubs as Eights Week became part of the summer social round, as useful club houses and grandstands.[6] However, in 1930 the Committee on the House Barge reported that 'The present barge is in a state of collapse and no further use can be made of it.'[7] A new barge was much the preferred option; when the idea was put to old members in 1933, they responded that they might be prepared to fund a large portion of, if not all, the cost of a new barge but not of a boathouse. As it turned out, the cost of a new barge, at £2,250, was prohibitively high, so the boathouse idea prevailed, although funds were indeed slow in coming in. The site was chosen quite quickly – in really the obvious place, at the end of what was once known as Earl's Ham alongside the New Cut – but it took another two years for Christ Church to decide to go ahead with the new brick boathouse, turned at a slight angle to look downstream. It was completed in time for Eights in the summer of 1936, and a ninety-nine-year lease was granted to the Christ Church Boat Club.[8] Even before Christ Church's facility was open, others were applying for permission to build. Magdalen College was the first, followed shortly by an application from the University Boat Club for permission for all colleges to be allowed to build on the land between the Cherwell and the New Cut. At the same time an application was received from Magdalen to do the same.[9] By the end of 1935 plans had been submitted by Magdalen, Trinity, Merton and Worcester colleges, all of whose boathouses were finished before war broke out in 1939.[10] The designs allowed for storage and maintenance of the boats on the ground floor, with club facilities and a balcony for spectators

Christ Church boathouse.

on the first floor. They were not universally popular; a traditional image of Oxford was lost when the barges departed from the Isis. However, they did find favour with the clubs themselves, and more colleges followed suit from the 1950s, the designs becoming progressively more modern and more functional. As these boathouses were going up, so Christ Church's was modernised and supplied with drying rooms and hot and cold water in 1955, and then extended in 1988 by Stroudley Brothers at a cost of £125,000.[11] In the early 1960s, after the septic tank was found to be defective, mains water and drainage were brought to all the boathouses on the island.[12]

As the new post-war boathouses were built, so the footbridge over the Cherwell was redesigned in 1949–50.[13] The original crossing appears to have been erected around 1885, once college barges were moored downstream of the Cherwell to a design by T. G. Jackson. The architect for the new bridge was Cecil Handisyde and the consulting engineer Felix Samuely, an Austrian who had worked with Erich Mendelsohn on such iconic buildings as the De La Warr Pavilion in Bexhill. By 2012 the structure of the

Cecil C. Handisyde was a specialist in the science of building materials. Felix Samuely (1902–59), conscious of the shortage of steel and timber in the years after the Second World War, promoted composite construction from pre-cast concrete. He engineered the Skylon tower, designed by Powell and Moya, for the Festival of Britain in 1951.

ODNB; Harwood (2015), 348

bridge, built using pre-stressed concrete, was causing concern, and for a short while it seemed that complete renewal would be necessary. In the end, after a summer persuading excited rowing fans not to jump up and down too enthusiastically, repairs were undertaken.[14]

Other sports were not neglected, with cricket receiving particular attention. The Christ Church cricket ground was originally closer to the Great Western Railway's first station in Oxford, near Grandpont, but by 1860 it had moved to its present location, in St Thomas's parish on the west side of the city, with a new pavilion. John Ambler, a cricketer who lived conveniently on Iffley Road, was employed as keeper of the ground, and as umpire and bowler to the club.[15] A century later, in 1972, the Cricket Club pointed out – and the Governing Body agreed – that the pavilion was now beyond repair. Costs to build a new one were high: estimates in 1974 ranged from £41,000 for a prefabricated building to £100,000 for the grand design submitted by Peter Bosanquet. The decision made was for a traditional design but incorporating a flat for the groundsman, and to a maximum cost of £80,000. The new pavilion was opened on 2 May 1976.[16] Alterations were made in 1981 and then again in 1990, mainly to make provision for sportswomen.[17] In 2014 there was another major overhaul. The pavilion had begun to look a bit tatty and rather dated, and major work was undertaken to bring the changing and catering facilities up to twenty-first-century standards.

Even getting to the pavilion has been made easier. For many years the only way from the Meadow to the sports ground was by a chain punt. The unstoppable rise of health and safety concerns put this out of use some

Squash courts were built just before the boathouse proposals were put to
the Governing Body, very soon after the game received its modern rules in
1928.

Christ Church 1929–30

decades ago, but it was not until 2014 that the Jubilee Bridge – a modern
steel single span – rose over the Cherwell.[18] The work involved in getting just
one (relatively) simple structure built demonstrates how modern planning
regulations can constrain development. The consultation process for the
Jubilee Bridge included: the preparation of a historic landscape appraisal; a
biodiversity mitigation and enhancement strategy (including a bat survey);
an arboricultural method statement; and talks with the Oxford Civic Society,
the Oxfordshire Architectural and Historical Society, the Oxford Preservation
Trust, conservation experts at the Environmental Agency, the City Council,
the City Conservation Officer and the City archaeologist.[19] All before a planning application could be submitted and any technical work could begin.[20]

The Second World War

The interruption of the Second World War put a stop to any major projects,
and to the recurring debate about the separation of college and cathedral,
but the buildings were affected in many ways by the outbreak of hostilities.[21]
The Governing Body and Chapter had begun to prepare, as did the nation,
two years earlier, but in August 1939 the new dean, John Lowe, 'rallied and
directed the staff with prompt alacrity'. The Steward, Harold Percival, gave
demonstrations on handling incendiary bombs with long-handled shovels
and ensured that all necessary precautions, including black-out blinds and
air-raid precautions, were put in place. Christ Church's sandbag barricades
were said to be the most scientifically constructed in Oxford. Fire-watching
rotas, which included two men being perched in a sort of crow's nest on the
roof of the Library, were established; treasures were moved to safe locations;

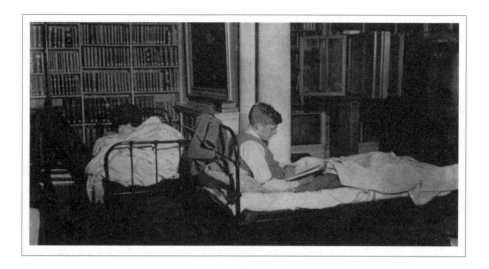

Fire-watching during the Second World War. Students and senior members took shifts to watch for fires from the roof of the Library. During the refurbishment of Peck 6–8 in 2016, two fire-watchers' helmets were discovered in the basement.

and the iron railings were soon removed from St Aldate's, Meadow gate and the Library.[22] More substantial alterations involved the construction of air-raid shelters in the basement of Canterbury 3 (which could accommodate seventy people) with a ramp down into the shelter from the gate protected by a blast wall and another under Tom 4 (to hold 146 people), accessed by a ramp under Tom Gate. The plans for these were drawn up by A. Carstairs, the City Engineer, in January 1940.[23]

The late 1940s were a period of reconstruction of Christ Church life, rather than of its buildings. Clubs were re-begun almost as soon as the war ended; the quatercentenary was celebrated with as much style as rationing would permit; and everyone battened down the hatches against the cold, gales and floods of the winter of 1946–7. It was not until 1949 that attention was turned again to the physical environment, with the conversion of the basement of the Anatomy School into a refectory, the construction of the new servery between the School and the kitchen, the building of a new west front to the buttery and Old Lecture Room, and the refurbishment of the Law Library in Tom 4. The following year Caröe's kitchen scullery was converted into a rest room for staff.[24] Darsie Rawlins, ecclesiastical sculptor, carved the memorial to Christ Church's war fallen,[25] and Tom was rehung in time to ring for the coronation of Elizabeth II.

Blue Boar Quad

Far bigger projects were afoot, however. Accommodation for an undergraduate population swelled by men from grammar schools became of increasing importance in the second half of the twentieth century. No new residential buildings had gone up since Meadow Buildings in the 1860s, and Christ Church has always tried to provide accommodation on-site for its students.[26] From the late 1950s future requirements both for student and teaching rooms were often on agenda. The old coal yard on the northern edge of Christ Church seemed an ideal location for a new building.

The coal yard, behind the north canonries, Killcanon and the west side of Peckwater, had been gardens when Loggan made his engraving of the site in 1673. The Brewhouse stood on one side and a racquet court on the other. The court was operated as a public facility and is mentioned in sixteenth-century leases of the public house that fronted on to St Aldate's.[27] At Lady Day 1832 the property was taken back in hand, and plans, which were no doubt unpopular with the sporting undergraduates, were drawn up to convert the court into stables and coach houses for the canons who lived on this side of the site. The conversion was complex, and the instructions for ensuring that each canon had both access and privacy were lengthy. The work cost a huge £1,200.[28]

The site was split in two, probably with the building of Killcanon, by a high wall, the westerly portion containing the domestic brewhouse and stables and the easterly a garden attached to Killcanon. By the early twentieth century the garden had gone, and the area was used for storage and coal until the 1950s. Proposals in the 1920s to turn the brewhouse into an elegant lodging for a canon, with the stables adapted as garages and domestic services, were never fulfilled.

As the Ministry of Fuel and Power continued to limit supplies of coal (which was rationed until June 1958), Peckwater was wired for electric

*The coal yard, photographed c.1960, looking west towards St Aldate's,
showing the north brewhouse and the stables; the site of Blue Boar Quad.*

heaters and the need for solid fuel declined. Various proposals were made,
divided between plans for the use of the site to fulfil Christ Church's needs
and those which might generate some revenue. Most importantly, it was felt
that the redevelopment of the site needed to be initiated by Christ Church
rather than risking a solution imposed by the council. Already the City
Architect had told the Governing Body that he wanted to see a widening of
Blue Boar Street, new offices for the Corporation, garages for the mayor and
the town clerk, and extra car parking.[29] Discussions were both influenced
and delayed by the city's Development Plan, which had significance for other
parts of Christ Church's property in Oxford, particularly around the railway
station, but within a few months it was decided that the city could use the
site for parking for a limited period while Christ Church's plans for the site
were finalised.

A committee was formed in February 1952 to 'consider what we could most usefully use the coal yard for, though any project would have to be weighed against such tasks as the Library in assigning priorities'.[30] One plan was to build new canons' houses to free up Tom Quad for other uses, but this was soon rejected. The committee decided that the needs were primarily for lecture rooms, Library storage, a caretaker's flat, guest rooms, a new Treasury and Student sets. Development was held up partly for financial reasons and partly because of the failure of the Governing Body and the Chapter, who still retained control over the site, to reach an agreement.[31] Another short-term lease for the city's use of the site was proposed in 1954, and it was not until 1958, when alterations were being made to one of the canon's houses closest to the coal yard, that serious discussions recommenced.[32]

It was at this point too that the Senior Censor, J. Steven Watson, reported to the Governing Body on student numbers. Things had been in a state of some flux since the war, with the complications of compulsory military service and then its sudden suspension. It seemed, said Watson, an ideal time to reassess and to take back some control. The aim was for a body of between 360 and 380 undergraduate members at any one time; a stable position he felt could be achieved within three or four years. Watson was actually calling for a decrease in numbers; censorial policy was for a 'community, loose-knit but intimate, upon our present site, and dining together in our present Hall'. The inflated numbers in college – approaching 500 undergraduates in 1959 – meant that there had been a loss of personal contact with students. Watson's campaign for a new building was not, then, to allow for increasing numbers but more to improve living conditions in college and to provide for more men to spend longer than one year in residence within the college walls. The coal yard – or Blue Boar site – was the obvious place to find the extra rooms that were needed. Watson also suggested that it could be possible to create lecture-room space and increase reader space in the Library by having dedicated law and science libraries, or even converting the ground floor of the existing Library into the working Library, moving the art collection into the Anatomy School.[33] Within a few months, by the end of 1959, more definite plans were drawn up for a four-staircase block

to accommodate both lecturers – in the 'penthouses' – and undergraduates. New offices for the Treasury and a store for the college and cathedral
archives were also to be included.[34] It was not until 1962 that the architects
Philip Powell and John Hidalgo Moya were selected. Powell and Moya had
designed the Skylon tower for the Festival of Britain in 1951, and had made
their names after the creation of the welfare state with their schemes for
schools and hospitals. New styles in architecture were embraced by all the
colleges at this time, and Powell and Moya were at the forefront. The first
college in Oxford to use the partnership was Brasenose, and the Governing
Body commissioned them soon after to design a similar Modernist structure for Christ Church, using the same Portland stone and large windows
with metal window frames, and combining the current taste for horizon-
tality with strong vertical piers to reduce scale.[35] The choice of architects
caused much discussion in Governing Body meetings, with Powell and Moya
approved partly because 'they had shown that they were good at dealing
with difficult people'.[36]

An appeal to old members was launched in October 1962, and within
three months £170,000 of the first £200,000 requested had been received.[37]
A timetable was drawn up for plans to be finalised, for tenders to be invited
and received and for building to begin. An announcement was made at the
June gaudy in 1963 that operations were to begin at once, with the intent
that actual construction should start in August 1965 and be completed by
May 1967.[38] Unsurprisingly, alterations were made to the plans, but the
final result was a structure that retained the traditional staircase format of
college buildings and which was given a slightly wavy form to reflect the
ancient wall separating it from Blue Boar Lane.[39] It was there, though, that
any sense of antiquity ended. It was faced in Portland roach bed stone, which
was filled with fossil shells. Opinions on its success as a building vary widely.
Disliked by many as an ugly 'concrete' block, out of kilter with its surroundings, it is seen by architects and architectural historians as a masterpiece of
modern design, and it has been listed Grade 2*.[40] Blue Boar was, however,
flawed from day one. A case against the architects and builders was made in
1975, when the roof failed; the under-floor heating was soon switched off

CHRIST CHURCH   OXFORD   NEW BUILDINGS   INTERIOR of A TYPICAL   BED-SITTING ROOM   Powell & Moya 155/24

CHRIST CHURCH OXFORD NEW BUILDINGS AERIAL VIEW FROM THE EAST   155/22

The architects Powell and Moya's sketches for Blue Boar Quad, dated January 1964.

214

Blue Boar Quad as built.

as it was unreliable and irreparable; and the dampness caused by the lack of 'breathing' materials has been a problem both for the human inhabitants and for the archive in the basement of staircase 4. Rainwater downpipes were constructed inside the structure of building and were lined with pitch fibre material. After a few years, accelerated by necessary rodding, these deteriorated and began to leak. This difficulty, along with the decay of the steel reinforcing rods in the concrete of the exterior construction, was resolved during the major refurbishment of 2007–9.[41] Architects Purcell Miller Tritton oversaw a sensitive renewal of the building that included additional rooms on the original but unused roof terraces, ensuite facilities in all rooms and a new lecture theatre, something that had long been needed and desired.[42]

St Aldate's Quad

Further student accommodation, this time predominantly for graduates, was provided in the 1980s across St Aldate's. In May 1979 the Accommodation Committee presented a report to the Governing Body suggesting that 89–91 St Aldate's and the area behind it be redeveloped. A structural surveyor had already said that £200,000 needed to be spent just to bring those houses into a 'sound tenantable condition', and, as extra rooms were needed, he proposed going a bit further.[43] The idea met with approval. Sympathetically converting the ancient buildings facing onto the street, the development spread out between the cathedral school and Rose Place, providing a modern quad in keeping with its locality. Once the Architects Design Partnership, a local company, had been chosen, yet another appeal to old members was launched in 1982.[44] The quad was built by Hinkins and Frewin and opened in 1986, receiving an award from the Royal Institute of British Architects.[45]

Liddell Building

Only a few years later, in 1991, still more residential facilities were provided on Iffley Road in a joint project with Corpus Christi College on the site of three Christ Church properties: the Red House, Christ Church House and a third residence, called Compas. Discussions about the use of Christ Church House had been a constant theme in Governing Body meetings for several years. In the early 1970s the premises had been taken over by squatters, and a decision was made in 1972 to demolish the building.[46] The first plan was to build four new houses for Students, but this was abandoned in 1975. A bid by St Hilda's College for the site was turned down in 1977, but it was not until 1987 that the proposal to use the site for junior members' accommodation was first laid on the table.[47] Bosanquet and Perryman proposed a modular arrangement of three-storey buildings providing up to 138 rooms. The architects would have preferred to demolish the Red House, but this was not approved, and so the plan included its restoration. In 1987 the estimated cost was £15,000 per bedsitter.

The site was too large for Christ Church alone, and so, as Corpus Christi College had expressed an interest in acquiring part of the land, negotiations began between the two colleges.[48] On 3 June 1987 an agreement was drawn up with Corpus Christi for a joint building scheme to which Corpus would contribute a considerable portion of the costs, and be granted in return a ninety-nine-year lease for its own discrete accommodation on the site.[49] Three years later, as construction began, the costs had risen to £33,000 for each bedsitter, with a total building cost of nearly £5.5 million.[50] In May 1991 the name for the new accommodation became the hot topic; the President of Corpus Christi, Sir Keith Thomas, took to his Governing Body a paper with various suggestions, including Ruskin (which 'might confuse'), Pococke ('too esoteric') and Buckland. More geographical names included St Clement's, Cherwell and Iffley ('too obvious'). Liddell was not one of the names put forward at that time, but on 17 June it was reported that it was the favourite at Christ Church and therefore would be supported.[51] By October 1991 the name was firmly in use.[52]

The Picture Gallery

It was not just the students who needed accommodation. Almost simultaneously with the building of Blue Boar, Powell and Moya turned their attention to a new art gallery to house Christ Church's large collection of paintings and drawings. Library provision within the colleges for undergraduates as well as senior members was increasingly expected as the twentieth century progressed, and the pictures, which had been housed on the ground floor of the New Library, had to be found a new home as books began to push them into an ever more confined space. There had been plans to incorporate a gallery into Blue Boar, but it was Powell and Moya's opinion that if this were done, the quad 'would be so crowded that it would scarcely be a quad at all'.[53] Two other sites were put forward as possibilities: 'Dr Jenkins's Garden', next to the deanery garden, and the east end of the deanery garden with an entrance through Canterbury Quad. The second proposal received universal approval from the Building Committee and was passed by the Governing Body, by twenty-nine votes to two.[54] Powell and Moya were

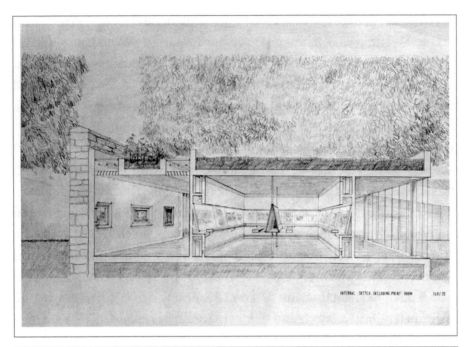

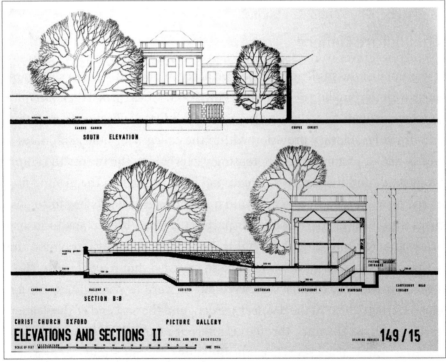

Powell and Moya's sketches for the Picture Gallery, dated June 1964

accepted as architects without any further discussion. A model was made and costs estimated at around £76,500 for the whole project. But it was put on hold for a while – 'not indefinitely', the dean reassured the Students, but because financing depended on the results of the Blue Boar Appeal.[55] Only a few months later the problem was solved when, in October 1963, Charles Forte came forward with an offer of £50,000 towards the building of the new gallery.[56] Plans could now be put into action under the watchful eye of the new Curator of Pictures, Daniel Bueno de Mesquita, and of James Byam Shaw, who had just been appointed to catalogue the drawings and engravings. The dean permitted the use of part of his garden, and the gallery was built semi-underground and almost invisible from anywhere in college, but still providing a light and airy space, with two principal top-lit galleries, one for early Renaissance art and one for the Old Masters, a wide corridor acting as a kind of long gallery, continuing the style of grand houses, and a print room with controlled light levels for the display of Renaissance drawings. The construction combined new and old, using both concrete and Portland stone. The window mullions along the cloister-like walk, which allows natural light into the gallery, are in bronze.[57]

The pictures were moved into their new space early in 1968, and both Blue Boar Quad and the Picture Gallery were opened by the Queen on 2 May that year. The grand event was preceded by much debate on all sorts of topics, not least whether the commemorative plaques should be in English or in Latin.[58] There were to be two plaques for each building: one commemorating the donors and the other the occasion of the Queen's visit. A postal vote came down in favour of an English inscription, but the committee preferred Latin 'for its neatness and elegance'. In the end the plaques to the donors were inscribed in Latin, and those celebrating the Queen's unveiling were in English. Structural problems have beset this building, too, with major repairs taking place in 1998, but its success as a gallery is unquestioned. It won an RIBA award, and has recently been listed.[59]

* * * * *

The second half of the twentieth century was a period of increasingly strict control over building and maintenance work on historic sites. The Ancient Monuments Protection Act of 1882 grew out of the attempts by Sir John Lubbock to set up a National Monuments Commission to protect ancient sites in private ownership or to acquire them by purchase. George Shaw Lefevre, the first Commissioner of Works, appointed in 1880, realised that it was perfectly legal for owners to do what they wished with remains on their land, including complete destruction, and there was a distinct reluctance to tell people what they could or could not do with their own property. The 1882 Act had far less power than either Lefevre or Lubbock would have liked; there was no clause allowing compulsory purchase of sites at risk. Rather, owners were encouraged to hand over remains voluntarily to the Office of Works. It did, however, set up an Inspectorate under General Pitt-Rivers.[60]

All sorts of heritage-saving bodies were formed in the late nineteenth century, but these were small, private concerns; even the National Trust, founded in 1895, had only 700 members by 1915. It was the Second World War and the effect of the German bombing campaigns that prompted the beginning of listing as a means of protecting properties of historical and architectural merit and interest. Scheduling of ancient monuments had begun before the First World War, but the new listing system, established by the Town and Country Planning Act of 1944, was to include inhabited properties. It was particularly concerned with the survival of original fabric and, in these early days, mainly with pre-Victorian architecture.[61] The government departments and quasi-governmental bodies that oversee listing have changed over the decades, but in essence almost every piece of work done on a listed building requires consent from Historic England and, very often, an archaeological watching brief and an historic impact assessment.

Although not an immediate reaction to the new listing regulations, Oxford responded to the needs of its architecture in 1957 with the establishment of the Historic Buildings Fund. The city had not suffered from bombs but, after the First World War, was increasingly industrialised and congested, both of which caused air pollution and resulting damage to its soft local stone that needed addressing as a matter of some urgency. An appeal aimed to raise £1,750,000 for the fund, to be topped up by the University and the colleges from their own reserves. Astonishingly, the fund reached its target within thirteen months. Christ Church, as we have seen, benefited from the fund to the tune of £501,000, which was put towards repairs to the Library, Tom Quad and Tom Tower, Hall, Fell Tower, Canterbury and Peckwater quads, Killcanon, Old Library, the Priory House and Chapter House, the cloisters, the kitchen and the cathedral.[62]

From 1990 an archaeological investigation was incorporated into all new development projects under the government's Planning Policy Guidance document 16 (PPG 16), and more general advice was given on the treatment of historic buildings and the environment in PPG 15.[63] From 1991 the Churches Fabric Commission required all cathedrals to employ an architect and an archaeologist to oversee any work done and fabric maintenance.[64] In 2007, however, the Governing Body considered a complete overhaul of the management of Christ Church's built environment. Prompted by the complexities of the renovation of Blue Boar Quad, and aware that maintenance and refurbishment would remain a significant aspect of Christ Church's expenditure for the long term, it was proposed that a Buildings Sub-Committee of the Finance Committee should be established and that a Surveyor should be appointed to oversee all planning and budgeting. There would also be a House Architect to 'provide a continuity of approach ... designing and implementing a philosophy of repairs and maintenance'.[65] Since 2008 a consultant conservation architect has been employed for the whole foundation, with a surveyor briefed to manage the maintenance programme for all the buildings in conjunction with the Clerk of Works.[66]

Other regulations, covering issues such as accessibility and public liability, also influence the maintenance, repair and use of Christ Church's buildings. Ramps have been installed on either side of Tom Gate to give easy access to the terrace; another gives access to the Lodge, and a further one to the cathedral. A long, inclined pathway has been installed outside the Library. The new lift to Hall was constructed for similar reasons, but all these improvements have to have the same archaeological investigation and listed building consent, and to be built of sympathetic materials, as well as conforming to all modern safety regulations. A task such as the improvement of water, gas and electricity services, which would once have been taken on internally and with little fuss, entailed a major archaeological study of both Tom and Peckwater quads. This is not all bad news, apart from the increased costs and extended deadlines, as the investigations reveal much about the site both before Christ Church was established and during its early days.[67]

But the buildings of Christ Church have always been a challenge. Building, refreshing, updating and maintaining while being hampered by the constraints of a city site (however big), by financial considerations and by rules and regulations has always been difficult. In 1530 the dean and canons were left with the grandest of structures only half-finished and with a budget severely diminished and insufficient to complete Wolsey's scheme. However, that incompleteness has meant that the college is now blessed with a variety of styles not only for the grand, imposing showpieces but also for the more functional, everyday buildings. As the needs of the college have changed, so the designers, whether gentlemen amateurs or professional architects, have kept Christ Church up to date. Christ Church has sometimes been at the forefront of fashion, leading the way with Peckwater Quad, for example, and at other times has followed close behind the pioneers, keeping up with trends such as the Victorian Gothic Revival or Modernism.

The Dean and Chapter and, later, the Governing Body have also kept *au courant* in their choice of architects. In the seventeenth and early eighteenth centuries it was the scholar designer whose knowledge of the classical led the way – men such as Henry Aldrich, George Clarke and their mason William Townesend. By the mid-eighteenth century, however, the professional architect began to come to the fore, and Christ Church picked the best of the day, men who were commissioned all over Oxford and the country, beginning with Christopher Wren, who straddled the divide as a scholar with tremendous scientific skill, and moving on to dedicated architects such as Keene and Wyatt. By the mid-nineteenth century, competitions between architectural practices were commonplace, and tenders for the commission for the Wolsey Tower, for example, saw the nation's big names battling it out before the Governing Body. And once chosen, particularly in the twentieth century,

Christ Church stuck with its decision for several projects, there being definite 'favourites' in different periods.

In the post-war period, as Geoffrey Tyack has concluded, 'The historic fabric of the city ... is cared for as never before.' [68] This is certainly true of Christ Church; there always seems to be one corner or elevation decorated with some scaffolding. But, in the constant effort to keep Christ Church standing, we need to remember not always to look backwards but to be pioneers.

Appendix: Deans

Richard Cox	1546		George Smalridge	1713
Richard Marshall	1553		Hugh Boulter	1719
George Carew	1559		William Bradshaw	1724
Thomas Sampson	1561		John Conybeare	1733
Thomas Goodwin	1565		David Gregory	1756
Thomas Cooper	1567		William Markham	1767
John Piers	1570		Lewis Bagot	1777
Toby Matthew	1576		Cyril Jackson	1783
William James	1584		Charles Henry Hall	1809
Thomas Ravis	1596		Samuel Smith	1824
John King	1605		Thomas Gaisford	1831
William Goodwin	1611		Henry Liddell	1855
Richard Corbett	1620		Francis Paget	1892
(also Bishop of Oxford, 1628–32)			(also Bishop of Oxford, 1901–11)	
Brian Duppa	1629		Thomas Banks Strong	1901
Samuel Fell	1638		(also Bishop of Oxford, 1925–37)	
Edward Reynolds	1648		Henry White	1920
John Owen	1651		A. T. P. Williams	1934
Edward Reynolds	1659		John Lowe	1939
George Morley	1660		Cuthbert Simpson	1959
John Fell	1660		Henry Chadwick	1969
(also Bishop of Oxford, 1675–86)			Eric Heaton	1979
John Massey	1686		John Drury	1991
Henry Aldrich	1689		Christopher Lewis	2003
Francis Atterbury	1711		Martyn Percy	2014

Conventions and monetary values

Conventions

All years, even those before 1732, are assumed to start in January.
All archival references, unless otherwise prefixed, are to Christ Church sources.
References to the *Oxford Dictionary of National Biography* are to the name in context unless otherwise indicated.

A note on monetary values

Calculations of equivalent values have been derived from Lawrence H. Officer and Samuel H. Williamson, 'Five Ways to Compute the Relative Value of a UK Pound Amount, 1270 to Present', *Measuring Worth* (2014). URL: www.measuringworth. com/ukcompare/. Hopefully, the correct relative value has been arrived at for each calculation.

Notes

Introduction

1. Pevsner (1973), 15.
2. Grose (1779), 52.
3. Thompson (1900); Warner (1924); Watson (1935); *History of the University of Oxford*, 8 vols (1984–2000).
4. Caröe (1923); Cook and Mason (1988); Bill (2013).

1. A college-in-waiting: St Frideswide's Priory and its environs

1. Ashdown and Hassall, in Rodwell (1975), 133; Hassall, in Briggs, Cook and Rowley (1986), 118; Boyle et al., *Oxoniensia*, 66 (2001), 337–68; Blair (1994), 100–101.
2. Blair (1990), 224, 231; Graham-Campbell, in Blair (1990), 259–63; Warner (1924), 15ff.
3. Evidence suggests that St Frideswide's monastery had become a royal minster or 'royal free chapel' in the eleventh century, with the original residents having been replaced by canons before Aethelred's refoundation: Blair (1990), 226–7. Soon after, in 1129, Oseney Priory was founded, also as an Augustinian house, soon to be raised to the rank of an abbey. Over the next two centuries Oxford was filled with religious houses and the early monastic colleges that formed the beginnings of the University. The city walls were altered and realigned several times between the eleventh century and the thirteenth. Hibbert (1988), 91.
4. The remainder of the Chapter House is later, *c.*1220–40. Warner (1924), 33.
5. Blair (1990), 238ff. The original grave is probably in roughly the position of the shrine now, rebuilt in 2002 using the pieces of a later (1289) Purbeck marble shrine base discovered in 1875 and 1985, and reconstituted in stone.
6. Blair (1990), 240. The evident fire damage around the door begins over a metre above the present ground level.
7. Chadwick et al. (2012), 16.
8. Tyack (1998), 16–20. Alternatively, the Lady Chapel may have been positioned to the north to be close to the shrine.
9. The pendants, or lanterns, were executed by William Orchard, and restored in 2014 by Cliveden Conservation. See Harvey (1984), 222.
10. The parish church of St Frideswide's, for which there is very little evidence, may have been just a chapel for the laity within the priory church. Either way, it may have been

the driving force behind Prior Robert's choice of location for the shrine chapel. Later, official papers required the absorption of the cemeteries into the new college to be undertaken with sensitivity. *L&P Henry VIII*, 4 (1), 1499 (1870).

11. The associated building may have been demolished by Wolsey during the construction of the quadrangle.

12. Warner (1924), 10; Clark (1889–90), 156–7. Virtually no archaeological evidence from the pre-Meadow Buildings period was found in the 2010–11 watching brief during work on staircase 3, and excavations prior to the construction of the building were concerned more with topography and the Thames river channels: Keevill (2011); *Proceedings of the Oxford Architectural and Historical Society* (1860–64), 217–22.

13. Blair (1990), 186–7; Dearmer (1899), 69.

14. Harvey (1984), 222. Orchard also worked at Balliol, Magdalen and Eton Colleges.

15. Blair (1990), 188–90.

16. Warner (1924), 169; CCA BR 1/2/16. Possibly the present Cloister House, although there are indications that this was built around 1636.

17. Blair (1990), 192.

18. In 2014 the Priory House, Cloister House and Priory Rooms were renovated and refurbished. A fire escape was created between the cathedral offices and the Priory House by relocating a lavatory.

19. CCA BR/1/2/16. Dendrochronological dating by Dan Miles; archaeological analysis by Julian Munby of Oxford Archaeology and Graham Keevill, foundation archaeologist.

20. CCA D&C xx.c.3/1. The Lady Margaret professorship, founded in 1502, was attached to a Christ Church canonry in 1840.

21. CCA Plans Priory 1.

22. CCA Plans CH 1, by Bosanquet and Perryman.

23. CCA D&C xx.c.3/1.

24. *Christ Church 1996.*

25. The garden was named after Edward Pococke, seventeenth-century regius professor of Hebrew, and after the huge plane tree, planted by Pocock in the 1640s, which still dominates the space.

26. RCHME (1939), 29.

27. The remains of both are still visible in the stonework.

28. Chadwick et al. (2012), 218; Salter (1960), Map SE VI.

29. Clark (1889–90), 158.

30. The position of the gate is uncertain but is probably somewhere under the deanery or its garden, close to the wall with the cathedral garden.

31. Oriel Square and the present St Edward Street were not laid out until the nineteenth century.

32. Chadwick et al. (2012). St Frideswide Lane was found during excavations in 1961–2 in the cathedral garden. Its line was confirmed during the 2005–7 excavations, which revealed a cobbled road surface with a central kennel, or open drain.

33. The entire Jewish population of England was expelled in 1290, not to return until invited to do so by Oliver Cromwell in the 1650s. In the sixteenth and seventeenth

centuries, however, Jewish converts were studying and working in the city, particularly on the Hebrew manuscripts held in the Bodleian Library.

34. There were two St Michael's churches in Oxford: one at the south gate and one at the north, the dedications possibly reflecting the archangel's role as protector and guardian.

2. 'So goodly and convenient': the buildings of the foundation period

1. The monastery was the only one entirely within the city walls and so was used by the university to store its crucial documents and money in a place of security; http://www.oua.ox.ac.uk/history.html (accessed 2 July 2016).
2. Everett (2015), 33.
3. Thurley, in Gunn and Lindley (1991), 78–81.
4. Richardson (2013), 58.
5. BL Cott. Vitellius B V, fols 8, 9.
6. Curthoys (2012), 3–5; *L&P Henry VIII*, 4 (2), 3141, 3190 and 3210, for example.
7. Newman, in Gunn and Lindley (1991), 109.
8. Duncan, in McConica (1986), 559. The tiny parish of St Michael's at the south gate was absorbed into St Aldate's: *L&P Henry VIII*, 4 (1), 1499 (1870). Although Balliol was not paid for these properties, Christ Church did give generously to that college when it was in dire financial straits in the 1660s. Perhaps, suggests John Jones, author of the Balliol College history, there was some residual guilt.
9. Probably the Dolphin and the Pike under new names. Salter (1960), 227–8.
10. If the inn was as large as it appears to have been, its site would have stretched south of the present quadrangle as far as the present deanery garden. Whether it was an inn in the sense of a hostelry, or just a large house, is not known.
11. Chadwick et al. (2012), 49, 50.
12. Possibly revealed in recent geophysics, 2014.
13. Pantin (1985), 155–66.
14. Chadwick et al. (2012), 235–7.
15. Tyack (1998), 71–3.
16. Newman, in McConica (1986), 598, 607–11. As soon as Corpus Christi was complete, Coke was diverted to the ill-fated St Mary Hall: see Blair (1978), 48–99. My thanks to Julian Reid and Barry Collett.
17. To calculate the modern equivalent of this figure depends on the choice of relative value, but it probably represents an annual income today of about £34 million.
18. Harvey, in Catto and Evans (1992), 768. Redman and his colleagues definitely saw and used drawings, but there are no surviving plots or plans.
19. Milne and Harvey (1943); Harvey (1943); Harvey (1984), 65.
20. Thompson (1900), 5; Hammer, in McConica (1986), 105.
21. *L&P Henry VIII*, 4 (1), 1499 (1870).
22. Milne and Harvey (1943), 137–53; Harvey (1943); *L&P Henry VIII*, 4(1), 1499 (1870).
23. *L&P Henry VIII*, 4 (1), 1499 (1870).

24. The location of the foundation stone is unknown; perhaps it was to be prominent in the planned chapel or, as Ingram suggests, close to the archway in the south-east corner of the Great Quadrangle: see Ingram (1837), 40–41. Longland did much to help Wolsey in the creation of his college (*ODNB*).

25. Milne and Harvey (1943); Richardson (2013), 58.

26. A perch is 16½ feet. The actual internal dimensions of the Great Quadrangle are 261 feet × 264 feet.

27. Newman, in McConica (1986), 613.

28. Arkell (1947), 62.

29. Arkell (1947), 44.

30. Arkell (1947), 72–4.

31. Horsfield et al. (2013), 115–26; Arkell (1947), 130.

32. *L&P Henry VIII*, 4 (2), 2734. Larke is likely to have been Thomas Larke, Wolsey's chaplain and brother of Joan, Wolsey's mistress between 1509 and *c*.1519.

33. The inner doorways of staircases 3 and 4, the only ones still in their original state, still carry Wolsey's devices, but they are no longer coloured.

34. Bod. MS Wood F.28, fols 169–70.

35. The lodgings in Canterbury Quad and Chaplains' Quad were demolished in the eighteenth and seventeenth centuries respectively, replaced by residences in the north side of the Great Quadrangle and in Killcanon. Those in Peckwater Inn were rebuilt with the rest of the quad in the early eighteenth century and now form Peck 9 staircase.

36. CCA xii.b.24, fol. 14v.

37. CCA xii.b.25, fol. 34v.

38. CCA xii.b.23.

39. CCA D&C i.b.2, 237.

40. Bod. MS Wood F.28, fol. 6.

41. Richard Thornton was appointed canon of the first stall in 1596. He died in January 1614–15. His brother Thomas, canon of the third stall from 1567, died in 1629 after a more illustrious church career. Thornton's report – Bod. MS Wood F.28 – appears to have been written around 1617 and to have been associated with proposed changes to the residence by the church.

42. Bod. MS Wood F.28, fols 169–70; CCA D&C i.b.2, 273.

43. CCA D&C i.b.2, 125.

44. CCA D&C i.b.3, 27.

45. CCA D&C i.b.5, fol. 36v.

46. CCA D&C i.b.5, 40.

47. CCA D&C i.b.6, 22.

48. CCA D&C xx.c.3/5.

49. Newman, in McConica (1986), 623–4.

50. Colvin (1983), 4. Another, matching, tower may have been intended for the south-east corner, at the other end of the Hall.

51. CCA DP vi.c.6.

52. Foster (1891).

53. *ODNB*. Chedsey may have died in the Fleet prison.

54. The Priory House garden was divided in the 1990s and the more easterly portion, containing the plane tree, set aside for staff use. The tree is said to be one of the first plane trees, if not the very first, in this country and possibly the father of all the London planes.
55. CCA GB i.b.2, 205; Crossley (1979), 303.
56. CCA i.b.2, 205; CCA D&C ii.b.1, 2.
57. Thompson (1900), 177–8; CCA MS Estates 144, fols 32–140.
58. Bod. MS Top.Oxon.d.247, fol. 130v.
59. Roberts (1814), p.116.
60. *Gentleman's Magazine*, c.1, v.105 (1809). A large proportion of Dr White's collection of valuable printed books and manuscripts was destroyed.
61. Wyatt died in 1813 (*ODNB*).
62. CCA MS Estates 144, fol. 140; CCA xxxiii.b.8.
63. Thompson (1900), 231.
64. CCA xxxiii.b.8.
65. CCA D&C i.b.8, 78v. Another new fire engine was purchased some years later, in 1831, at a cost of £46. Proper pipes or hoses were to be provided and a small copper hand-engine was to kept in the Lodge ready for use at any time: CCA D&C i.b.9, 122v.
66. Four rooms were transferred from the lodgings to the staircase Tom 3 in 1936 for £500.
67. CCA GB i.b.41/10718 & 42/11131; *Christ Church 2007*, 37.
68. Work on the exterior masonry on the south face of the canonry and attached staircases was carried out in 2011.
69. Most of the visible 'remains' of the cloister – the arches and springers – are nineteenth-century, reconstructed at the command of Dean Henry Liddell. Before this date, the walls were worn almost smooth.
70. Martyr built a study or 'fabrick of stone' in the garden of the Priory House, evident in Loggan's engraving. It was demolished in 1684. Bod. MS Rawl. B. 407a.
71. Hiscock (1946), 200; Bod. MS Wood F.28.
72. Batey and Cole, in Blair (1990), 213. Batey's suggestion is further scuppered by the location of the blocked doorway on the east side of the building, not the west. Christ Church is officially designated as an unoccupied royal palace – see http://www.royal.gov.uk/TheRoyalResidences/FormerRoyalResidences/Historicresidences.aspx (accessed February 2014)
73. OUA Hyp/B/13, fols 35–6. The description is from Dean Goodwin's will preserved in the University Archive.
74. Historic Manuscripts Commission, *Portland*, vii, 152–3.
75. CCA D&C ii.b.1. John Conybeare was installed as dean in January 1733.
76. In 1744 repairs to the deanery roof formed part of a larger restoration of the battlements around the whole of the Great Quadrangle – CCA D&C ii.b.2.
77. CCA D&C i.b.5; CCA D&C ii.b.5. The following winter was equally severe.
78. The Hinksey conduit is on the hills to the west of the city. Built in the early seventeenth century, it collected water from local natural springs and fed it down to the central conduit at Carfax. From there, water was piped around Oxford until it was

taken out of action in 1868. The Bell Yard is probably School Yard, and the supply may well have been for the kitchen. See CCA xii.c.187.

79. CCA D&C i.b.9.

80. Possibly using a company called Dudley and Bowler, which, according to the 1831 disbursement book, was paid considerable sums for plumbing work that year. No details of the company can be found.

81. CCA D&C ii.b.2, 8.

82. Law (1998), 15; Thompson (1899), 147–8. The deanery may always have had a small gallery. There is an account in 1670 for the cost of the picture, frame and boards for a portrait of Henry VIII, which was then placed in the gallery: CCA xii.b.113. If not in the deanery, then the gallery was probably in the Audit House.

83. Thompson (1899), 163; Thompson (1900), 208, 232, 245; *ODNB*. A statue of Fell that occupied this site before the restoration of the quad was moved to Nuneham Park. Bodley was evidently in tower-building mode: in June 1875 he proposed that there should be a small tower erected over the new entrance to the cathedral – CCA xlix.a.1, fol. 24 – a suggestion that was not taken up.

84. CCA GB i.b.8/152, 154, 174; *Christ Church 1901/2*.

85. CCA GB i.b.8, 47.

86. CCA GB i.b.10/95, 96; GB i.b.15/276; GB.i.b.17/277, 291; GB i.b.18/284; GB i.b.19/27.

87. A raised walkway is illustrated on both Loggan's 1670s engraving of Christ Church and on Edmund New's early twentieth-century version. Recent archaeological investigations have shown a possible surface that would fit with a bowling alley, and the disbursement books include at least one entry for turves for the alley. CCA xii.b.75.

88. *ODNB*.

89. CCA GB i.b.8, 276. £5,000 was spent on dealing with the rot.

90. The deed of agreement between the Chapter and the Governing Body was signed on 1 March 1973, to take effect on 1 April, by Peter Baelz (canon in residence, and first canon into the much-reduced residence on the north side), Keith Batey (Treasurer and member of GB) and Carl Witton-Davies (archdeacon, for the Chapter). The garden would remain Chapter property. CCA xx.c.66, 48.

91. CCA GB i.b.11, 192–3.

92. Bosanquet and Diplock were the architects responsible for the division of the central lodgings on the north side of Tom, of which more below.

93. The lodging was empty following Thomas Thornton's upgrading to better accommodation – see above.

94. D&C i.b.2, 149.

95. Bod. MS Wood F.28.

96. Wakeling (2001), 265.

97. The new bay was paid for, in part, by Canon Edward Dowdeswell and was, for a period, known by his name.

98. CCA MS Estates 144, fols 267–9. Still two lecture rooms now, and the offices of the Senior Censor, Admissions and the Tutors' Administrators. The lecture rooms were refurbished recently.

99. CCA BR 2/1/1/4.
100. Williams produced engravings of the ground plans of all the existing Oxford colleges for a volume called *Oxonia Depicta*.
101. *Christ Church 1932/3*.
102. CCA S xxxiii.a.1/2, 42.
103. Borrett [1962].
104. CCA GB i.b.11, 250; GB i.b.12, 171, 206, 220; GB i.b.13, 48; BR 2/1/1/3. The cost of the work was now just £2,500.
105. CCA GB i.b.17, 29, 75, 109, 250, 311. The tender was from Fisher and Townsend, and the final cost of the lodge was £46,500, excluding VAT and fees.
106. The picture for the screen was taken by David Stumpp, of David Stumpp Photography.
107. Newman, in McConica (1986), 629; CCA xii.b.20.
108. CCA D&C vi.c.6.
109. Newman, in McConica (1986), 617, 627.
110. CCA xii.b.21, 37.
111. Newman, in McConica (1986), 614.
112. As far as we can tell, without technical dating evidence, the gate under Tom Tower today is the original.
113. Newman, in Gunn and Lindley (1991), 112.
114. Notes and news, *Oxoniensia* (1964/5), 192; Newman, in Gunn and Lindley (1991), 110; Chadwick et al. (2012), 234.
115. Harvey (1984), 65. It is possible that the roof is the one now in the chapel at Hampton Court, which bears considerable resemblance to the stone vault in the cathedral, and would confirm that the new chapel at Cardinal College was planned to be 33 feet wide.
116. Colvin (1983), 4; Newman, in McConica (1986), 614.
117. J. Gutch (1781), 204–8.
118. Newman, in Gunn and Lindley (1991), 111. Although the removal of the old spire evidently never took place, its tip did fall down, or was taken down, at a later date and is currently a rather large ornament in the garden of the arch-deaconry.
119. *L&P Henry VIII*, 4 (1), 1707, 1836, 2258 (1870); CCA DP iv.b.2, 15.
120. Batey and Cole, and Biddle, in Blair (1990), 211–12.
121. Biddle and Scull, in Blair (1990).
122. The Hall compares with those at Hampton Court (106 feet by 40 by 45) and Trinity College, Cambridge (100 feet by 40 by 50): Skelton (1823), plate 107. It can seat 300 people, even with chairs rather than the benches with which it was equipped until the 1990s.
123. Hiscock (1946), v; Keevill and Underwood (2010).
124. RCHME (1939), 33–4.
125. Strong's painting of Wolsey suggests that the original kitchen louvre was taller and more elaborate in design than the present one, but when it was replaced is unknown.
126. Wayment, in Gunn and Lindley, 116–18. See http://vidimus.org/issues/issue-11/feature/ (accessed February 2014). Wolsey's coat of arms was granted to Cardinal College by the College of Arms on 4 August 1525: *L&P Henry VIII*, 4 (1), 1548 (1870).

127. Why Clare is represented remains a mystery. Thompson thought that it might have come from Gloucester College, which was the bishop's palace for a while. The Clare family held the earldom of Gloucester during the medieval period. Elizabeth de Clare, a grand-daughter of Edward I, endowed Clare Hall (later College) in Cambridge.

128. Most of these are self-explanatory. Presumably the Tudor rose and the fleur-de-lys represent Wolsey's royal patron, the portcullis the cardinal's high secular office, and the staves his pastoral roles. Two silver pillars were carried before Cardinals Pole and Wolsey as emblems of that high ecclesiastical office.

129. CCA BR 2/2/1/10.

130. Hiscock (1946), 53; Thompson (1900), 147–8; Historical Manuscripts Commission, *Portland*, iii (1901), 268–9. The flues for the modern gas fires in Hall are hidden inside the nineteenth-century pinnacles.

131. CCA xlv.b.1. The surplus of the 'King's Bounty', £186 15s. 2½d., was transferred to the Library building fund. CCL Library Building Accounts, fol. 11v; CCA MS Estates 144, fol. 22v; Bod MS Ballard 35, fol. 87.

132. *Christ Church 1980*.

133. CCA D&C ii.b.5.

134. CCA MS Estates 144, fol. 27; Thompson (1900), 235.

135. *Christ Church 1980*.

136. CCA MS Estates 144, fols 156, 246.

137. CCA MS Estates 144, fols 236, 246, 271, 391; CCA GB i.b.2, 230, 231, 250, 331. The stonework of the noblemen's oriel was repaired by Bodley in 1878–9, and the glass fitted in 1883.

138. Charles Clerke was archdeacon of Oxford from 1830 to 1877 as well as sub-dean. Sampson and Salwey were both Students, heavily involved with the changes to Christ Church's constitution in the 1860s. Thomas Vere Bayne was Dean Liddell's 'right-hand man' and a great benefactor to Christ Church.

139. Two windows were restored by Goddard and Gibbs, of London.

140. Horner (2013), 169–77.

141. The pesky death-watch beetle had also done its work. For a summary of the work undertaken in Hall in 2014–15, see *Christ Church Matters*, 35 (Trinity term 2015), 2–3; CCA BR 2/2/1.

142. The capsule includes, among much else, a Christ Church tie, pictures and a video recording of the hall roof on CD, a Christ Church tourist guide, lists of staff, members and all the people who worked on the restoration project, a recording of the choir and a copy of the Annual Report for 2014. A list of the contents is retained in the archive. The capsule rests on the wall plate beneath the final roof truss in the north-east corner.

143. CCA D&C i.b.5, 103.

144. Thompson (1900), 234; CCA Cen 1.a.2, 3.

145. [Swinstead] (1900), 7.

146. Mr and Mrs Potts were the resident housekeepers of St Aldate's Quad before it was redeveloped in the 1980s. Mrs Potts moved into the cottage (formerly Holloway Cottage, after the long-serving verger, and Stable Cottage before that) after her husband's death. One or two students lodged with her.

147. CCA BR 2/1/1/1.
148. CCA GB i.b.13, 261; Cartwright and Burn, in Butler (2006), 158. The library was refurbished by Luke Hughes & Co. in 2003. The 'No Peel' door with its inscription commemorating the anger of Christ Church men over Robert Peel's bill for the emancipation of Catholics, which leads into the library from the lobby by the Hall stairs, was preserved.
149. Now known as the Dodgson Room.
150. Now known as the Bayne Room.
151. Thompson (1900), 234; Grossel et al. in Butler (2006), 107–10; CCA GB i.b.3, 227; GB i.b.4, 227.
152. CCA CR 86/1. The Common Room toilets, once a coal shed and butler's office converted in the mid-twentieth century, were refurbished in 2011: CCA BR 2//1/6/3, 5.
153. Batey and Cole, in Blair (1990), 211–20.
154. Munby (2004).
155. Batey and Cole, and Biddle, in Blair (1990), 211–12.
156. Campbell et al. (2014), 88–9; Batey and Cole, in Blair (1990), 211–20.
157. MS Bod1.13, fol. 5v; Newman, in McConica (1986), 614.
158. *ODNB*.
159. Girouard, in Butler (2006), 51; Ingram (1837), 51n. The stairs themselves were probably rearranged at this time too.
160. This chapter house at Hereford was demolished in 1769.
161. Viscount Paul Bayning was the grandson of an Essex merchant. He came up to Christ Church in1632 and died, aged only twenty-two, in 1638.
162. Bod. MS Top.Oxon.d.287, fol. 34v; Girouard, in Butler (2006), 49–51; Hiscock (1946), 207–8; Thompson (1900), 234–5; Tyack (1998), 112–14; Thurley, *Building of England*, 243. It is possible that the curtain wall between the Hall stairs and the rest of Hall was erected at this time. It survived until the creation of the belfry in the 1870s.
163. Robinson (2012), 210.
164. Keevill and Underwood (2010); Curthoys (2012), 211.
165. RCHME (1939), 34–5.
166. Brears (2008), 180.
167. Brears (2015), 350–51.
168. Bod. Add. MS 27591, fol. 93.
169. Jacobs (September 1950).
170. Lyte (1886), 447.
171. Brears (2015), 37–8.
172. Bod. MS Top.Oxon.d.287, fol. 36.
173. According to the *OED*, spicks were probably long nails.
174. CCA xxxiii.b.11, fol. 28.
175. CCA D&C i.b.4, 145; D&C i.b.5, fol. 53.
176. CCA D&C ii.b.2.
177. Unfortunately, the records do not record the purchase of the firebricks. See http://www.stourbridge.com/stourbridge_fireclay.htm

178. CCA xii.c.221, term 4.

179. CCA GB i.b.4, 197, 245.

180. CCA GB i.b.4, 252; Maps ChCh 109 & 110.

181. Law (1998), 129–30.

182. CCA S.xxxiii.a.1/2, 212, 223; GB.i.b.8, 347–54; CCA S.xxxi.a.3.

183. CCA S.xxiii.a.1/2, 238, 240–41; S.xxxi.a.3. None of the records actually states what was installed.

184. CCA GB i.b.10, 111, 112. The boiler was replaced again in 2008: GB.i.b.46, 13229, 13662.

185. CCA GB i.b.15, 297; *Christ Church 1981*.

186. CCA GB i.b.18, 110, 284, 344.

187. *Christ Church 1992*. Nearly all the modernisations of the catering facilities coincide with the arrival of a new Steward or a new Head Chef.

188. *Christ Church Matters*, 36 (Michaelmas term, 2015).

189. TNA E101/479/10.

190. TNA E/101/479/9.

191. BL Harley MS 599, fols 5, 37, 42.

192. *L&P Henry VIII*, 4 (3) (1876), 5714, 6023, 6131, 6184.

193. Newman, in McConica (1986), 614–15.

194. Aubrey's drawings, best known for the sketch of the base of the new chapel walls, also show a window which must have been inserted into the north end of the west frontage some time after Wolsey's fall: Colvin (1983), 5.

195. Biddle (1988), 205–10; Thompson (1900), 239. The foundations of the bell-tower have been recreated in the paving around the new fountain, dedicated in June 2008.

196. Perhaps in the region of £50 million.

197. *L&P Henry VIII*, 4.2, no. 4135.

198. Newman, in Gunn and Lindley (1991), 109. Any calculation of the modern equivalent of this figure is fraught with problems. According to the Measuring Wealth website, just the labour cost could be in excess of £120 million. See <http://www.measuringworth.com/ukcompare/index.php>

199. *L&P Henry VIII*, 4 (2), 2734.

3. The almshouse: 'an original endowment close to our Gate'

1.   RCHME (1939), 96.

2.   Curthoys (1995).

3.   CCA MS Estates 142, fol. 168ff.

4.   CCA MS Estates 142, fol. 176.

5.   CCA MS Estates 142, fol. 214. The Commissioners for Mileways offered £600 towards the £2,500 that was necessary to purchase and demolish the four tenements, but it could only be used on the condition that the almshouse was taken down as well.

6.   Christ Church still has almsmen. Today the small annual gift is made to selected long-serving members of staff.

7.   CCA MS Estates 142, fol. 344.

8. CCA xlix.a.1, fols 81v–84v. Bayne's report was actually printed on 15 November 1886, two days before the vote against the sale, but was not considered until the following week.
9. CCA xlix.a.1, fols 86v, 87v. The recommendation was adopted by the Governing Body on 23 November 1887, and the plans were discussed the following February.
10. CCA xlix.a.1, fols 89v, 90.

4. A cautious start: Christ Church at the end of the sixteenth century

1. Records Commission (1814), 250–53.
2. Colvin (1983), 3–6; CCA P.TOP.TQ 26; Thompson (1900), 227–8. Pieces of St Frideswide's shrine were found in the rubble of the wall, which suggests that the north side was closed 'temporarily' soon after 1538, the date when the shrine was destroyed. Thompson suggests that the northern turrets were built around this period, too, although they are not shown on Agas's map of 1578.
3. Ingram (1837), 54.
4. Remains of a cobbled surface were uncovered in recent archaeological excavations (2006) running underneath the west side of Peckwater Quad, along the edge of the old inn, which could be interpreted as the extension to the street.
5. A rule honoured more in the breach in the early twenty-first century, when almost every department seems to have its resident canine.
6. CCA D&C i.b.2, 227.
7. CCA xii.b.24, fol. 34v.
8. Tyack (1998), 39.
9. CCA xii.b.25, fol. 51v.
10. CCA D&C vi.c.4, fol. 24.
11. CCA xii.b.24, fol. 74v; Bod MS Wood F.28, fols 169–70. Little of Oseney Abbey remains today.
12. CCA xii.b.24, fol. 74v; xii.b.25, fols 15v, 16; MS Estates 142, f.1.
13. CCA xii.b.25, fol. 16, 51v, 69v; Warner (1924), 36. Christopher Wilson has argued that the work on the chapel roof was done in the mid-fifteenth century rather than in the later part, as was previously thought.
14. CCA xii.b.23; xii.b.24, fol. 14v; xii.b.45, fol. 61v.
15. The thatched barn on the Meadow was, according to markings on one roof timber, built in 1851. Recent investigations, as well as old pictures, suggest that it stands on or close to eighteenth-century footings for a coach-house. Keevill (2014); CCA BR 3/2/14.
16. RCHME (1939), 48; CCA1.c.2, fols 171–6; *Christ Church 1965*.
17. CCA Maps ChCh 31, 32; GB i.b.5, 200.
18. CCA GB i.b.8, 464.
19. Although there was an archaeological watching brief on the conversion, no evidence was found of early brewing or of much else.
20. In fact, evidence suggests that each of the canonries had individual brewhouses for their own domestic needs.
21. CCA GB.i.b.11, 250.

5. Expansion: the seventeenth century

1. Newman, in Tyacke (1997), 135.
2. McConica (1986), 50, 51; Williams, in McConica (1986), 413.
3. Newman, in Tyacke (1997), 146–9.
4. Rundle and Hanna [2016]. At least 174 books with gift inscriptions dating from the reign of Elizabeth are still in the library today, with the earliest given in 1562. The books of Cardinal College, which included over 300 manuscripts, were largely dispersed after the dissolution of the college.
5. Skelton (1823), plate 124.
6. *Christ Church 1976*; CCA Plans OL 1. The upper portion of the arcading was discovered in 1975, having been plastered over probably in the eighteenth century.
7. Sturdy et al. (1961–2).
8. CCA xii.b.23–34, 45; Ker, in McConica (1986), 443–4, 514; Hiscock (1946), 4.
9. CCA xii.b.4; D&C i.b.2, 277. John Taylor, the mason, was paid 15s., and Francis Robinson, the plumber, received 3s. 9d. for filling the joints between the stones.
10. Hiscock (1946), 215; CCA xii.b.57, fols 41v, 42, 56v.
11. CCA xii.b.56; Sturdy et al. (1961–2).
12. CCA D&C i.b.2, 277; Cole, in *Oxoniensia*, xxix–xxx (1964/5), 142–68.
13. Sturdy et al. (1961–2).
14. Newman, in McConica (1986), 62; Newman, in Tyacke (1997), 147.
15. CCA xx.c.3, 175.
16. The library's benefactors' book dates from 1614, with Nicholson's name and crest prominent – Christ Church Library Records 1.
17. Burton's gift is now at the British Library, having been stolen from Christ Church at some time in the early nineteenth century. He was librarian from 1626.
18. Chichester (1977); Hiscock (1946), 6, 7; CCA D&C i.b.2, 278–9. During the medieval period the pawning of library books appears to have been a common means of raising cash.
19. Hiscock (1946), 6; CCA xii.b.57, 59. Nicholson's monument cost £6, and a further 20s. to erect. It did not survive very long in the library; a further entry in the disbursement books records its removal in 1615 at a cost of 26s. 8d. It is now in the cloister.
20. Rundle and Hanna [2016]. Windows were blocked by Townesend to allow for this.
21. Sturdy et al. (1961–2).
22. The remainder of the total cost of £2,300 came from Dr Lee's estate and a small legacy from Canon Burton.
23. Hiscock (1946), 74; CCA MS Estates 144, fol. 25; D&C i.b.6, 296; D&C i.b.7, 321.
24. Sturdy et al. (1961–2); CCA Plans OL 1. One panel, bearing the Scottish royal arms, was given to the National Trust for Scotland, and another (with the Jacobean royal arms) to Fulmer church, which was built in 1610. Modernisation was undertaken in 1975 by Bosanquet and Diplock (architects) and Biscoe-Taylor (surveyors). The bay with the painted panels became the Art Room in 2007.

25. Keevill et al. (2014). The room has remained untouched apart from redecoration in the early 1980s and in 2011–12, when the opportunity was taken to improve the environmental conditions and monitoring.
26. CCA xii.b.112. The organ had been removed in 1649: D&C i.b.3, 2.
27. Beddard (1976/77).
28. Hiscock (1946), 201. Samuel Fell died on 1 February 1649, allegedly of a broken heart on hearing the news of the execution of Charles I. John matriculated from Christ Church in 1637, aged eleven.
29. BL MS Add. 22602, fols 26v–27.
30. Morley remained dean only until October 1660, when he was appointed bishop of Worcester.
31. Wood states that the earldom was supposed to go to Francis Lutterel, gentleman commoner of Christ Church: Clark (1891–4), vol. ii, 421.
32. CCA xi.b.32, fol. 63ff.
33. Beddard (1976/7); CCA DP ix.b.1; Dunbabin, in Sutherland and Mitchell (1986), 270.
34. CCA D&C i.b.3, 108.
35. CCA D&C i.b.3, 108; xi.b.32, fol. 85.
36. The residences on the north are slightly narrower than those on the other three sides.
37. CCA1.c.2, 179. As a consequence of the demolitions, the street was widened by about 11 feet.
38. Today Fell's balustrade survives only on the street side of Tom Quad.
39. Grose (1779), 52.
40. At the back of the house is a small residence known as Demant's Cottage. Canon Demant occupied the lodgings from 1949, but the cottage evidently dates from much earlier than this, probably from the late seventeenth century or early eighteenth (it appears on Williams's plan in the 1730s): Keevill (*Demant's*, 2011).
41. CCA Maps ChCh 56–8; D&C xx.c.1 & 2. The building work was done by Symm and the electrical engineering by A. Dean & Co. of Victoria Street, London.
42. The leadwork was done by Collett Bros.
43. Jenkins died in 1959.
44. CCA D&C xx.c.3/1. Not entirely at college cost, as the accumulated income of the sixth canonry, which had been vacant since 1959, would be applied as well.
45. CCA Plans Canons 1; Law (1998), 106. Bosanquet and Diplock were the architects. Symm undertook the masonry work. A fireplace, inserted in the 1930s and covered during the 1972 conversion, was opened up again in 2016 to provide a fire escape between the Fell Tower and the canonry: CCA BR 2/1/5/7 and 8.
46. Curthoys, in Brock and Curthoys (2000), 251; CCA GB i.b.3, 20.
47. Moore (1850–1915) was a local architect, designing many houses in north Oxford and the bridge over Logic Lane at University College.
48. CCA xlix.a.1, fol. 98; GB i.b.3, 113.
49. CCA GB i.b.4, 254, 274; GB i.b.5, 201, 222, 280. Warren (1856–1937) was the brother of Herbert Warren, President of Magdalen College. He worked all over the country. In Oxford he is known for, among other things, the Victoria Fountain at

Magdalen Bridge, the outpatients' block at the Radcliffe Infirmary and the Eastgate Hotel.

50. CCA GB xiii.c.4; GB i.b.9, 586.
51. CCA GB i.b.9, 658; GB i.b.15, 334; GB i.b.16, 37.
52. CCA Gb i.b.16, 194; Plans JCR 1.
53. CCA GB i.b.23, 220, 390. Most recently, the tutor's set on the top floor of Tom 6 has been renovated and divided into two.
54. Glaziers certainly seem to have been paid well in 1669–70: CCA xii.b.112, 113.
55. Clark (1891–4), vol. ii, 175, 176; Thompson (1900), 89; CCA xii.b.112, 113; MS Estates 126, fol. 309; xii.b.113. Fire was a constant risk; in 1771 the Treasurer paid 5 guineas for five new fire engines for use in St Aldate's parish: CCA D&C i.b.6, 212.
56. Colvin (1983), 4.
57. It probably lay immediately to the south of the Priory House; remains of doors and windows can be seen in the end wall facing Meadow Buildings.
58. CCA xii.b.49.
59. CCA D&C i.b.3. Washbourne was appointed a chaplain of Christ Church in 1641.
60. CCA xii.b.47, 48; D&C ii.b.1, 2; D&C i.b.5, 145.
61. Ingram (1837), 62.
62. CCA xxxiii.b.11, fol. 10; Thompson (1899), 160–61; Warner (1924), 10.
63. CCA xxxiii.b.11, fol. 38.
64. Thompson (1900), 87–8, 217, 232.
65. There are no specific details about the building of Killcanon.
66. This passage has been recreated slightly further to the south in the redevelopment of Blue Boar Quad by taking a small portion of the garden of one of the canonries.
67. Keevill (2012).
68. Sherwood and Pevsner (1974), 125.
69. The southernmost portion of the mansard roof was probably rebuilt around 1979: Keevill (2012).
70. This may not be completely true. Building work is mentioned all the time in the Chapter minutes; it is just impossible to determine, on many occasions, which building is meant.
71. CCA D&C i.b.11. Tom 8:4 was set aside for the other censor in 1878.
72. Curthoys (2012), 240–50.
73. CCA D&C xx.c.3/1. Part of the proceeds of the sale went towards making a third canonry on the north side of Tom Quad.
74. CCA GB i.b.2, 374, 375. Some of these changes, particularly the new Blue Boar gates, were kick-started by the need for more storage for coal, especially after the cellars under the Porter's Lodge had been converted to enlarge the porters' accommodation.
75. CCA xlix.a.1, fol. 69v; GB i.b.3, 259. At the same time part of the deanery was granted to the college as a house for the fire engine.
76. Oakeshott (1975), 59.
77. CCA BR 2/12.
78. CCA xi.b.32, fol. 87; xii.b.112; xii.b.43; Clark (1891–4), vol. ii, 188. £110 in 1668 is equivalent to around £15,000 today.

79. Details on Christ Church's plumbing and water supply can be found in Curthoys (2012).
80. CCA xi.b.32, fols 89–92; Hiscock (1946), 156, 202; Colvin (2008); Bod. MS Rawl. B. 407a, fol. 233. The pond is said to be on the site of a preaching cross at which Wycliffe is said to have proclaimed the Gospel in English: Ingram (1837), 55.
81. The Fettiplaces were an old English family who settled in Berkshire and Oxfordshire. Sir Edmund's son John was MP for Berkshire in the mid-seventeenth century, and supported the Royalist cause during the Civil War.
82. CCA xii.c.139; Bod. MS Top. Oxon.d.247, fol. 38v; Ingram (1837), 55.
83. CCA MS Estates 144, fols 185–97, 211; CCA D&C i.b.10, 37v–38; CCA GB i.b.2, 174, 240.
84. CCA xlix.a.1, fol. 23 ff.
85. Caröe (1923); Bod. MS Tanner 147, fol. 71.
86. Newman, in Tyacke (1997), 160, 163–4, 171–2; Colvin (2008) 560.
87. Hiscock (1946), 202; CCA xii.b.107; Mrs Jackson received £5 early in 1664.
88. Hiscock (1946), 143; Curthoys (2012), 134.
89. CCL MS 376; Caröe (1923); Newman, in Tyacke (1997), 171–2; CCA MS Estates 143, fols 2–29. This was the cost of the masonry and plant required. The total cost was reckoned to be £2,098 18s.
90. Summerson (1993), 236; Caröe (1923), 23.
91. Thurley, *Building of England,* 266; Newman, in Tyacke (1997), 176; Caröe (1923), 23; Thompson (1900), 229. The vault is full of armorial bearings, the majority of which are those of men with some connection to Christ Church and who, possibly, contributed to the cost of the tower.
92. Kempster's younger brother John had matriculated at Christ Church in 1647 and had been a chaplain during the Commonwealth: Caröe (1923), 83.
93. Mobus (2013), 99–114; Arkell (1947), 67ff.
94. CCL MS 376; Caröe (1923), 23.
95. Tyack (1998), 142; White, in Green and Horden (2007), 107; Colvin (2008), 608.
96. Caröe (1923), 25, 29.
97. CCA MS Estates 144, fol. 14; Caröe (1923), 33.
98. *Christ Church 1959.*
99. Thompson (1900), 116; Hiscock (1946), 206; CCA xlix.a.1, fol. 26; CCA GB i.b.2, 184.
100. CCA GB i.b.2, 184, 197.
101. CCA xxxiii.b.13. Only the bills for the final part of the work, dated 1684, survive.
102. Curthoys (2012), 134.
103. In the region of £95 today.
104. Legend has it that the central newel post came from a warship. This seems most unlikely; long timbers for masts were much prized and would have been salvaged. Much more likely is that the tree was felled on one of Christ Church's timber estates (Chandence and South Stoke were the closest) specifically for the purpose.
105. For information on the clock and the bell itself, see Curthoys (2012).
106. CCA MS Estates 144, 369. The work was funded by Student, tutor and Censor Thomas Prout. Doulting, in spite of being the stone of which Wells Cathedral and

Glastonbury Abbey had been constructed, had been found to be highly permeable to water and liable to split in five degrees of frost.

107. Law (1998), 81. The work on Tom Tower prompted publication of Caröe's book *'Tom Tower', Christ Church, Oxford* (1923).
108. Arkell (1947), 27, 103; Caröe (1923), 75; Law (1998), 81.
109. Oakeshott (1975), 57–8.
110. Sharpe (1953).
111. John Fell had been consecrated bishop of Oxford in 1676.
112. Thompson (1899), 147–8.
113. CCA xxxiii.b.11, fol. 39.
114. This may well have been Oliver's last commission. He died in 1701, well into his 80s: *ODNB*.
115. *ODNB*.

6. The 'Great Rebuilding': Christ Church's eighteenth-century renaissance

1. Colvin, in Sutherland and Mitchell (1986), 831–2.
2. Salter (1960), 221, 260. Recent archaeological excavations (2006) have shown the western wall of Peckwater Inn against the cobbled street that continued the present Alfred Street further south into the Great Quadrangle: Chadwick et al. (2013); see also Chapter 1.
3. CCA xii.b.45, fols 13v, 26, 46, 61v.
4. CCA D&C i.b.2, 244.
5. CCA D&C i.b.2, 151; Thompson (1900), 115–17. Certainly, by the time of Hollar's Oxford map of 1643 all four sides of Peckwater Quad were built.
6. Hiscock (1960), 15–31; Brittain [2012], 10; Colvin (1983), 9; Summerson (1993), 291. Hiscock also credits Aldrich with influence, at the very least, in the design for the Old Ashmolean and renovations to St Mary's Church.
7. Tyack (1998), 142–3; Thompson (1900), 116; CCA xxxiii.b.15; E. G. W. Bill, 'The rebuilding of Peckwater Quadrangle at Christ Church' (unpublished paper) in CCA MR iii.c.1/1/8. Radcliffe's will was proved on 3 November 1706; Brittain [2012].
8. The stone laid by Salisbury is said to have described Aldrich as the architect of the quadrangle – Colvin, in Sutherland and Mitchell (1986), 832. The location of the foundation stones is unknown; they were already lost by 1900 (Thompson (1900), 117).
9. Bod. MS Rawl. Letters 37, 75, cited in Bill, 'The rebuilding ...'.
10. Doble, i (1885), 168.
11. CCA xxxiii.c.1; CCA xxxiii.b.17, fols 140–42; Colvin, in Sutherland and Mitchell (1986), 836. The archive of the Townesend family is a recent acquisition of the Bodleian Library. It covers the period 1687–1804 and is concerned principally with their work in Oxford.
12. Colvin, in Sutherland and Mitchell (1986), 832. The design anticipated developments such as Queen's Square in Bath, which also bears a distinct resemblance to the new quad: Thurley, *Building of England*, 297, 310.

13. Tyack (1998), 142–3.
14. Brittain [2012], 1.
15. Townesend's account book for 1707–8 records stone, including pilaster bases and capstones, and lime delivered for the west side: Bod. MS Don.e.223. 'STP' stands for 'Sacrae Theologiae Professor', an abbreviation once used on monuments and inscriptions to indicate that the subject was a Doctor of Divinity.
16. Bill, 'The rebuilding ...'.
17. Portland MSS, vii, 15, cited in Bill, 'The rebuilding ...'. Stratford lived in the east end of the north side of the Great Quadrangle.
18. CCA xxxiii.c.1.
19. Servants of noblemen and 'privileged Scholars' were not permitted to lodge in college after 20 May 1773. CCA D&C i.b.6, 243; xxxiii.c.1.
20. Hiscock (1946), 41; CCA D&C i.b.5, fols 7v, 8; xxxiii.b.17, fol. 128; D&C i.b.4, 131. A monument to Somerset was ordered by the Chapter in August 1713: CCA D&C i.b.5, fol. 5.
21. CCA D&C i.b.4. Later, rules were laid down about meeting the costs of new sashes and any breakages of windows, following an outbreak of undergraduate vandalism in 1771, when a notice had to be placed in Hall warning of punishment and stigmatisation of anyone found to be breaking windows or lamps: CCA D&C i.b.6, 216, 197.
22. CCA D&C ii.b.1.
23. CCA D&C i.b.6, 212; D&C i.b.10. The privies were rebuilt in 1849 by Trehearne of Drury Lane.
24. CCA D&C ii.b.2. The privy behind Peck 6 was where the unfortunate Francis Bayly drowned: see Curthoys (2012), 155.
25. CCA D&C ii.b.4.
26. CCA D&C ii.b.5.
27. Ingram (1837), 57.
28. Oakeshott (1975), 57–8.
29. Vyner offered himself as a hostage to ensure the safety of his travelling companions. After ten days in captivity, he was murdered. There is also a window by Burne-Jones in the cathedral in his memory.
30. Some of the repairs, particularly to the balustrade and entablature, appear to have been done quickly with an artificial or reconstituted stone. It is this which has caused some of the present problems and is being replaced in the 2016 refurbishment.
31. Christ Church 1958; CCA Plans PQ 1. The architects were Bosanquet and Diplock, and the work was carried out by Symm.
32. The Peck 9 renovation was undertaken through the generosity of Peter Moores (ChCh 1952)
33. Project surveyors: Sidleys; contractors: Knowles.
34. Colvin (1983), 26; Weeks (2005), 107–38; Colvin, in Sutherland and Mitchell (1986), 832. This fourth side had to be separate from the other three in order to maintain a clear route through to Merton Street.
35. Summerson (1993), 290; Weeks (2005), 110–11.
36. Weeks (2005), 115.

37. Historical Manuscripts Commission (1901) iii, 217. In between the completion of Peckwater Quad and the commencement of work on the New Library, Townesend was kept busy on other projects around Christ Church, including the repair of the Hall roof in 1720, and on the repair and construction of chimneys and fireplaces: Bod. MS Don.c.209.

38. Chichester (1977), 9, 10; CCA D&C i.b.2, fol. 383.

39. Hiscock (1946), 18; CCA D&C i.b.5, fol. 5v; Chichester (1977), 7; Rundle and Hanna [forthcoming]. Kneller's portrait of Aldrich hung at one end of the library and a smaller watercolour of the beneficent dean in the 'place where they lock up their Rarities': Bod. MS Top.Oxon.d.287, fol. 35.

40. Cook and Mason (1988), 3; ODNB; Colvin (1995). The contract was signed on 10 January 1717.

41. Other projects included the Front Quad of The Queen's College, the Clarendon Building and the Robinson Building at Oriel College. Townesend also had a hand in the construction of Shotover House and worked at Blenheim Palace. Hiscock (1946), 38–62; ODNB; Colvin, in Sutherland and Mitchell (1986), 830ff.

42. Hiscock (1946), 52; CCA MS Estates 127, fols 3–11; Colvin, in Sutherland and Mitchell (1986), 840; xxxiii.a.2. The library plans form part of the Aldrich print and engraving collection. The contract for the roofing of the library specifically mentions drawings made by Townesend.

43. Colvin, in Sutherland and Mitchell (1986), 840; McKitterick (1995), 35.

44. Arkell (1947), 81–2; Bod. MS Don.e.226, fol. 11.

45. Cook and Mason (1988), 15 and CCL MS 373.

46. Both the Queen's College library and the Radcliffe Camera in Oxford were designed with open spaces beneath. It was practical, protecting the precious books from damp and rats.

47. Campbell et al. (2014), 99–102. The use of iron balustrades on stone staircases was for practical reasons: an iron balustrade could be fixed using molten lead, impossible on a wooden staircase, and was lighter than stone.

48. Cook and Mason (1988), 4. John Mason compares this with the funding for All Souls' library, which *began* with a lump sum of £12,000 from Christopher Codrington.

49. Caution money was an insurance payment made by undergraduates, or their sponsor, on matriculation, against damages or non-payment of battels. The amount varied, depending on status. It was usually returned to a graduate on going down, but many allowed college to keep it against projects such as the building fund. As late as 1772 Dean Markham redirected surplus unreclaimed caution money towards the library building fund. CCA D&C i.b.5, fol. 96; CCA xxxiii.b.18; CCA D&C i.b.6, 242.

50. Hiscock (1946) 53; CCL MS 373, fol. 10v.

51. John Urry was elected a Student of Christ Church in 1682 until his expulsion on refusing the oath of supremacy on the accession of William III: ODNB.

52. Urry had died leaving debts associated with the preparation of the text.

53. Cook and Mason (1988), 5; CCA D&C i.b.5, fol. 37v.

54. CCA D&C i.b.5, 36.

55. CCA xxxiii.a.2. Charles Cole was responsible for the leading of the roof. In 1844 the college plumber, on pain of dismissal, was forbidden to light any fire on the roof

of college buildings, and was ordered to do any leadwork on the ground: CCA D&C i.b.10, 69. An order probably honoured more in the breach. The lead guttering on the library roof was, until Health and Safety regulations complicated everything, repaired 'in-house'.

56. CCA D&C ii.b.1.

57. Bod. MS Top.Oxon.d.287, fol. 34v.

58. In 1921 the floor of the Upper Library was found to have dry rot, and was completely replaced: *Christ Church 1921/2*.

59. CCA MS Estates 127, fol. 1; CCA D&C i.b.5, 132; CCA D&C ii.b.1; Chichester (1977), 12.

60. Another five thousand volumes, plus manuscripts and Wake's coin collection.

61. Hiscock (1946), 64–7; CCA D&C i.b.5, 157. The two ousted Students were given rooms 2 and 3 on staircase 7, which had previously not been allocated for Student use.

62. Weeks (2005), 129; Hiscock (1946), 69.

63. Weeks (2005), 131–3.

64. Eric Halfpenny, 'The Christ Church trophies', in *Galpin Society Journal*, xxviii (1975) [on the musical instruments]; CCA D&C i.b.6, 104, 193, 242.

65. Tyack (1998), 179–81.

66. Painting was done by the Green family, whose business was on the High Street. The iron balustrade was manufactured by Nathan Cooper, for which he was paid £90. Cooper also made sconces for the cathedral in 1765.

67. CCA D&C i.b.6, 8. The statue of a rather gaunt Locke, given by William Lock (probably a relative), was placed in the library in 1754. Although, appropriately, a bust of Aldrich now stands in the opposite niche, in 1946 the space was occupied by the ample Proserpine: Hiscock (1946), 103.

68. CCL MS 373 Library Building Accounts, fols 23–8.

69. BL Add. MS 27591, fol. 93. Until 1956 Carracci's *Butcher's Shop* (JBS 181), which is now in the Picture Gallery, hung above one of the fireplaces in the kitchen. The collection was not always so highly appreciated; in 1844 Carus, the personal physician to Frederick Augustus II, described it as 'mere rubbish', with only one picture worth saving 'come the deluge', in his account of Frederick's travels, *The King of Saxony's Journey through England and Scotland in 1844* (1846), 185.

70. CCA MS Estates 127, fols 17–52.

71. Tyack (1998), 181.

72. *ODNB*. The employment of Keene marked a move towards professional architects from the gentleman-amateur. He and James Wyatt dominated the second half of the eighteenth century: Colvin, in Sutherland and Mitchell (1986), 848.

73. CCA MS Estates 127, fols 28–58. Guise's collection was sent from John Prestage's warehouse in London on 17 March 1767 and presumably stored in crates until such time as the space was ready. The first catalogue of Christ Church's pictures was printed in 1776 at a cost of £1 17s.

74. The order to pay Keene was made in November 1769: CCA D&C ii.b.4.

75. Cook and Mason (1988); CCA xii.c.213; D&C i.b.7, 368. William Pound was one of the longest-serving members of staff at Christ Church; when he died, in 1787, he

was honoured with a plaque in the cloister commemorating his 'honest attention to the Duties of his Station', by which he 'deserved and obtained the approbation and esteem of the whole Society'. It was not until 1866 that warm-air heating was proposed for the library to maintain a temperature of 60–68 degrees 'for reading purposes': CCA MS Estates 127, fol. 121.

76. Smallwell had come up to Christ Church in 1739 and was made a canon in 1775. In addition to the living at Batsford, he was also chaplain to the king from 1766 and bishop of St David's 1783–8 and of Oxford from 1788 until his death in 1799.

77. Hiscock (1946), 72; CCA D&C i.b.6, 163.

78. CCA MS Estates 127, fol. 64. The document is actually an estimate, and there is an endorsement 'to be done'.

79. CCA GB i.b.3, 10.

80. CCA MS Estates 127, fol. 162; GB i.b.3, 216; GB i.b.2, 76. Room 10 in the old library was also constituted as a lecture room on the same date.

81. CCA MS Estates 127, fols 162, 163. If Bayne's plan had been adopted, there would then have been five lecture rooms: the Old Lecture Room by the Hall (built in 1829 by Hudson and now known as the McKenna Room), the two lecture rooms in Tom VIII, one in Peck 2 and the new proposed room in old library. This last was finally done in the 1990s, but on the ground floor.

82. CCA GB i.b.3, 216. Occasional lectures in the west and east libraries had been sanctioned from as far back as 1870 (CCA GB i.b.2, 76), but this was only intended as a temporary measure.

83. CCA MS Estates 144, fol. 213; MS Estates 127, fol. 65.

84. CCA MS Estates 127, fol. 124.

85. McMullin, in Butler (2006), 81; Chichester (1977), 19, 63–7; Hiscock (1946), 107–10. The Reading Room by the great gate became the first Law Library. There was also, very briefly between 1958 and 1969, a Science Reading Room. A surprising number of the books from the Undergraduate Reading Room are still on the shelves in the main library today.

86. Warner (1924), 140; *Christ Church 1921/2.*

87. Chichester (1977), 19.

88. *ODNB.* Jackson's memorial, commissioned after his death and paid for by subscriptions from old members, and which had cost 2,000 guineas, 'exclusive of package, conveyance and erection', was originally installed in the cathedral. It was moved to the library in 1871, and then to the ante-Hall in 1960. The Epstein bust of Dean Lowe was a gift of Israel Sieff in 1956.

89. Arkell (1947), 152–4.

90. Gates was unable to undertake the repairs as he had a permanent contract with the Metropolitan Railway, so the work fell to Symm: MS Estates 127, fol. 154.

91. Kay, in Harrison (1994), 507; Arkell (1947), 82. The refacing was completed in 1962. The capitals on the front were carved by a Mr Adams, and those on the east and west ends by E. J. and A. T. Bradford of London.

92. *Times*, 15 May 1963. The cost of the library renovation, inside and out, was £212,000.

93. CCA GB i.b.9, 608. Some pictures had been moved to the old Anatomy School in 1949.

94. A softer version, in which Fowler allegedly used 'lingerie pink' instead of 'knicker pink', is also quoted in some sources. The gold-leaf work was undertaken by Clark & Fenn.

95. The discussions on the Library redecoration are recorded in the reports of the Library Committee to the Governing Body. There is, however, a summary by John Mason in the *Christ Church Library Newsletter*, vol. 2, issue 3 (Trinity 2006). The lighting was redesigned at the same time so that it could be switched between low and high intensity (basically a choice between one or two sets of fluorescent tubes!): *Christ Church 1964*.

96. CCA GB i.b.9, 608.

97. *Christ Church 1965*. The editor was, of course, Dr John Mason, Librarian.

98. The need for these more stringent rules becomes painfully evident when it is revealed that the Upper Library hosted a drinks reception in 1966 for 700 guests – CCA LR (S) 11. The maximum permitted in the library at any one time now is around fifty, including staff.

99. The building contractors were Knowles; Sidleys were project surveyors, and Giffards handled the mechanical and electrical work.

100. Each light fitting weighs 8 stone, and hanging them was quite a feat of sheer muscle power. The dimming system works but has had its problems.

101. Painting the walls in the entrance hall required several teams on several layers of scaffolding. If the painting had stopped, and the paint been allowed to dry before completion, lines would have been very evident.

102. CCA GB i.b.5, 165; *Christ Church 1934/5*.

103. The shape of the grassed areas and of the pond were copied when the quad was relaid in 1978. Batey (1989), 90.

104. CCA MS Estates 144, fol. 16; *Alumni Westmonasterienses* (1852), 149–50. Hammond had come up to Christ Church in 1658. He was appointed a canon in 1679 and held various clerical posts until his death, aged eighty-three, in 1723.

105. *Christ Church 1949*.

106. Pantin (1985), 137–9.

107. Thompson (1900), 165. What evidence Thompson had for this is hard to say.

108. Clark (1891–4), vol. iii, 215; Beddard, in Tyacke (1997), 936.

109. CCA D&C i.b.7, 457.

110. Chadwick et al. (2012), 49, 240.

111. *ODNB*; Malcolmson (2003), 45.

112. Tyack (1990), 184; Colvin (1986), 850; Greenwold [forthcoming]; Robinson (2012), 195; Summerson (1993), 426.

113. CCA DP ix.b.1, 80, 82; D&C i.b.6, 280.

114. Bod. MS Top.Oxon.d.247, fol. 40v.

115. CCA D&C i.b.7, 368–9; xxiii.b.3; DP ix.b.1, 90; xxxiii.a.1. Thomas Walley Partington was the father of Thomas Partington, Student 1776, who became a barrister and chairman of the Lewes Quarter Sessions. Robert South died in 1716 and left to Christ

Church the reversion of his properties in Kentish Town (Middlesex) and Caversham (Oxfordshire).

116. CCA D&C i.b.7, 389, 390, 396. Six months after the loan had been taken out, in February 1779, Canon Benjamin Kennicott advanced the Dean and Chapter £500 to discharge part of the loan. In 1785 a decrement was placed on all resident members of the House to be added to the fabric fund: CCA D&C ii.b.5.

117. CCA D&C i.b.6, 366; D&C i.b.7, 497. The quit-rent was finally redeemed on 29 November 1878, when the arrangement of Oriel Square was decided between Christ Church and Oriel.

118. Robinson (2012), 196.

119. Greening Lamborn (1912), 80.

120. Robinson (2012), 197.

121. Bod. MS.Top.Oxon. d. 247, fol. 54v; the remains were collected and reburied in the cathedral.

122. Thompson (1900), 165–6; CCA xxiii.b.3; CCA MS Estates 144, fol. 24; CCA D&C i.b.7, 451, 454.

123. *Christ Church 1926–7*; CCA GB i.b.5, 316.

124. *Christ Church, 1930–31* and *1931–2*.

125. *Christ Church 1958*.

126. Oakeshott (1975), 58.

127. *Christ Church 1987* and *1989*. The architects were Bosanquet and Perryman.

128. *ODNB*; CCA D&C i.b.6. 134.

129. *ODNB*.

130. The Murder Act of 1752 allowed the dissection of hanged murderers to be used for anatomical research.

131. CCA D&C i.b.6, 135, 148. The organist's house had to be demolished to allow the construction of the Anatomy School. The college mason and carpenter were ordered to erect 'a proper convenience' in compensation.

132. Hiscock (1946), 210.

133. Thompson (1900), 159–60; CCA MS Estates 127; D&C ii.b.5.

134. CCA Maps ChCh 13.

135. CCA D&C i.b.7, 526, 573. In 1821 a gas pipe was laid to the Anatomy School: CCA D&C i.b.9, 18v.

136. CCA MS Estates 127, fol. 425.

137. CCA MS Estates 127, fol. 425.

138. CCA MS Estates 144, fol. 244.

139. CCA MS Estates 144, fol. 450; Fox, in Brock and Curthoys (1997), 673.

140. Bod. G.A. Oxon.b.113, 270.

141. CCA MS Estates 127, fols 446–56.

142. Fox, in Brock and Curthoys (1997), 674.

143. CCA MS Estates 127, fol. 515.

144. CCA MS Estates 127, fols 515–24.

145. *Christ Church 1929/30*.

146. Evelyn's printed books were sold by the Trustees in the 1970s, and the manuscripts and estate papers were removed to the British Library in 1994.

147. The takeover of the Lee Building by the Senior Common Room had first been proposed in 1862 after the scientific specimens had been moved to the new University Museum: Grossel, Mason and Truman, in Butler (2006), 107–10.
148. CCA GB i.b.9, 586, 661, 778.
149. CCA CR 86/1; CCA Plans SCR 2.
150. CCA GB i.b.9, 808, 812.
151. CCA GB i.b.10, 14. Collie was Dr Lee's Reader in Physics, and had been elected a Student in 1930.
152. CCA GB i.b.10, 12, 14, 23, 54.
153. Architects: Purcell; Contractors: Knowles.
154. CCA D&C i.b.5, 36. There were between thirty and forty men coming up each year. After the rebuilding of Peckwater Quad, there were 145 chambers available. With some men permitted to pay for several rooms in order to make suites – such as the Duke of Queensberry, who had laid out nearly £300 to refurbish his rooms on Peck 7 and paid £22 10s. chamber rent per annum (CCA xxxv.c.1) – accommodation must have been incredibly tight.
155. CCA D&C i.b.6, 305. The valuation was £21,600 and the annual premium £24 19s. 6d. In 1782 the Dean and Chapter decided to discontinue insuring the buildings: CCA D&C ii.b.5.
156. This is the number of residents during the week 14–21 May 1779. The battels books show many men, perhaps the same number again, who could be resident but were just absent this week. The 1849 chamber rent book shows 105 rooms residential rooms, but Peck 7 and Peck 8 are not included. These would add probably another sixteen rooms. Canterbury 4, the Westminsters' staircase, is also excluded. There were evidently not enough rooms for all the resident members.

7. The Gothic revival

1. CCA MS Estates 144, fol. 211; D&C i.b.7, 597; DP ix.b.1. The interest was to go to the Repair Fund but principal not to be touched except for rebuilding Chaplains' Quad.
2. CCA D&C i.b.7, 603.
3. CCA xxxiii.b.4.
4. CCA D&C i.b.8, 70v; xxxiii.b.4 and xxxiii.b.8; *Six Etchings by William Crotch, from Sketches by Mr. O'Neill, of the Ruins of the Late Fire at Christ Church, Oxford* (1809). After 1798 Land Tax could be redeemed either by paying a lump sum or by purchasing government stock which would yield an annuity. Surpluses in the Land Tax Fund had previously been paid to the poorer college livings, so, in order that they would not lose out under the new arrangements, the dean and canons doubled their own personal subscriptions to the Small Livings Fund. No leases of tithes, or the increasingly common tithe rent charge, in poorer livings were to be made without ensuring that an augmentation was built in.
5. CCA D&C i.b.10, 32v.
6. CCA D&C i.b.9, 125. Admission fees would now range from £26 5s. to £10 10s., according to status, exclusive of their caution money and lecture fees. Rooms rates varied from 18 to 6 guineas a year, an increase of between 20 and 50 per cent.

7. CCA MS Estates 127, fol. 65.
8. This is now the McKenna Room, refurbished through the gift of Stephen McKenna (ChCh 1906) in 1983.
9. CCA MS Estates 144, fol. 147ff.
10. Probably Skidmore's of Coventry, who were later to do the decorative ironwork for Scott's restoration of the cathedral.
11. CCA Maps ChCh 4, and 8–11; MS Estates 144, fols 162–73.
12. The Governing Body order to demolish the stables and retain the stone for building garages close by was made on 16 June 1925: CCA GB i.b.5, 285.
13. Curthoys, in Brock and Curthoys (1997), 481.
14. Brock, in Brock and Curthoys (1997), 27; Curthoys, in Brock and Curthoys (1997), 481.
15. Curthoys, in Brock and Curthoys (1997), 147–8.
16. A drawing of this is held at the Irish Architectural Archive. Deane and Woodward had designed the University Museum on Parks Road. Woodward died in 1861.
17. Thompson (1899), 161.
18. CCA GB ii.b.10, 148, 162; Law (1998), 13, 47–9. There is no surviving archive of the Deane and Woodward practices. The Irish Architectural Archive has only a few references in an account book belonging to the firm and in a letter book of the Dublin quantity surveying firm Patterson Kempster Shortall.
19. There is little, if any, written evidence to prove Ruskin's influence. In fact, his own letters indicate that he was rather hurt not to have been included in the discussions.
20. Crossley (2016).
21. Tyack (1998), 227 (although Law says fifty-one); Colvin (1983), 141–2; Law (1998), 49, 52. In the 1970s many of the double-sets were converted into single rooms. By 1975 all but Meadows 1 had been completed, providing an additional thirty-seven 'units'.
22. CCA MS Estates 126, fols 115–18. Part of the construction included work on the sewer during which the old Trill Mill was discovered, the oak still in perfect condition. Three hundred cartloads had been removed from the sewer and buried in Dean's Ham, and it was said that anyone could walk out of college through the sewer without any more inconvenience than walking 'half up to the knees in water'.
23. CCA MS Estates 126, fol. 312; GB i.b.2, 89.
24. CCA MS Estates 144, fols 253–63.
25. Law (1998), 49.
26. Arkell (1947), 152.
27. Thompson (1899), 165; CCA Maps ChChM 14.
28. *Christ Church 1959, 1973, 1975.*
29. *Christ Church 2011.*
30. CCA MS Estates 143, fols 46–55, 118–34, 162; D&C i.b.8, 50v. The repairs included cleaning, the installation of German pedals from GG to C and altering the touch. Further changes were proposed after Charles Corfe, appointed in 1846, was employed as organist when the compass was extended to FFF and a double diapason was installed. The work was undertaken by John Gray.
31. CCA D&C i.b.8, 43v, 50v.

32. CCA MS Estates 143, fol. 103. Possibly Henry Coddington, for whom see *ODNB*.
33. Except the first organ, which was installed in the cathedral in 1608.
34. Hiscock (1946), 213; CCA xi.b.35, fol. 83v.
35. It is likely that the monuments were later medieval, rather than pre-Conquest. Similarly old slabs were removed from the cloister at the same time. Browne Willis, writing about a century later, suggests that there were only around eighteen or nineteen of these slabs, which were, in fact, placed in the aisles rather than thrown out altogether. He did admit, however, that only two – those of John Fitzalyn and Edward Courteney – were left with their brasses intact. Both are still in the cathedral.
36. Some stalls were moved to Cassington church.
37. *ODNB*; Bussby (1967); Thompson (1900), 63; Jones (2005), 98; Darwall-Smith (2008), 162.
38. CCA xi.b.35, fols 79–86; Hiscock (1946), 213. This rather odd use of the receipt books is not unique. All the building accounts for the north side of the Great Quadrangle are in the 1628 receipt book. Most receipt books had space at the back, and were evidently used rather than create a fresh series of accounts for extraordinary work. The structure of the disbursement books did not readily allow for unusual expenditure.
39. Warner (1924), 77.
40. Another van Linge window was the memorial window to Bishop King, the last abbot of Oseney and first bishop of Oxford. This was removed during the Civil War, by his descendants, for safety, and returned at the Restoration.
41. Wright (1656).
42. CCA D&C i.b.3, 40. There are fragments of others in the upper windows of the north transept, and there is some indication that some survived *in situ* at the time of the nineteenth-century restoration. Still more fragments were discovered recently in a coal hole. The van Linges also created the window showing the first bishop of Oxford, Robert King, which survived the Commonwealth, having been removed by the family for safe-keeping in 1648.
43. Much of the following is derived from E. G. W. Bill's paper on the restoration of the cathedral, written in 1956 but only published, edited by Peter Howell, in *Oxoniensia*, 78, in 2013.
44. Thompson (1899), 149.
45. CCA DP vii.c.1, fol. 4.
46. Much of what follows on the cathedral restoration is derived from Dr Bill's paper, cited in Note 43 above.
47. CCA DP vii.c.1, fols 2–18; CCA DP vii.c.1, fols 1, 19; CCA MS Estates 143, fols 168–79. Some of this work was paid for by a bequest of £1,000 left in 1848 by Edward Christopher Dowdeswell (mt. 1749, Canon 1799) for use 'out and about the cathedral'. In 1873 G. Haden & Son proposed adapting the warm-air heating to a hot-water system: CCA MS Estates 143, fol. 271.
48. CCA DP vii.c.1, fol. 21.
49. Hugall's 1867 report does not appear to have survived.
50. CCA D&C i.b.2, 22 and DP vii.c.1, fol. 23.

51. The OAS, later the Oxford Architectural and Historical Society, had begun as the Society for promoting the study of Gothic Architecture.

52. CCA DP vii.c.1, fols 9, 297. Total expenditure between 1870 and 1877 was £18,451 11s. 10d. After the funds from the Chapter and the Governing Body the remainder was donated by members of the House.

53. CCA DP vii.c.1, fol. 71; GB i.b.2, 47, 59.

54. CCA DP vii.c.1, fol. 23.

55. CCA MS Estates 143, fol. 231; DP vii.c.1, fol. 39; D&C xix.b.1–75.

56. Report of George Gilbert Scott, Esq., R.A. on the Cathedral of Christ Church, Oxford, 3 June 1869. Printed for private circulation only.

57. In actuality, the amount spent on the restoration was under £20,000, the extension of the nave not being as long as initially proposed.

58. CCA GB.i.b.2, 59.

59. CCA xlix.a.1, fol. 11.

60. Law (1998), 51; CCA DP vii.c.1.

61. This window had already been altered with the removal of two mullions in the seventeenth century: Tyack, in Barnwell et al. (2014), 132.

62. Thompson (1899), 157; Warner (1924), 94.

63. Scott retained much of the original stonework, which gave, to his eyes, the evidence for the Norman round window, and displayed it in a gallery in the south transept.

64. Archdeacon Clerke's gift of £100 towards a proper vestry was withdrawn. He felt that the Scott/Liddell solution was mean.

65. CCA xlix.a.1, fols 30, 42v. Some of the woodwork and other discarded items were offered for sale. The church at Easthampstead, which was then undergoing some restoration, was given some panels, and six of the stalls went to Cassington.

66. Law (1998), 51, 68. By the end of the 1870s Symm had three yards in the city, including one in Brewer Street. which was almost exclusively for work for Christ Church.

67. Barnwell et al. (2014), 133.

68. CCA DP vii.c.1, fols 138–43; Bill, 'Report to the Friends of the Cathedral' (internal publication, 1956); Pevsner (1979), 118; Hall (2914), 250; CCA DP vii.c.1, fols 246, 277, etc.; CCA xlix.a.1, fols 32, 34, 38 . Brindley and Farmer were responsible for other woodwork in the restoration, including that in the cloisters. Other carving was undertaken by Chapman of St Clement's, Oxford, who was contracted by Symm for the work.

69. CCA xlix.a.1, fol. 24.

70. Wakeling (2001), 265.

71. The new bay was paid for, in part, by Canon Edward Dowdeswell and was, for a period, known by his name.

72. CCA MS Estates 144, fols 267–9. Still two lecture rooms now, and the offices of the Senior Censor, Admissions and the Tutors' Administrators. The fireplace had been acquired from Grimbly and Hughes, a high-class grocer's shop on Cornmarket where McDonald's is today.

73. CCA MS Estates 144, fols 268–70.

74. Dodgson wrote a pamphlet, *The Vision of the Three T's*, which derided the 'tunnel', the 'trench' and the 'tea-chest'. Published in Wakeling (1993).

75. The replacement of the gable roofs on the cathedral, and the suggestion that the internal stone vaulting be extended, were also victims of either common sense or impecuniosity.

76. CCA MS Estates 143, fols 58–73, 112–17, 188–92; Warner (1924), 95–9. Vyner is also commemorated outside the door to staircase 3 in Peckwater Quad. Little remains now except the protective cover for the stone. See Chapter 6.

77. *Christ Church 1926–7*.

78. Oakeshott (1975), 60. In 1960 roofs were restored and the interior washed at the same time. See also Law (1998).

79. CCA BR 2/5/8, 12.

80. CCA BR 2/5/8.

81. The work was done by Cliveden Conservation and Price and Myers Engineers, under the guidance of Purcell as architects.

82. Heathcote (1999), 56–7.

83. CCA GB i.b.38, 9729 etc. The doors were partly funded with a gift of £5,000 from the PF Charitable Trust. A hearing loop was installed at the same time.

84. *Christ Church 2013*. Opening out the crossing, by removing the pews, was first proposed in 2005: CCA GB i.b.38, 9729.

85. Repairs to the tower and spire had been done by Fell, in 1701 and between 1734 and 1736; the belfry had needed attention in 1741: CCA D&C ii.b.1; xii.c.144.

86. CCA MS Estates 143, 74–8.

87. CCA MS Estates 143, fols 141–4; Colvin (1983), 17.

88. CCA D&C i.b.2, 99. It is possible that Boswell's expertise did not run to the stonework supporting the frame, but equally likely that Scott exaggerated the state of the spire to improve his chances of opening up the interior of the crossing.

89. Dodgson (1873); Wakeling (1993).

90. CCA MS Estates 144, fol. 278.

91. CCA GB i.b.2, 143; xlix.a.1; BR 2/2/2/1. Much of what follows on the construction of the belfry derives from Bill (2013), 157–73.

92. *ODNB*; Colvin (1983), 137n; CCA MS Estates 3, fol. 157. Hugall was working at East Garston and Easthampstead.

93. CCA GB xv.c.1.

94. CCA xlix.a.1, fols 1, 2.

95. CCA xlix.a.1, fol. 5.

96. Wolfe-Barry was the youngest son of Charles Barry, architect of the Houses of Parliament: *ODNB*.

97. Bill argued that, if Wolsey had completed his scheme, there might well have been further accommodation on the site of the cloister, which would have provided a buttress for this side of the tower.

98. Nearly all the designs, with the exception of one of Scott's and Jackson's, seem to have accepted that the bells would remain within the tea-chest, rather than incorporated in a belfry constructed as part of the tower.

99. Jackson (1950), 127. Jackson's design was rejected because of its height; the tower would compete with the cathedral spire.
100. CCA xlix.a.1, fol. 8; Howell, in Brock and Curthoys (2000); CCA xlix.a.1, fol. 19; Hall (2014), 310–12. The vote was carried in the Governing Body on the following day by twelve votes to five, with three abstentions. It was probably the enormous height of Jackson's tower that put off the committee; it would have overpowered the spire and been in stern competition with Tom Tower.
101. CCA xlix.a.1, fol. 20ff; GB i.b.2, 184. The statue of Wolsey, created by Francis Bird in 1719, had been moved to the front of Tom Tower in 1872.
102. CCA MS Estates 144, fol. 278.
103. Colvin (1983), 140; Law (1998), 51.
104. Hall (2014), 312. Christ Church's finances were in a pretty dire state in the last decades of the nineteenth century. It was overstretched after all its building work, and income was suffering while old beneficial leases were run out, and as a result of the agricultural depression.
105. Thompson (1899), 159.
106. Law (1998), 51. Two new bells were added in 1897, to celebrate Queen Victoria's sixtieth jubilee, bringing the peal to twelve.
107. Law (1998), 97; Oakeshott (1975), 57–60.
108. Much depended on which level was accepted as the correct one. John Mason argued that the sixteenth-century height of the tower was higher than the nineteenth-century one, probably using the Bereblock drawing as evidence. CCA GB i.b.12, 279.
109. CCA GB .i.b.12, 303.
110. CCA GB i.b.13, 295 and GB i.b.15, 5. A grant for some of the work was given by the Secretary of State for the Environment and the Historic Buildings Council. Many of the gargoyles on the tower were completely renewed.
111. CCA BR 2/2/2/2. The quarries were Ancaster, Ketton, Taynton and Weldon.
112. The stonework was undertaken by Stone Firms Ltd of Bath in Phase I and by Axtell Perry Symm Masonry Ltd for Phases Ii and III. The leadwork was by Collett Bros. The Historic Buildings Council for England contributed £140,000.
113. Thompson (1899), 162; Wakeling (2001), 366–7. It was decided anyway that to complete the cloister would make the ground–floor rooms too dark for comfort.
114. One of the arches in the south-west corner was left unfinished as the long window was, apparently, the only source of light into the study of Edward and Philip Pusey: Thompson (1900), 232.
115. Hall (2014), 328. The statues of Fell and Liddell on either side of the Fell Tower are unattributed.
116. CCA D&C i.b.2, 180.
117. CCA MS Estates 144, fol. 285.
118. The footpath and railings between Canterbury Gate and King Edward Street were ordered by the Governing Body on 15 October 1879: CCA GB i.b.2, 250.
119. CCA xlix.a.1, fol. 33; MS Estates 144, fols 283–327; OCA EST A 2 A7 and Drawer 37 (exchanges): no.3; Oriel Record (1989), 35.
120. Warner (1924), 37–8. A watercolour hanging in the Old Common Room shows the entrance into the cloister opposite the Chapter House door.

121. Hiscock, 215; CCA xii.b.57, fols 41v, 42, 56v.
122. CCA D&C i.b.4, 146.
123. CCA xii.c.215; D&C i.b.6, 226.
124. CCA MS Estates 143, fol. 30; D&C i.b.8, 12v. The room was to have a double-headed Gothic door. Chapter records were kept in small rooms off the Chapter House.
125. Thompson (1900), 240; CCA MS Estates 143, fols 346–9; Hiscock (1946), 215. Only one of the two canonries that had been suppressed under the 1858 Act had fallen vacant. The second lapsed after the death of Richard Jelf in the summer of 1871, so he made it into the cloister by the skin of his teeth.
126. This extension of the cloister originally ran past the front of the Priory House between Chaplains' Quad and Fell's Buildings towards the Meadow. Most of this had been demolished to allow the building of Meadow Buildings, but one of the central decorative arches is dated 1891. No evidence can be found in minutes or accounts for this work.
127. Thompson (1900), 208, 227–8, 239.
128. Thompson (1899), 163.
129. CCL MS 101.
130. CCA1.c.2, 115. St Bernard's College was sold to Sir Thomas White by Christ Church in 1555 as the site of White's new foundation, St John's College. One of the conditions of the sale was that the Dean and Chapter retained the right to confirm the elections of the presidents of St John's College. An example of the procedure in 1747 is given in the Chapter Book: CCA D&C i.b.5, 230.
131. The Chapter's wine investment kept the choir school afloat, so to speak, for some years: Curthoys (2012), 91.
132. Thompson (1899), 163–4; Thompson (1900), 244; CCA D&C ii.b.11.
133. Munby, in Blair (1990), 192. A fire escape was built in 2005 into the Priory House garden: CCA GB i.b.38, 9729.
134. CCA MS Estates 143, fols 34–44; Ingram (1837), 63. The stone was originally just inside the Chapter House door to the right. The bishop who laid the stone at Ipswich and who is cited on it as 'Episcopus Lidensis' was John Holt, titular bishop of Lydda, who may have supplied cash for the building of Cardinal College: ODNB.
135. It was evidently a chilly place, as in 1899 Haden's were called in to improve the heating: CCA D&C xix.c.1.
136. CCA GB i.b.12, 133. Chapter meetings have been held since in the deanery dining room.
137. Ove Arup was the design engineer for the Sydney Opera House.
138. Architectural Review (1976). The Chapter House Treasury included the cathedral shop from 1980. In 1999 it was proposed that the room be restored to its original state for meetings or lectures, but at the time of writing, in 2010, this has not been achieved: CCA GB i.b.31, 533–4.
139. Private Eye (3 March 1989), 9; CCA GB i.b.31, 5334.

8. Regeneration and new responsibilities

1. CCA MS Estates 144, fols 360–68, 383, 391; S xviii.c.1.

2.   *Christ Church 1901/1902*. Annual reports at this period consisted of no more than a single page. The report for 1901–2 announced the deaths of C. H. Hoole and S. R. Gardiner, the election of Francis Paget to an Honorary Studentship, the appointment of C. D. Fisher and R. F. McNeile to tutorships, the restoration of the east side of the great gateway, the presentation of the portrait of Charles Sandford, bishop of Gibraltar (which currently hangs in the Development Office), and the installation of electricity.

3.   CCA GB.i.b.4, 56; MS Estates 130, fols 258, 264. The Library was not lit until 1928: CCA GB i.b.5, 373.

4.   CCA GB i.b.4, 197.

5.   CCA MS Estates 126, fol. 279; GB i.b.4, 156.

6.   Diana Rowntree (1956).

7.   CCA GB i.b.6, 18.

8.   CCA GB i.b.6, 139, 145.

9.   CCA GB i.b.6, 199, 208.

10.   CCA Maps ChCh Meadow 15–17; Diana Rowntree (1956).

11.   *Christ Church 1955*; CCA GB i.b.20, 47, 53.

12.   CCA GB i.b.8, 564, 604. Further renewal and refurbishment are scheduled imminently.

13.   CCA MS Estates 134, fol. 295; CCA Maps ChCh M 19.

14.   *Christ Church 2012*. A further bridge was proposed by the City Architect in 1979 to join Boathouse Island to Aston's Eyot to make a safe cycle route from Folly Bridge to Donnington Bridge. The Governing Body turned down the idea: CCA GB i.b.15, 130.

15.   CCA SOC v.c.1.

16.   CCA GB i.b.11, 250; GB i.b.12, 208; GB i.b.13, 225.

17.   CCA GB i.b.16, 34; GB i.b.22, 35. In 1981 a new house for the groundsman was included in the plans for the Iffley Road residential development.

18.   The bridge was funded by donations from Christopher Ainsley and Martin Alderson Smith.

19.   CCA BR 3/2/15.

20.   The lead consultants were the Morton Partnership. Albury S. I. Ltd were geo-technical specialists.

21.   The First World War appears to have had little effect on the site itself, just on its occupants.

22.   Curthoys (2012), 312–17. The portraits in Hall were moved to the cellars under the SCR and Killcanon; other pictures, manuscripts and incunabula were stored in the basement under Peck 9; Renaissance drawings and the coin collections went to the Ashmolean, the coins on permanent loan. A photographic survey was made of the library 'just in case'.

23.   CCA Maps ChCh 67, 68. Both shelters are now used as bicycle stores.

24.   *Christ Church 1950*. Other parts of the Caröe kitchen extension were turned into new freezers in 2013.

25.   http://sculpture.gla.ac.uk/view/person.php?id=msib4_1273849641 [accessed 3 July 2016].

26. Even so, in 1932, 1 Brewer Street had been converted to accommodate students, and in 1957 the Governing Body had been forced to rent fifteen rooms at the Castle Hotel: *Christ Church 1932/3* and *1957*.

27. Potter (1994), 44–5, 63–6. The tennis court was included in a list of the property of Cardinal College in 1546; it was rebuilt in around 1670, and given a new dressing room as late as 1829. There was another court, behind staircase 6 in Peckwater Quad, which was outdoor, and exclusively for college use. When this went out of use is uncertain; it is not on the plans for the alteration of King Edward Street and Oriel Square in the 1870s.

28. CCA MS Estates 144, 164–8.

29. CCA GB i.b.8, 46.

30. CCA GB i.b.8, 116.

31. CCA GB i.b.8,119, 237.

32. CCA GB i.b.8, 416–17.

33. CCA GB i.b.8, 452.

34. The provision of a Muniment Room in the basement was not popular with the then archivist, E. G. W. Bill, who suggested several alternatives, including what is now the Law Library and the room immediately below Tom. Presumably he was not intending to work in the latter. A temporary muniment room had been established in Peckwater in 1952, soon after Bill was appointed to catalogue the Treasury deeds, but was acknowledged as inadequate for the purpose: *Christ Church 1952*.

35. Tyack (1998), 313–14; Kay, in Harrison (1994), 510–11.

36. CCA GB i.b.9, 589; Harwood (2015), 220.

37. *Christ Church 1965* and *Christ Church 1967*. The Blue Boar Appeal was for £300,000 in total. This figure was reached in 1965, but building was delayed by government regulations, which required a licence on new building projects costing over £100,000. The first staircase was available for use in October 1967 and the second in Hilary term 1968.

38. CCA GB i.b.9, 642, 660.

39. The wall was retained at the insistence of Powell and Moya, against the preference of the City Council: *ODNB*; Jack, in Butler (2006), 191–2.

40. Tyack (1998), 315–16. In the 1960s Corpus Christi College hired Powell and Moya to design a new residential block, and Wolfson College commissioned the partnership to design all the buildings on its new north Oxford site.

41. Personal communication with Richard Benthall, Treasurer emeritus.

42. A lecture theatre had been proposed in 1991, when Perryman Associates were commissioned to draw up plans for a conversion of Mrs Potts's Cottage by the Memorial Garden.

43. CCA GB i.b.15, 48.

44. CCA GB i.b.16, 83, 84, 196, 230, and GB i.b.17, 255. The appeal raised over £1 million, including a huge donation from Harry Oppenheimer.

45. CCA GB i.b.20, 188.

46. CCA GB i.b.14, 135, 386.

47. CCA GB i.b.19, 41.

48. CCA GB i.b.19, 41.

49. CCA GB i.b.19, 96.
50. CCA GB i.b.22, 194. Christ Church's share of the cost amounted to *c*. £2.5 million, funded by a premium from Corpus Christi College, the Building Fund and a capital loan taken out in 1991.
51. CCCO B/4/1/27,
52. CCA GB i.b.23, 141, 227, 229.
53. One proposal was to put the gallery on the top floor of the new Blue Boar building: Thalmann (2008), 9.
54. CCA GB i.b.9, 605, 606.
55. CCA GB i.b.9, 649, 653. An appeal to the Wolfson Foundation had been unsuccessful.
56. CCA GB i.b.9, 666, 668. Building on the Gallery actually started before Blue Boar Quad as it was not constrained by the government regulations on high-cost new buildings: *Christ Church 1965*.
57. Tyack (1998), 314–15; *Architectural Review* (1968); Harwood (2015), 513. The gallery won a RIBA award. The lawned area within the confines of the gallery still belongs to the deanery.
58. CCA GB i.b.10, 7–10. There were two plaques for each building, one commemorating the donors and the other the occasion of the Queen's visit. A postal vote came down in favour of an English inscription, but the committee preferred Latin 'for its neatness and elegance'. In the end, the plaques to the donors were inscribed in Latin, and those celebrating the Queen's unveiling were in English.
59. Baker and Thalmann, in Butler (2006), 68–72.
60. Thurley, *Men from the Ministry*, 38–42.
61. Thurley, *Men from the Ministry*, 201.
62. Oakeshott (1975), 57–60.
63. In 2012 both of these guidance documents were replaced by Planning Policy Statement 5 (PPS 5), 'Planning for the Historic Environment'.
64. CCA GB i.b.22, 7. Martin Stancliffe from 1990 and then Robert Montgomery from 1996.
65. CCA GB i.b.43, 12046ff.
66. There is also a consultant archaeologist, Graham Keevill.
67. For example, one major change has been the withdrawal of the VAT zero-rating on approved alterations to listed buildings that are either dwellings or used for residential or charitable purposes with effect from 1 October 2012.
68. Tyack (1998), 343.

Bibliography

Manuscript sources

Bodleian Library (Bod.):
 MS Ballard 19
 MS Ballard 35
 MS Bodl.13
 MS Don.c.209
 MS Don.e.223
 MS Don.e.226
 MS G. A. Oxon.b.113
 MS Top.Oxon.d.247
 MS Top.Oxon.d.287
 MS Rawl. B. 407a
 MS Rawl. Letters 37
 MS Wood F.28
 Roberts, B. C., 'Letters and Miscellaneous Papers' [printed but not published, 1814]
  (Bod. 270 c.396)

British Library (BL):
 Add. MS 27591
 Cott. Vitellius B V
 MS Add. 22602

Christ Church Archives (CCA):
There are few sections of the archive that do not contain some information about work on Christ Church's buildings. Archival documents used are referenced throughout the text, prefixed with CCA. However, the principal series used are as follows:

Annual Reports	Series cited as *Christ Church [date]*
BR	Building Records series (including commissioned reports listed below)
D&C i.b.1–12	Dean and Chapter act books
D&C ii.b.1–15	Dean and Chapter minute books
Maps and plans ChCh	Architectural drawings, etc.

MS Estates 127, 142–4	Estates correspondence relating to the main site and surroundings
Prints	Engravings, etc.
xii.b.1–119	Disbursement books
xii.c.120–308	Disbursement books
xxxiii.b.1–19	Historic building accounts (C17/18)

Many have written on aspects of Christ Church's history, whether as part of academic research, as commissioned reports or as personal memoirs, but few of these works have been published. Many of the following form part of the college's archive and are indicated as such with a CCA shelfmark. Others are research-in-progress which the author has generously given permission to use.

Borrett, F. V., 'Sitting on the Fence' [an unpublished account of Borrett's experiences as Head Porter from 1936 to 1962] (S xxxiv.a.3)

Brittain, Kate, 'The Classical Rebirth of Oxford: A Reappraisal of Peckwater's Palladianism' [unpublished undergraduate thesis, 2012] (BR 2/7/3)

Crossley, F., 'Ruskinian Gothic in Oxford: A Study of the Meadow Building at Christ Church' [unpublished dissertation, 2016] (BR 2/4/8)

Greenwold, Steve, 'The Origins of Pugin's Rationalist Revolution at the University of Oxford: A Micro-History of Architectural Thought and Practice, 1772–1844' [forthcoming DPhil thesis]

Haigh, C. A., '1546, Before and After: The Making of Christ Church' [unpublished lecture given to celebrate the 450th anniversary of the foundation of Christ Church, 1996]

Hawkins, John W., 'A Synoptic Study of Visual Representations of Some Oxford Buildings from 1566 to 1751' [Oxford University DPhil working paper, 2014]

Heard, Kate, 'Christ Church, Oxford, and the English Reformation, 1546–1576' [unpublished undergraduate thesis, 1998] (D&C viii.b.2)

Keevill, G., 'The Meadows Building, Christ Church, Oxford: Report on an Archaeological Watching Brief during Refurbishment of Staircase 3' [2011] (BR 2/4/2)

Keevill, G., 'Demant's Cottage, Christ Church, Oxford: Archaeological Appraisal and Preliminary Record' [2011] (BR 1/2/6)

Keevill, G., 'Christ Church, Oxford: Archaeological Appraisal of Proposed Fire Safety Works on the Upper Floors of Killcanon' [2012] (BR 1/2/7)

Keevill, G., 'The Porter's Lodge at Christ Church Oxford: Proposals to Provide Inclusive Access: Heritage Impact Assessment' [2013] (BR 2/1/1/4)

Keevill, G., 'Report on an Archaeological Watching Brief and Building Record in Fell Tower, Christ Church, Oxford' [2016] (BR 2/1/5/8)

Keevill, G. and Underwood, C., 'Christ Church, Oxford: Report on Archaeological Mitigation of the New Access Lift from the Buttery Cellar to the Ante Hall' [2010] (BR 2/2/1/3)

Mason, J. F. A., 'Christ Church Common Room and Its Possessions' [unpublished paper, February 1991] (CR 84)

Scott, G. G., 'Report of George Gilbert Scott, Esq., R.A. on the Cathedral of Christ Church, Oxford' [3 June 1869, printed for private circulation only] (D&C xix.b.1)

Christ Church Library (CCL):
     MS 373   Library Building Accounts
     MS 376   Correspondence concerning Tom Tower etc.
     Chichester, Morna, 'Christ Church Library, *c.*1562–1976' [unpublished dissertation, 1977] (MS 686)

Corpus Christi College Library and Archives:
     MS 565   Dean Higdon's daybook
     CCCO B/4/1/27   College Meeting Minute Book, October 1990–June 1991

National Archives:
     E101/479/9–11   Accounts for the building of Cardinal College

Oriel College Archives (OCA):
     A 2 A7 and Drawer 37 (exchanges): no. 3 Oriel Square alterations

Oxford University Archives:
     OUA Hyp/B/13   Will of Dean Sampson

Pembroke College Archives:
     PCA 18/12/15   A. H. Lawes, 'Historical Notes on the Almshouse'

Online sources

http://www.ipswich.suffolk.sch.uk/about/a-brief-history/wolsey-patron-of-ipswich-school.
     aspx_
http://www.measuringworth.com/ukcompare/index.php
http://www.oua.ox.ac.uk/history.html
http://www.royal.gov.uk/TheRoyalResidences/FormerRoyalResidences/Historicresidences.
     aspx
http://sculpture.gla.ac.uk/view/person.php?id=msib4_1273849641
http://www.stourbridge.com/stourbridge_fireclay.htm
http://vidimus.org/issues/issue-11/feature/

Printed sources

Abbreviations

L&P Henry VIII *Letters and Papers, Foreign and Domestic of the Reign of Henry VIII* (London, 1870 and 1872)
ODNB   *Oxford Dictionary of National Biography*, ed. H. C. G. Matthew and B. Harrison (Oxford, 2004) [If the relevant article has been updated in the online version, this has been recorded in the notes.]

Architectural Review, vol. cxlv, no. 886 (April 1968), 269–72
Architectural Review, vol. clx, no. 958 (December 1976), 363–6
Arkell, W. J., *Oxford Stone* (London, 1947)
[Arnold, Frederick,] *Christ Church Days: An Oxford Story*, 2 vols (London, 1867)

Barnwell, P. S., Tyack, Geoffrey, and Whyte, William, *Sir George Gilbert Scott, 1811–1878* (Donnington, 2014)

Barrett, Philip, *Barchester: English Cathedral Life in the Nineteenth Century* (London, 1993)

Batey, Mavis, *The Historic Gardens of Oxford and Cambridge* (London, 1989)

Beddard, R.A., 'Christ Church under John Fell', in a supplement to *Christ Church 1976/77*

Biddle, M., and Kjølbye-Biddle, B., 'An early medieval floor-tile from St Frideswide's minster', in *Oxoniensia*, 53 (1988), 259–63

Biddle, Martin, 'Wolsey's bell-tower', in *Oxoniensia*, 53 (1988), 205–10

Bill, E. G. W. (ed. Hall, Michael), 'The belfry at Christ Church', in *Oxoniensia*, 78 (2013), 157–73

Bill, E. G. W. (ed. Howell, Peter), 'Sir Gilbert Scott's restoration of Christ Church cathedral', in *Oxoniensia*, 78 (2013), 127–55

Blagden, Claude M., *Well Remembered* (London, 1953)

Blair, J., 'Frewin Hall, Oxford: a Norman mansion and a monastic college', in *Oxoniensia*, 43 (1978), 48–99

Blair, J., 'St Frideswide reconsidered', in *Oxoniensia*, 52 (1987), 71–127

Blair, J. (ed.), *Saint Frideswide's Monastery at Oxford: Archaeological and Architectural Studies* (Gloucester, 1990)

Blair, J., *Anglo-Saxon Oxfordshire* (Gloucester, 1994)

Boyle, A., et al., 'Excavations in Christ Church cathedral graveyard, Oxford', in *Oxoniensia*, 66 (2001), 337–68

Brears, Peter, *Cooking and Dining in Medieval England* (London, 2008)

Brears, Peter, *Cooking and Dining in Tudor and Early Stuart England* (London, 2015)

Briggs, G., Cook, J., and Rowley, T. (eds.), *The Archaeology of the Oxford Region* (Oxford, 1986)

Britton, John, *The History and Antiquities of the Cathedral Church of Oxford* (London, 1821)

Brock, M. G., and Curthoys, M. C., *History of the University of Oxford*, vol. vi: *Nineteenth-Century Oxford, Part 1* (Oxford, 1997)

Brock, M. G., and Curthoys, M. C., *History of the University of Oxford*, vol. vii: *Nineteenth-Century Oxford, Part 2* (Oxford, 2000)

Brockliss, L. W. B., *The University of Oxford: A History* (Oxford, 2016)

Bussby, F., 'Brian Duppa, Bishop of Winchester, 1660–1662' in *Winchester Cathedral Record* (1967)

Butler, C. (ed.), *Christ Church, Oxford: A Portrait of the House* (London, 2006)

Campbell, James W. P., Tutton, Michael, and Pearce, J., *Staircases: History, Repair and Conservation* (London, 2014)

Caröe, W. Douglas, *'Tom Tower', Christ Church, Oxford: Some Letters of Sir Christopher Wren to John Fell, bishop of Oxford, hitherto unpublished, now set forth and annotated* (Oxford, 1923)

Catto, J. and Evans, T .A. R., *History of the University of Oxford*, vol. ii: *Late Medieval Oxford* (Oxford, 1992)

Chadwick, A, Gilbert, D. R., and Moore, J. (eds.), *'Quadrangles where wisdom honours herself': Archaeological Investigations at Tom Quad, Peckwater Quad and Blue Boar Quad, Christ Church, Oxford* (Oxford, 2012) [A succinct summary of this report can be found in *Current Archaeology*, 280 (July 2013), 34–41.]

Clark, A. (ed.), *Survey of the Antiquities of the City of Oxford, Composed in 1661–6, by Anthony Wood* (Oxford, 1889–90)

Clark, A. (ed.), *Life and Times of Anthony Wood, Antiquary, of Oxford, 1632–1695, Described by Himself*, 3 vols (Oxford, 1891–4)

Cole, Catherine, 'Carfax conduit', in *Oxoniensia*, xxix–xxx (1964/5), 142–68

Colvin, H., *Unbuilt Oxford* (New Haven, CT, and London, 1983)

Colvin, H., *A Biographical Dictionary of British Architects, 1600–1840* (London, 2008)

Cook, J., and Mason, J. F. A. (eds.), *The Building Accounts of Christ Church Library, 1716–1779* (Oxford, 1988)

Crossley, A. (ed.), *History of the County of Oxford*, vol. iv: *The City of Oxford* [VCH] (London, 1979)

Curthoys, J., '"To perfect the college …": the Christ Church almsmen, 1546–1888', in *Oxoniensia*, 60 (1995), 379–95

Curthoys, J., *The Cardinal's College: Christ Church, Chapter and Verse* (London, 2012)

Darwall-Smith, Robin, *A History of University College, Oxford* (Oxford, 2008)

Dawson, J. E. A., 'The foundation of Christ Church, Oxford, and Trinity College, Cambridge, in 1546', in *Bulletin of the Institute of Historical Research*, lvii (1984), 208–15

Dearmer, P., *Oxford: The Cathedral and See* (London, 1899)

Doble, C. E. (ed.), *Remarks and Collections of Thomas Hearne* (Oxford, 1885–1907)

Dodgson, C. L., *The New Belfry at Christ Church* (Oxford, 1873)

Durand, W. Y., 'Palaemon and Arcyte, Progne, Marcus Geminus, and the theatre in which they were acted, as described by John Bereblock (1566)', in *Proceedings of the Modern Language Association of America*, xx (1905), 520–28

Everett, Michael, *The Rise of Thomas Cromwell: Power and Politics in the Reign of Henry VIII* (New Haven, CT, and London, 2015)

Foster, Joseph, *Alumni Oxonienses: The Members of the University of Oxford, 1500–1714*, 4 vols (Oxford, 1891)

Gaskell, Charles Milnes (ed.), *An Eton Boy: Being the Letters of James Milnes Gaskell from Eton and Oxford, 1820–1830* (London, 1939)

Gibson, Strickland, *Statutes of the Colleges of Oxford* (Oxford, 1853)

Green, S. J. D. and Horden, Peregrine (eds.), *All Souls under the Ancien Régime: Politics, Learning, and the Arts, c.1600–1850* (Oxford, 2007)

Greening Lamborn, E. A., The *Story of Architecture in Oxford Stone* (Oxford, 1912)

Grose, Francis, *The Antiquarian Repertory*, ii (London, 1779)

Gunn, S. J., and Lindley, P. G., *Cardinal Wolsey: Church, State, and Art* (Cambridge, 1991)

Gutch, A. (ed.), *History and Antiquities of the University of Oxford, in Two Books, by Anthony à Wood, MA of Merton College* (Oxford, 1796)

Gutch, John, *Collectanea curiosa*, i (Oxford, 1781)

Gwyn, Peter, *The King's Cardinal: The Rise and Fall of Thomas Wolsey* (London, 1990)

Halfpenny, Eric, 'The Christ Church trophies', in *Galpin Society Journal*, xxviii (1975)

Hall, Michael, *George Frederick Bodley and the Later Gothic Revival in Britain and America* (London, 2014)

Harrison, Brian (ed.), *History of the University of Oxford*, vol. viii: *The Twentieth Century* (Oxford, 1994)

Harrison, James Park, *An Account of the Discovery of the Remains of Three Apses at Oxford Cathedral* (London and Oxford, 1891)

Harvey, John, *English Mediaeval Architects: A Biographical Dictionary down to 1550* (Gloucester, 1984)

Harvey, John H., 'The building works and architects of Cardinal Wolsey', in *Journal of the British Archaeological Association*, viii (1943), 48–59

Harwood, Elain, *Space, Hope, and Brutalism: English Architecture, 1945–1975* (London, 2015)

Heathcote, Edwin, 'Christ Church cathedral, Oxford: lighting scheme by Ecclesiastical Lighting', in *Church Building*, 59 (1999), 56–7

Hibbert, C. (ed.), *Encyclopaedia of Oxford* (London, 1988)

Hiscock, W. G., *A Christ Church Miscellany: New Chapters on the Architects, Craftsmen, Statuary, Plate, Bells, Furniture, Clocks, Plays, the Library, and Other Buildings* (Oxford, 1946)

Hiscock, W. G., *Henry Aldrich of Christ Church, 1648–1710* (Oxford, 1960)

Historical Manuscripts Commission, *Report on the Manuscripts of His Grace the Duke of Portland, KG, Preserved at Welbeck Abbey*, vii (London, 1901)

Horner, Libby, *Patrick Reyntiens: Catalogue of Stained Glass* (Bristol, 2013)

Horsfield, W. T., et al., 'The building stones of Oxfordshire villages', in *Oxoniensia*, 78 (2013), 115–26

Ingram, James, *Memorials of Oxford*, i (Oxford, 1837)

Jackson, Basil H. (ed.), *Recollections of Thomas Graham Jackson, 1835–1924* (London, 1950)

Jacob, E. F., *St Frideswide: The Patron Saint of Oxford* (Oxford, 1953)

Jacobs, M., 'Christ Church kitchens', in *Institutional Management Association Journal* (September 1950)

Jones, John, *Balliol College: A History*, 2nd edn (Oxford, 2005)

Keevill, G., Mellor, M., and Curthoys, J., 'The Allestree Library at Christ Church Oxford, and its tiled pavement', in *Oxoniensia*, 79 (2014), 31–46

Keevill, G. and C., *Christ Church, Oxford: The Thatched Barn. NGR SP 515 058. Archaeological Evaluation Report* (July 2014)

Kennedy, Jane, 'Vault repairs to the tomb of Sir Robert Danvers, Christ Church Cathedral, Oxford', in *Transactions of the Association for Studies in the Conservation of Historic Buildings*, 35 (2012), 18–22

Kent, P. W., *Some Scientists in the Life of Christ Church, Oxford* (Oxford, 2001)

Ker, N. R., 'Oxford college libraries in the sixteenth century', in *Bodleian Library Record*, vi (3) (January 1959)

Knowles, D. and Hadcock, R. N., *Medieval Religious Houses: England and Wales* (London, 1971)

Law, Brian R., *Building Oxford's Heritage: Symm and Company from 1815* (Oxford, 1998)

Letters and Papers, Foreign and Domestic of the Reign of Henry VIII (London, 1870 and 1872)

Lowe, J., *Handbook to the Cathedral Church of Christ in Oxford* (Oxford, 1949)

Lyte, H. C. M., *A History of the University of Oxford from the Earliest Times to the Year 1530* (Oxford, 1886)

Malcolmson, A. P. W., *Primate Robinson 1709–94* (Belfast, 2003)

Mason, J. F. A., 'Pink v. white: the redecoration of the Upper Library in 1964–5', in *Christ Church Library Newsletter*, vol. ii, issue 3 (2006)

McConica, J. (ed.), *History of the University of Oxford*, vol. iii: *The Collegiate University* (Oxford, 1986)

McKitterick, David (ed.), *The Making of the Wren Library, Trinity College, Cambridge* (Cambridge, 1995)

Milne, J. G. and Harvey, J. H., 'The building of Cardinal College, Oxford', in *Oxoniensia*, 8 (1943), 137–53

Mobus, Melody, 'The Burford School of masons', in *Oxoniensia*, 78 (2013), 99–114

Morgan, Paul, *Oxford Libraries outside the Bodleian: A Guide* (Oxford, 1980)

Morrell, Jack, *Science at Oxford, 1914–1939: Transforming an Arts University* (Oxford, 1997)

Morris, James, *Oxford* (Oxford, 1965)

Munby, Julian, *Christ Church Oxford: The Hall Stairs and Proposed Lift Access. Historic Building Assessment* (2004)

Munby, Julian, *The Bishop, the Shopkeeper and the Cloister: Robert Shirborne and St Frideswide's* [forthcoming]

Nichols, John, *The Progresses and Public Processions of Queen Elizabeth* (Oxford, 1823)

Nichols, John, *Progresses, Processions, and Magnificent Festivities of King James the First, His Royal Consort, Family, and Court* (Oxford, 1823)

Oakeshott, W. F. (ed.), *Oxford Stone Restored: The Work of the Oxford Historic Buildings Fund, 1957–1974* (Oxford, 1975)

O'Dwyer, Frederick, *The Architecture of Deane and Woodward* (Cork, 1997)

Pantin, W. A., 'Before Wolsey', in Trevor-Roper, H. R. (ed.), *Essays in British History Presented to Sir Keith Feiling* (1964)

Pantin, W. A., *Canterbury College Oxford*, vols i and iv (Oxford, 1947 and 1985)

Pevsner, N., *An Outline of European Architecture* (London, 1973)

Pevsner, N., *Oxfordshire* (Harmondsworth, 1979)

Postles, D., 'The foundation of Oseney Abbey', in *Bulletin of the Institute of Historical Research*, liii, no. 128 (November 1980), 242–4

Potter, Jeremy, *Tennis and Oxford* (Oxford, 1994)

Powell, Ken, *Powell & Moya: Twentieth Century Architects* (London, 2009)

Proceedings of the Oxford Architectural and Historical Society (Oxford, 1860–64)

RCHME (Royal Commission on the Historical Monuments of England), *An Inventory of the Historical Monuments in the City of Oxford* (London, 1939)

Records Commission, *Valor Ecclesiasticus*, ii (London, 1814)

Rex, Richard, *Henry VIII and the English Reformation* (Basingstoke, 2006)

Richardson, Glenn, *The Field of the Cloth of Gold* (New Haven, CT, and London, 2013)

Richardson, Walter C., *History of the Court of Augmentations, 1536–1554* (Baton Rouge, LA, 1961)

Robinson, John Martin, 'A great architectural family: the rise of the Wyatts', in *Country Life* (13 and 20 December 1973), 2006–9 and 2098–101

Robinson, John Martin, *The Wyatts: An Architectural Dynasty* (Oxford, 1979)

Robinson, John Martin, *James Wyatt: Architect to George III* (New Haven, CT, and London, 2012)

Rocheford, Torevin de, *The Antiquarian Repertory*, ii (London, 1779), 52. Translated from *Travels of Monsieur Torevin de Rocheford* (1672)

Rodwell, Kirsty (ed.), *Historic Towns in Oxfordshire: A Survey of the New County* (Oxford, 1975)

Roscoe, Ingrid, *A Biographical Dictionary of Sculptors in Britain, 1660–1851* (New Haven, CT, and London, 2009)

Rowntree, Diana, 'Oxford college barges: their history and decay, and their successors the boathouses', in *Architectural Review* (July 1956), 37–42

Rowntree, John, 'The organs of Christ Church cathedral' [printed as a supplement to the Annual Report, *Christ Church 1980/1981*]

Roy, Ian (ed.), *The Royal Ordnance Papers, 1642–1646* (Wheatley, 1963–4)

Rundle, David, and Hanna, Ralph, *Descriptive Catalogue of the Western Manuscripts, up to c. 1600, of Christ Church, Oxford* [forthcoming, Oxford, 2016]

Salter, H. E., *Survey of Oxford*, vol. i (Oxford, 1960)

Sharp, Thomas, *Oxford Replanned* (London, 1948)

Sharpe, Frederick, 'Re-hanging Great Tom', in *Country Life* (28 May 1953)

Sherwood, Jennifer, and Pevsner, Nikolaus, *The Buildings of England: Oxfordshire* (London, 1974)

Skelton, John, *Oxonia Antiqua Restaurata* (Oxford, 1823)

Stenton, F., *St Frideswide and Her Times* (Oxford, 1953)

Sturdy, D., Rouse, E. Clive, and Cole, J. C., 'The painted roof of the Old Library, Christ Church', in *Oxoniensia*, 26 and 27 (1961–2)

Summerson, John, 'The changing face of Oxford', in *The Times* (15 May 1963)

Summerson, John, *Architecture in Britain, 1530–1830* (London, 1993)

Sutherland, L. S., and Mitchell, L. G. (eds.), *History of the University of Oxford*, vol. v: *The Eighteenth Century* (Oxford, 1986)

[Swinstead, J. Howard], *Christ Church Cathedral School, Oxford: Register of Choristers, Probationers, Masters, Precentors, Organists from 1837–1900* (1900)

Thalmann, Jacqueline (ed.), *40 years of Christ Church Picture Gallery* (Oxford, 2008)

Thompson, H. L. *Henry George Liddell, DD, Dean of Christ Church, Oxford: A Memoir* (Oxford, 1899)

Thompson, H. L., *Christ Church* (Oxford, 1900)

Thurley, Simon, *The Building of England: How the History of England Has Shaped Our Buildings* (London, 2013)

Thurley, Simon, *Men from the Ministry: How Britain Saved Its Heritage* (New Haven, CT, 2013)

Trevor-Roper, Hugh, *Christ Church Oxford: The Portrait of a College*, 3rd edn (Oxford, 1989)

Tyack, G., *Oxford: An Architectural Guide* (Oxford, 1998)

Tyack, G., Bradley, S., and Pevsner N., *Berkshire* (London, 2001)

Tyacke, N. (ed.), *History of the University of Oxford*, vol. iv: *Seventeenth-Century Oxford* (Oxford, 1997)

Wakeling, E. (ed.), *Lewis Carroll's Diaries*, vol. vi (Luton, 2002)

Wakeling, E. (comp.), *The Oxford Pamphlets, Leaflets, and Circulars of Charles Lutwidge Dodgson* (Charlottesville, VA, 1993)

Ward, G. R. M., *Foundation Statutes of Bishop Fox for Corpus Christi College in the University of Oxford, AD 1517. Now first translated into English, with a life of the founder* (London, 1843)

Ward, W. R., *Georgian Oxford: University Politics in the Eighteenth Century* (Oxford, 1958)

Ward, W. R., *Victorian Oxford* (Oxford, 1965)

Warner, S. A., *Oxford Cathedral* (New York, 1924)

Watson, E. W., *The Cathedral Church of Christ in Oxford* (London, *c.* 1935)

Weeks, James, 'The architects of Christ Church library', in *Architectural History*, 48 (2005), 107–38

Weinstock, *Hearth Tax Returns, Oxfordshire, 1665* (Oxford, 1940)

Welch, J., *List of the Queen's Scholars of St Peter's College, Westminster* [*Alumni Westmonasterienses*] (London, 1852)

Winkles, Benjamin, *Architectural and Picturesque Illustrations of the Cathedral Churches of England and Wales*, ii (1851)

Wright, Abraham, *Parnassus biceps* (London, 1656)

Wright, Abraham, and Beal, Peter (ed.), *Parnassus biceps* (Aldershot, 1990)

Youings, Joyce, *The Dissolution of the Monasteries* (London, 1971)

Index

All places are in Oxford unless otherwise stated. *Italic* page numbers refer to black and white illustrations and their captions; colour plates are indicated by 'Pl.'

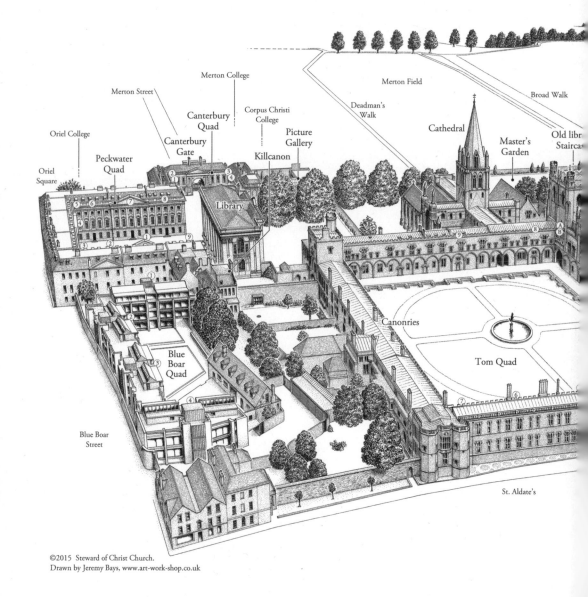

Oriel College

Merton Street

Merton College

Canterbury Quad

Canterbury Gate

Corpus Christi College

Merton Field

Deadman's Walk

Broad Walk

Cathedral

Master's Garden

Old libr Staircas

Oriel Square

Peckwater Quad

Killcanon

Picture Gallery

Library

Oriel Square

Canonries

Blue Boar Quad

Tom Quad

Blue Boar Street

St. Aldate's

©2015 Steward of Christ Church.
Drawn by Jeremy Bays, www.art-work-shop.co.uk

Liddell Building

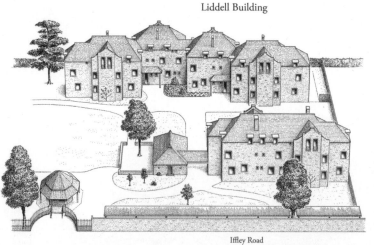

Iffley Road